THE CAUSES
of
WORLD HUNGER

THE CAUSES
of
WORLD HUNGER

edited by
William Byron

PAULIST PRESS
New York / Ramsey

Library of Congress
Catalog Card Number 82-60591

ISBN: 0-8091-2483-1

Published by Paulist Press
545 Island Road, Ramsey, N.J. 07446

Printed and bound in the
United States of America

Contents

for
those who know hunger
inside out

Preface

Descriptions of hunger and the hungry poor of our world are readily available. Discussions of the causes of their hunger are harder to come by. This book discusses causes. In doing so, it provides the reader with a framework for continuing causal analysis.

Each of the writers participating in this project is a past or present member of the Board of Directors of Bread for the World, the Christian citizens' movement dedicated to the reduction of hunger in the world through redirection and creative application of U.S. policy. All too frequently in this nation, the discussion of policy tends to encourage the substitution of blame for analysis. It is not the purpose of this book to lay blame. This project attempts rather to identify and discuss distinct causal influences that produce the hunger all of us want to see eliminated.

To say that third world hunger is not a U.S. problem exclusively is true but dangerous. It tends to overlook or dismiss the fact that our own domestic hunger is part of the world hunger problem. It tends as well, and more seriously, to ignore the range of possible causal links between U.S. power and affluence over against foreign poverty, hunger and even starvation. Finally, it tends to ignore both the opportunity and the responsibility we in the U.S. have to exercise true world leadership in a campaign to end hunger everywhere. To ignore these considerations is—there is no other word for it—ignorance. Books are written to assist those who want to overcome ignorance. And knowledge always prevails over ignorance whenever prejudice is not permitted to stand in the way. In the pages which follow, interested readers can meet knowledgeable writers in prejudice-free analysis. The meeting is important and, perhaps, overdue. Time is running out on the hungry poor in all parts of the world.

1

"The profound promise of our era," said U.S. Secretary of State Henry Kissinger to the World Food Conference in Rome in 1974, "is that for the first time we may have the technical capacity to free mankind from the scourge of hunger. Therefore, today we must proclaim a bold objective—that within a decade no child will go to bed hungry, that no family will fear for its next day's bread, and that no human being's future and capacities will be stunted by malnutrition."[1] Secretary Kissinger pledged his nation's willingness to "work cooperatively" with other nations toward achievement of the "bold objective." He added that the nations gathered there in Rome should "resolve to confront the challenge, not each other. . . . And let us make global cooperation in food a model for our response to other challenges of an interdependent world—energy, inflation, population, protection of the environment."[2] Cooperation toward these great goals has been less than remarkable. But the possibility remains that in bearing down together on the hunger issue, some of the leading actors in the world community may indeed find a way to work together to remedy some of society's other pressing problems.

Bread for the World, like other citizens' movements in representative democracies, believes that elected leaders can be persuaded to follow the will of the people who vote them in or out of power. In sponsoring this book, the Bread for the World Educational Fund hopes to increase citizen understanding, raise citizen consciousness and stimulate a stronger citizen resolve to banish hunger from the world community. Once the citizens have the resolve, which is largely a question of political will, measurable progress will be made toward a solution to the problem of world hunger. This nation is becoming less of a representative democracy and more of a participatory democracy. Informed action is the goal of this book.

The idea for the organization of this book emerged as I was sitting at a meeting of the Board of Directors of Bread for the World in New York City several years ago. I thought of the causal complexity of the hunger problem and the possibility of inviting some of the many talented people seated around that table to write, out of their own reflection and experience, on a single causal factor. We had a sufficiency both of causes and directors to produce a book-length treatment of the problem.

Each contributor to this volume worked without reimbursement for talent, time and other costs incurred in writing a chapter manuscript. All proceeds from the sale of this book will support the Bread for the World movement, specifically the Educational Fund.

A grant from the Raskob Foundation made it possible for many of the authors to participate in a critique session at the University of Scranton Conference and Retreat Center at Chapman Lake near Scranton, Pennsylvania. In light of comments and suggestions exchanged in that session, manuscript revisions were made by individual authors and the essays were collected again for editing. Marilyn Coar, my Executive Assistant at the University of Scranton, made her contribution to the project by typing the final manuscript. With thanks to all who helped and without apology for the book's shortcomings (it is our hope that reader reaction will promote more refined analysis and better understanding of the causes as a prelude to more effective action), this effort is dedicated to the hungry everywhere and to those who are working to help them.

William J. Byron, S.J.

NOTES

1. For a full text of Dr. Kissinger's speech, see *War on Hunger,* A Report from the Agency for International Development, Vol. VIII, No. 12 (December 1974); the portion I cite appears on p. 24.

2. *Ibid.*

1
The Causes of World Hunger

William J. Byron, S.J.

It is always a mistake to substitute blame for analysis. Pinning blame is much simpler than analyzing the relatedness of factors that impinge on any problem. This is particularly true of the hunger problem with its economic, political, social, cultural, natural and technological complexities.

One of the contributors to this volume, C. Dean Freudenberger, co-authored a book with Paul M. Minus, Jr., which started me thinking about the multiple causes of world hunger.[1] Their basic list includes:

1. The colonial legacy.
2. Resource abuse.
3. Complexity of agricultural development.
4. False assumptions on the part of Americans.
5. Low status for agricultural (as compared with industrial) development.
6. Recent business expansion.
7. The dearth of agricultural and rural community leadership.
8. The arms race.
9. Disenchantment with international assistance programs.
10. Population growth.

The list is not exhaustive. In teasing it out with the benefit of student and colleague discussion, I have constructed a chain of causes that constitutes the table of contents of this book. And even that list admits of extension and subdivision. In a very real sense, this book provides a workshop experience for the reader. Additional causes can be added to the list. Causes on the list can be separated into distinct elements important enough to justify more extensive treatment. The discussion of a given cause provided here may prompt agreement or disagreement, satisfaction or dissatisfaction with the thoroughness of analysis. The "workshop" character of the book invites reader engagement with a view to producing an even more complete understanding of the problem. Although this particular project is aimed at improved understanding, the Bread for the World movement, in general, aims at converting understanding into responsible citizen action.

To the Freudenberger-Minus list posted above one would have to add a reminder that the basic cause is poverty. Other causal contributors are (1) tradition; (2) considerations of geography and climate; (3) trade barriers to development and the tendency of poor nations like Mexico to "cash crop" for export to wealthy nations leaving insufficient produce for the domestic market; (4) the inequality of wealth and income distribution in the world; (5) overconsumption in the developed nations; (6) the absence of political will in nations strong enough to do something about hunger; (7) the absence of an effective international system of grain reserves; (8) the uprooting of people from the soil and the consignment of these people to refugee status, driving them into areas of overcrowding and short supplies of just about everything needed to sustain life; and, from the perspective of a Christian nation where hunger is acknowledged to be a moral problem; (9) a condition of theological underdevelopment and ethical insensitivity (the "Dives and Lazarus" problem) must be called a cause of hunger.

No specific mention has yet been made of land reform, although the land problem—its use, ownership, abuse and transfer—is woven in and out of many of the chapters in this book. The land issue is of such overarching importance to the hunger problem that it really requires a book-length treatment of its own.

All of the issues mentioned thus far relate to hunger. Each of these issues merits study. The direction of such study encouraged here will follow the following pattern:

- Poverty is the basic cause of hunger. Arthur Simon almost

stumbled upon the hunger issue around 1970 as he searched for a way to bring Christian communities together to make "common cause" against the problem of *poverty* in the U.S. and the world. Since founding Bread for the World a decade ago he has reflected daily on the relationship between poverty and hunger. He is ready to concede that the link between poverty and hunger is self-evident to the persons most likely to read this book, but "it is manifestly not a part of common public awareness." He then takes the reader behind the episodic, extreme starvation events that capture media attention, to the problem of chronic undernutrition, to the "invisible hungry" whom we never see on television screens or in news magazines.

• Tradition, constantly under threat in a world of technological change, is a previous influence not to be devalued, certainly to be preserved. Why, then, list tradition as a cause of hunger? Kristen Wenzel explains how tradition, important for the guidance of human progress, can also impede human progress by blocking the acceptance of new technologies and new ways of doing things. The "new" need not negate the central values of a tradition. The cultural problem is, of course, to identify genuine central values and to prevent mindless superstition from impeding the embodiment of those values in new forms conducive to the fuller realization of human potential. It is possible to permit the dead weight of unexamined tradition to crush human life. Tradition has in fact caused, and continues to cause, hunger in the world.

• Theological underdevelopment is not to be regarded lightly by Christians concerned about hunger. Those who profess and proclaim the tenets of Christianity might reasonably be expected to recognize hunger as a moral problem. Edward Brady suggests that in a world where Christian believers still exercise significant business and political leadership, insufficient theological awareness can function as a cause of continuing hunger.

Theology is an exercise of human understanding applied to the data of divine revelation. What do our Christian symbols and Scriptures tell us about hunger? As answers to that question engage the Christian theological imagination, theological development will be underway in the minds of reflective Christians. Given the appropriate moral sensitivity, action will be the logical consequence of such reflection. If the late Peter Maurin's view of our general predicament is true, namely, that "the trouble with the world is that the people who do all the thinking never act, and the people who do all the acting never think," then a serious effort to overcome theological underdevelopment and heighten ethical sensitivity will surely help.

• Agricultural development is indeed complex. Douglas Ensminger, writing out of many decades of experience on the farm, in the classroom, and on long-term overseas technical assistance missions, outlines the complexities and explains the consequent neglect of agricultural development in places where it is needed most. The circumstances he describes function as a cause of continuing hunger. Sufficient understanding of these circumstances can, however, remove some important barriers to increased food production in the food-deficit nations.

• Richard Neuhaus cautions against misunderstanding and abuse of the term "colonialism" but does indicate that the colonial powers "frequently failed to encourage, and often actively discouraged, the development of native leadership." This would be one of several "causal connections between past behavior and present sorrow" since it meant that former colonies, upon achievement of independent statehood, found themselves without the political and agricultural leadership required to meet the problems of hungry people.

• Geography and climate are well understood by Warren Henegar who is a farmer and county commissioner in Bloomington, Indiana. Weather plays tricks and geography places constraints upon the farmer. The relative fertility or infertility of different soils and the virtual impossibility of restoring most impoverished soil to productive status are considerations to be noted in an on-going analysis of the reasons for hunger in our world.

Each agricultural region of the world has its own unique environment. Everywhere, however, there is a common dependence on water. Hence, the analysis must extend to variations in rain patterns, the sources of supplemental water, the problems of drainage and flood control. Careful management of the constraints imposed by geography and the conditions produced by climate can contribute significantly to the reduction of hunger.

• "Resource abuse" is an expression that speaks directly to the problem of hunger. Grassland, cropland, and forest resources around the world are undergoing ruthless exploitation. They stand in need of repair. In some cases the damage is irreversible. Arable land is shrinking at an alarming rate. Deforestation and desertification are widespread. Dean Freudenberger wonders whether the world has sense enough to preserve the basic biological systems needed to sustain life on this planet. He calls attention to abuse of our woodlands, croplands, grasslands, and oceanic fisheries. Damage to our lands and waters is a direct cause of hunger.

• Norman Faramelli analyzes trade relationships with an eye to adverse effects on the poor nations struggling to come up from hunger. Trade affects development of both the agricultural and industrial sectors in poor countries. Barriers to trade in world markets deny the developing countries the kind of participation that will reduce their need for aid. Such exclusion (or inclusion on blatantly unequal terms) amounts to a basic denial of life chances to the poor. Patterns of domination and dependency, which perpetuate income inequalities, can be broken by just trade relationships. Unjust trade relationships serve to keep people hungry. One such relationship is "export cropping" which benefits affluent importing nations at the expense of the landless laborers who produce crops for export in many poor countries.

• If food reserves are inadequate, victims of drought, famine and other disasters will have no security. The absence of reserves will also foster price instability and discourage production. Jayne Millar-Wood explains the function and stresses the importance of an international system of reserves which will benefit both producers and consumers of grain and other important crops. A reserve system is a good example of a structural remedy to the problem of hunger. Reserves, it should be noted, are not there just for emergencies. Their presence helps to guarantee efficient food production for normal times as well.

• James Cogswell puts foreign aid in perspective. He locates it in the larger "causal" context provided by the other chapters in this book. "Without a prior consideration of these root causes (the other chapter topics) of world hunger," writes Cogswell, "development assistance becomes charity without justice, and makes a mockery of all our good intentions." Granted all that, we must still deal with the problem of disillusionment or a "crisis of confidence" on the part of U.S. citizens regarding the effectiveness of their government's foreign aid programs. Despite its shortcomings, development assistance remains one of the positive bridges between the first and third worlds. U.S. failure to keep that bridge in reasonable repair and, more important, to move assistance across that bridge to places of greatest need would constitute another cause for the continuation of hunger in the world—not a root cause, but a real cause nonetheless.

• Senator Mark Hatfield is in a good position to reflect on the importance of political will in a nation in order to make things happen in that nation's capital. If the people of this country neither know nor care about the problems of hungry people, the elected officials who serve our people will be unresponsive to the problem of hunger—not only unresponsive, but likely to aggravate the problem of hunger through actions taken on other fronts. This is possible where a sensitivity to the hunger issue is not present as other issues are under consideration. In any case, the absence of political will in the U.S. can become a continuing cause of hunger.

• Eileen Egan is an expert on the problems of refugees. In a world of political upheaval, she argues, every year is a refugee year. The relationship between refugees and hunger is interesting. Food production requires a stable planting, cultivating and harvesting population. Uprooted from the land, refugees not only produce no food, they are driven into centers and clusters where food is in short supply. Their very presence in such centers makes the food supply there grow shorter. Refugees are not only victims of hunger, their condition is itself a cause of hunger.

• The arithmetic of expenditures for armaments in the United States and virtually every other nation is so staggering that it eludes practical comprehension. The common-sense conclusion that would footnote the bottom line of any consolidated defense-expenditure statement for the nations of the world is simply this: if less were spent to purchase or produce arms, more would be available to purchase or produce bread for the world. Eugene Carson Blake probes the arms-hunger relationship in the context of the Christian conscience. His reflections should be read with the realization that no less a patriot, pragmatist and military expert than Dwight D. Eisenhower said less than two months after he became President of the United States: "Every gun that is made, every warship launched, every rocket fired signifies, in the final sense, a theft from those who hunger and are not fed, those who are cold and are not clothed."[2]

• In countries where social security systems and pension plans are non-existent, a large number of offspring provides the hope for security in a parent's declining years. In such countries, moreover, infant mortality rates are high (a condition not unrelated to the hunger issue) and consequently more children are brought into the world in hopes that a sufficient number will survive to work the tired soil. So goes the cycle of poverty, and so grows the population dilemma. Bryan Hehir explains how population growth is an aggravating cause, not a primary cause of the hunger problem.

• John Calhoun maps the uneven distribution of wealth and income in the world and shows how the inequalities translate themselves into power gaps and calorie deficiencies. Anyone who undertakes analysis along these lines must juggle statistics, clarify concepts, resist ideological biases and avoid both prosecution and defense of the multinationals. All the while, however, the fact remains that statistics are dry, the concepts are technical, ideologies are at work in the world of political and economic decision making, and the multinational corporations are there, for good or ill, on the side of wealth and power.

As the world moves toward equality, the poor will be better off. It is thus easier to talk about equality to the poor than to the rich. But the rich must tune in more closely to what the poor are saying if there is to be a genuine "north-south" dialogue. The hunger problem presents an interesting laboratory for experiment as the dialogue goes on. For the food problem is far less one of production than of distribution. If redistribution of food produced works in favor of the hungry poor, the other unsolved problems of redistribution of wealth and income may become more manageable and thus less threatening to world security.

• Lifestyle links between overweight Americans and malnourished Asians must undergo the scrutiny of anyone attempting to understand the causes of world hunger. Overconsumption in the developed nations happens, to some extent, at the expense of poorer nations. Life in the affluent society has put unprecedented demands on natural resources and food supplies. Grain reserves are down as energy consumption is up in the United

States. As fuel and fertilizer prices hit new highs, poor nations become less agriculturally secure.

Myron Augsburger shows how consumption patterns in wealthy populous nations can have causal links to hunger abroad. He raises a Christian call for a simpler life here so that others elsewhere may simply live.

• Bishop Thomas Gumbleton provides a closing chapter to this book. He suggests that Bread for the World is one way of taking a few important steps toward a solution to the problem under analysis.

As I indicated earlier, our analysis is incomplete. This reflects both the limits of our competence and the virtual absence of limits to the complexity of the problem of world hunger. Hence, the importance of the "workbook" character of this collection. It enlarges understanding as it invites further investigation and deeper reflection.

Before releasing the reader for interaction with the chapters which follow, I want to end this introductory overview of "the causes" with a thought about research. The search for knowledge about all aspects of reality is, of course, endless. Our identification and analysis of the causes of world hunger is inadequate. Those interested in eliminating hunger must become more interested in promoting research. Indeed, those who read this book could serve the cause of the hungry poor by asking those in academic settings, particularly their Church-related colleges and universities, what they are doing to discover and communicate a fuller understanding of world hunger.

I like to think of research as the discovery of new understandings. If the discovery is absolutely new, in the sense that no one has grasped that understanding before, I would call it *original* research. If the discovery is new for me and nuanced by me to broaden or update an older understanding, I would call it *derivative* research. Finally, if a discovery in one sphere of knowing, say, chemistry, can be joined to a discovery in another sphere, say, economics, and then in combination the two understandings generate a new understanding of an old problem, I would call that *conjunctive* research.

The traditional categories of "basic" and "applied" research are, of course, both valid and useful in the context of the hunger issue. The problem that I have with them, however, stems from the fact that "basic research" tends to be associated with high-powered, generously funded centers in government, isolated institutes, or research-oriented universities. And "applied research" relative to hunger is easily presumed to belong in experimental stations overseas. Opportunities as well as responsibilities for hunger research in mainstream and mainstreet American colleges, in faculties of arts and sciences, in ordinary libraries and laboratories, will be largely ignored if we are content to let the search for a better understanding of the world hunger problem reside in the basic research centers at home and application stations overseas.

Daydreaming, "What if?" and "Why not?" questions— first turned over quietly in the individual mind and later shared with others—provides an agenda for research. Academic people follow their disciplines in framing the questions. The academic imagination is stretched by interdisciplinary stimulation whenever more than one mode of discovery promises to enlarge our understanding of a problem or issue. But academic people must be encouraged to move closer to the hunger issue.

It is not my intention to outline an organized research agenda here. There are simply too many disciplines that are capable of focusing the academic imagination on hunger. There are, moreover, too many interactive issues relative to hunger that invite interdisciplinary research but defy orderly cataloguing. Politics, economics, ethics, biochemistry, history, biological science— the list of disciplines could run on and on. Energy, land, trade, weather, fertilizer, capital, culture—the list of relevant issues is endless. Case studies, all too readily dismissed by sophisticates who say they pollute the groves of academe and appear only to salvage studies grounded in fragile theory—such case studies, it must be said, are necessary to advance our understanding of what helps or hinders human efforts to eliminate hunger. Who really knows which projects in our much maligned U.S. foreign aid program have helped the poor and which have not? More important, who can tell us why? The data are there at the World Bank and at the Agency for International Development. In some cases, supplementary and evaluative data will be available from other sources. Senior theses, master's theses and other student and faculty research papers could be produced from these data.

This is derivative research, of course, but not the least of the benefits to be derived is a better understanding of one element of an extraordinarily complicated problem. Not to be able to deal directly with the central element (which I would identify as the problem of activating agricultural development along a self-propelling path in the food-deficit nations themselves) is no excuse for not dealing at all with any related element.

Both conjunctive and derivative research could involve the historian who wonders these days, more often than in the recent past, about relevance and survival in the face of declining enrollments, rising career concerns on the part of collegians and mounting evidence of a weakening commitment to the humanities on the part of liberal arts colleges themselves. An imaginative historian might organize a survey course or even a textbook around incidents of famine, drought, malnutrition and hunger-related events. Most adult Americans have pegged their historical memory to dates of wars and the development of weaponry. The possibility of pegging the story to developments in food and famine is worthy of a place on the historian's research agenda.

Similarly, American and world literature, either in survey form or in microscopic examination of metaphor, might be organized in terms of food and hunger. It is worth a try, in any case, unless humanistic researchers are prepared to concede that the hunger issue belongs exclusively within the domain of scientific and technological research.

Poets, philosophers, artists, theologians, historians and litterateurs must be sensitive to the hunger issue and communicate that sensitivity if a foundation is to be laid for the political will to act on the hunger issue.

Action—world-wide action—must be taken on five fronts over the next quarter century. As Henry Kissinger told the World Food Conference, these action-imperatives are:

1. Increasing the production of food exporters.
2. Accelerating the production in developing countries.
3. Improving means of food distribution and financing.
4. Enhancing food quality.
5. Ensuring security against food emergencies.[3]

The original, derivative and conjunctive research activities in America's colleges and universities over the next twenty-five years could facilitate or impede the realization of these goals. Action without appropriate understanding is not likely to help very much. And blame without analysis is likely not to help at all. The reader is therefore invited to reflect, in the following chapters, on the causes of world hunger.

NOTES

1. *Christian Responsibility in a Hungry World* (Nashville: Abingdon, 1976). See especially Chapter Two, "Causes of Hunger," pp. 21–30.

2. Address entitled, "The Chance for Peace," presented to the American Society of Newspaper Editors, April 16, 1953; cited by Arthur Simon, *Bread for the World* (New York: Paulist Press, 1975), p. 130.

3. *Op. cit.*, p. 3.

2
The Basic Cause: Poverty

Arthur Simon

The Presidential Commission on World Hunger concluded in its March 1980 report that "the central and most intransigent cause (of hunger) is poverty."

People are hungry because they are poor.

That single conclusion points to the complexity of hunger in terms of both its causes and its solutions. The causes of hunger and the ways of ending hunger are as complex and intertwined as the causes of poverty and the ways of overcoming poverty. It is no accident that the table of contents of this book could just as easily lead you to conclude that the book's title is "The Causes of Poverty" rather than "The Causes of Hunger," because poverty *is* the basic cause of hunger and, therefore, the causes of poverty are also the causes of hunger.

The connection between hunger and poverty may seem self-evident to many readers of this chapter, but it is manifestly not a part of common public awareness. Why is this so? Public attention is usually drawn to the presence of hunger only when it reaches extreme proportions. I remember hearing British economist Barbara Ward describe the situation in India during the mid-1960s, when the severity of famine had reached such a level that massive deaths by starvation seemed imminent. Western television crews moved their equipment to strategic locations, waiting to beam into our living rooms the specter of people starving to death by the thousands. But thanks to heroic efforts by the Indians and by international rescue workers, the deaths never reached the proportions that had been anticipated—so the television people picked up their equipment and left. Massive deaths by starvation would have been a media event, but anything less than that is seldom able to compete with other stories for time on the evening news or space on the front page of our newspaper.

Unfortunately, the public learns from this, first, that hunger is an extreme but occasional and localized problem usually caused by bad weather; and, second, that the primary solution to hunger is emergency food relief. Consequently another conclusion of the Presidential Commission on World Hunger needs to be placed alongside its conclusion that poverty is the basic cause of hunger: namely that "the major world hunger problem today is not famine or starvation, but the less dramatic one of chronic undernutrition."

Famine is only the tip of the iceberg. It is the most visible part of the problem. Below the line of visibility the tragedy of hunger reaches truly mammoth proportions, with estimates ranging from four hundred and fifty million to a billion or more persons worldwide who suffer from chronic malnutrition. These are, for the most part, the "invisible hungry." We never see them on our television screens or on the printed page. U.S. tourists seldom notice their hunger. They simply suffer in quiet obscurity, get sick too often and die too soon. They do so because they are desperately poor.

When millions of Cambodians are starving, our nation can be aroused to take action, as well it should. But according to the United Nations Children's Fund (UNICEF), a million children under the age of five die each month from hunger and hunger-related causes. In effect, "Cambodias" are occurring all the time and we rarely hear about them. We fail to hear because those who die are victims of chronic malnutrition that pervades much of the inhabited world. They do not have the good fortune to be perishing under circumstances that are sufficiently dramatic to catch the media's, and consequently our own, attention. Yet their persistent malnutrition is far more pervasive and destructive of lives than are periodic famines. It is *this* dimension of hunger above all that needs to be addressed. And it can only be addressed by dealing with the poverty that lies behind it.

The thirty-one countries listed by the U.N. Food and Agriculture Organization (FAO) in April 1981 as having abnormal food shortages illustrates the relationship between hunger and poverty. According to World Bank figures, in 1978 those thirty-one countries, including China, had a combined population of 1.3 billion people, more than thirty percent of the world's population. The same countries had a combined average per capita gross national product (GNP)—roughly the same as the average income per person for a year—of $215.

The FAO list did not include many countries such as India and Bangladesh in which poverty and malnutrition are widespread, because they were experiencing no abnormal food shortages during early 1981. If India and Bangladesh were added, the list would include approximately half of the world's population and the 1978 average per capita GNP for those countries would drop to about $198 annually. (Averages conceal disparities, of course, which makes the actual situation worse than the figures indicate.) By comparison, the per capita GNP in the United States for 1978 was $9,590 or about forty-eight times that of the thirty-one countries with abnormal food shortages, plus India and Bangladesh. Nations such as these with extremely limited resources often lack facilities, services and materials that provide basic opportunities for people. These include roads, transportation, available markets, access to credit, water and fertilizer, basic health services, and—as the FAO list indicates—an adequate supply of food.

The World Bank estimates that more than eight hundred million people, roughly twenty percent of the world's population, live in "absolute poverty." Robert S. McNamara, who served as president of the World Bank from 1968 to 1981, describes absolute poverty as "a condition of life so degraded by disease, illiteracy, malnutrition and squalor as to prevent realization of the potential with which each individual is born." Clearly, where that degree of poverty prevails, hunger prevails as well. Each is causally related to the other.

Hunger and food surpluses can exist side-by-side—further evidence of the relationship between hunger and poverty. That was true in the United States during the 1950's and 1960's when large grain surpluses piled up. Investigations in the late 1960's astonished the nation with evidence that millions of U.S. citizens were seriously malnourished, some to the point of starvation. The incidence of malnutrition has substantially dropped since then, though in the absence of a systematic inventory of the nutritional status of our most vulnerable population groups, we still do not have adequate information on the extent and severity of hunger in the United States. It is clear enough, however, that almost all malnourished U.S. citizens come from the ranks of the very poor. Their hunger cannot be attributed to a national shortage of food.

India illustrates the same point even more vividly. By 1977, this nation, then with a population of six hundred and thirty million persons, had accumulated a grain reserve of more than eleven million tons. Although by 1981 India's reserve had dropped below three million tons of wheat and was considered to be critically low, nevertheless India achieved "self-sufficiency" in grain for a number of years and was able to store rather than import grain. The reserve demonstrated self-sufficiency, however, only in relation to market demand, not in relation to actual need, for with an average per capita income of $180 a year in 1978, much of India's population remains malnourished. In September 1980, Michael T. Kaufman reported in the *New York Times* that despite impressive gains in food production, per capita grain consumption in India had dropped since 1950. Kaufman noted that almost half of the population lived below the poverty line, which the government set at $8 a month for a household living in the countryside and $9 a month for an urban household.

The relationship of market demand to food supplies is crucial, because it means that purchasing power, not need, usually determines how food is distributed. Worldwide, enough food can be produced to give every person at least a minimally adequate diet. But doing so would require both a system of distribution and sacrifices so extraordinary as to make it an almost academic matter. Consequently, increased production of food in developing countries is a critical aspect of improving the distribution of food. But increased production by itself will not greatly reduce hunger, because those with money can buy the food they need, while those with too little money cannot.

Access to land, of course, can enable one to produce and consume food either as a supplement to earnings or even in place of it altogether. Normally, however, even those who farm will not be adequately nourished unless they earn enough to buy tools and other materials and resources needed to use the land well.

Three-fourths of the population in developing countries is rural and most of the world's hungry people live in rural, not urban areas. Like their urban counterparts, the rural hungry are hungry because they are extremely poor.

The relationship between income and hunger helps us to understand the accompanying graph which shows per capita food production slightly rising over the years in developing countries. Even considering the drop in per capita food production between 1979 and 1981, the graph appears to indicate that the problem of hunger is easing, and in some countries that is the case. The graph, however, fails in two respects. First, it shows overall averages and therefore does not reflect the fact that many countries, notably most of those in Africa, are steadily dropping in per capita food production. Second, it does not take into account the fact that as some people in the developing countries become affluent or even less poor, they buy more food. Increases in food production do not necessarily provide more food for those who are malnourished. Sometimes more food produced means more export sales or more food for a minority of persons with rising standards of living, but less food for the rest of the population. In developing countries as a whole the demand for food (that is, effective market demand, reflecting purchasing power) is rising faster than food production. That explains why developing countries are importing food at an alarming rate of increase.

In short, adequate nourishment for a family depends upon its ability either to produce enough food for its own needs or to earn enough money to buy the food—or some combination of the two. Without this ability, color the family hungry.

For many of us, hunger conjures up images of famine and the need to ship relief supplies. Because relief supplies are crucial for sustaining life in emergencies, they have an importance that greatly exceeds the usual measurement of food in tons or dollars. Nevertheless relief shipments account for only a tiny fraction of world food distribution. What is the mechanism for most food distribution? Money. The free market. For a vast majority of the world's inhabitants, income determines in whole or in part how well they can nourish themselves. Without an income that enables a family to buy enough food for an adequate diet, some or all of its members go hungry. Put another way, they are hungry because they are poor.

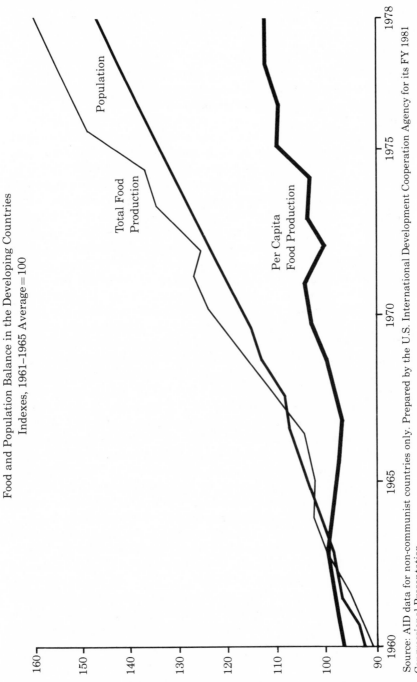

Food and Population Balance in the Developing Countries
Indexes, 1961–1965 Average=100

Population

Total Food
Production

Per Capita
Food Production

Source: AID data for non-communist countries only. Prepared by the U.S. International Development Cooperation Agency for its FY 1981
Congressional Presentation.

22

Why are they poor?

Other chapters in this book describe many of the causes and suggest steps that can—and must—be taken to change the situation. Here I will briefly sketch several of the more basic reasons for poverty.

1. *Powerlessness.* One of the underlying causes of poverty and hunger is the view held by many of the world's poor that they are victims of fate and there is little or nothing they can do to change their lot in life (their version of "You can't fight city hall"). Although this viewpoint is losing adherents, it is still widespread. The view is not irrational. It is rooted in extensive personal and collective suffering that over the centuries has produced a sense of powerlessness. As long as impoverished people look at life fatalistically or are prevented by others from taking steps that would enable them to improve their circumstances, they will remain powerless—and poor.

2. *Dependency.* Too often people and poor countries find themselves locked into a situation of permanent dependency on others. I am not objecting here to legitimate and growing forms of interdependence that increasingly characterize relations between people and nations. I am not suggesting, for example, that countries should not specialize in areas of comparative advantage, and trade with each other, or that they should produce only what they consume and consume only what they produce. I only want to emphasize that individuals as well as developing countries should use their own resources and ingenuity to the utmost. They may need assistance in order to develop those resources, but they should avoid inordinate and prolonged dependence on others. For developing countries "others" could mean other countries, financial institutions or transnational corporations, excessive dependence on whom is apt to skew their development efforts away from the meeting of basic human needs.

3. *Neglect of Agriculture.* If agriculture is given the emphasis it deserves, not only are people better fed, but the agricultural sector acts as a spur to the growth of related industries and provides a ready market for various products such as clothes, tools and furniture that can be produced domestically. That is the way industrial economies developed in the northern countries, and efforts so far to take short-cuts to industrial development by neglecting agriculture have failed impressively. Yet such neglect is

widespread in developing countries and its consequences are all too evident in the lives of poverty-stricken people. Another consequence is that the importing of grain by developing countries moved from scarcely a trickle in the early 1950's to about ninety-six million tons in 1981. The U.N. Food and Agriculture Organization (FAO) reports that the current trend would lead developing countries as a whole to import one hundred and eighty-five million tons of grain a year by the turn of the century. The trend is not expected to prevail, because the poorest half of the world cannot continue for long to increase food imports at the current rate. Meanwhile, the increases aggravate worldwide inflation, divert funds that should be used for internal development, and invite catastrophic famines during periods when global food production drops.

4. *Inequitable Growth.* In many developing countries, economic growth bypasses most of the poor, creating a prosperous elite but often leaving in its wake more hungry and impoverished people than before. Brazil, for example, experienced dramatic economic gains for almost two decades, but the disparity between the rich and the poor became more extreme. Not surprisingly, malnutrition is still widespread in Brazil.

5. *Unemployment.* A large portion of the poor and hungry of the world come from the swelling ranks of unemployed and underemployed people. The labor force in developing countries is growing much more rapidly than are available jobs. Related to this, the migration to the cities of rural families—often those without land or employment—continues unabated. This situation exists partly because developing countries often attempt to utilize more what they lack (capital) than what they have (an abundant supply of labor). In agriculture, as in industry, the failure to emphasize and improve small-scale, labor-intensive technologies, at least in the earlier stages of development, has been a costly mistake.

6. *Slow and/or Unsustainable Economic Growth.* Unsustainable growth is growth that fails to conserve a country's natural resources or to use its non-renewable resources in ways that will ensure the country's continued development after they are used up. Growth is also unsustainable if a country goes heavily into debt for development gains that in the long run cannot be supported or provide continued momentum to the economy. Yet

poor countries may feel under enormous pressure to incur such debts in order to avoid a sluggish growth rate. Although the *kind* of growth they engage in is the more important consideration, the rate of growth also makes a difference. In 1979, the World Bank projected several hypothetical economic growth rates for the developing countries as a whole and estimated the impact of each on the number of persons who would be living in absolute poverty by the year 2000:

Annual Growth Rate	Persons in Absolute Poverty by 2000
4.8%	710 million
5.6%	600 million
6.6%	470 million

There is nothing sacred about these projections. They do not take into account the differences between Brazil and Taiwan, for example. Brazil has a higher per capita income, but in proportion to the population it has three times as many people living in absolute poverty as does Taiwan. Changes in national policies can substantially affect the outcome no matter what the rate of economic growth. On balance, however, it would be foolish to ignore the difference that the rate of growth is apt to make regarding the incidence of hunger and poverty in developing countries.

As the chapter titles of this book indicate, there are significant causes of hunger that I have not mentioned. Without slighting them in the least, I want to elaborate on powerlessness as a cause of hunger and poverty because it is so easily overlooked and misunderstood.

People mired in poverty and hunger often need to begin thinking differently about themselves, their surroundings and the opportunities they could have for shaping the future. This changing awareness can and should take place with the encouragement of a government which, as the central characteristic of its development policy, sees its people as the nation's most valued resource, the end as well as the means of development. But real participation of the poor in their development involves a role in making decisions about their own and their nation's future. That kind of participation begins to shift some economic and political power toward them. Inescapably, those who have an economic or political stake in the status quo will find such a shift threatening. Consequently, it does not come about without controversy or political struggle. It does not, however, have to be understood in terms of an ideology or brought about by means of a revolution.

For example, on a recent visit to India I spent several days in some tribal villages about one hundred miles from Calcutta. The villages were gradually becoming small centers of production and their people were turning barren land into small productive plots by building irrigation systems. Next to one village was a huge reservoir that villagers had dug with hand tools as part of a food-for-work project. The villagers told me that a nearby landowner, who owns much more land than is legally permitted and who also serves as the local moneylender, tried, with a promise of water, to discourage them from digging the reservoir. They all owed him money. I asked them how much interest he charged. They replied by citing bags of rice and days of labor, which translated into interest rates ranging from two hundred to three hundred percent. Digging that reservoir and bringing barren land into production was a way of getting out from under the moneylender and moving up to an improved level of nutrition and poverty. In the process, they were also developing new self-esteem and economic power, as well as a stronger sense of community.

Events in Central America since 1979 remind us that where peaceful participation is impossible, violent revolution may become inevitable. Writing in *The New York Times Magazine* ("Guatemala: State of Siege," August 24, 1980), Alan Riding describes poverty in Guatemala:

> Some 350 people, who abandoned their shacks at the bottom of muddy ravines after the fierce February 1976 earthquake, now live in highly visible hovels beside a six-lane highway in Guatemala City. In the countryside, the Indians live in wooden huts with mud floors and no light or water, illiteracy reaches 80 percent, unemployment is chronic, infant mortality exceeds 100 per 1,000 live births, and four out of five children are undernourished. Generations of poor health have caused impaired eyesight and an above-normal rate of mental retardation, while babies are often born with tuberculosis, con-

tracted inside the womb from their mothers. The
Indians, according to a recent United Nations report,
are as poor as the poorest in Bangladesh, Somalia or
Haiti.

Riding reported that government repression combined with extreme poverty is moving politically passive Indians, who comprise fifty-five percent of Guatemala's population, to turn increasingly to those who see armed rebellion as the solution.
The lesson is clear: When participation of the poor is not permitted and peacefully encouraged, it may take the form of violence.
That is why a much more determined effort on the part of the
United States to help people overcome hunger and to avoid
strengthening governments that resist reforms toward that end
is not only ethically imperative, but in the interest of global security as well.

The overcoming of hunger and poverty depends predominantly on efforts made by and within each country. However,
crucial cooperative steps are possible and necessary on the part
of the United States and other prosperous nations. As special ses-
sions of the United Nations General Assembly have repeatedly
emphasized, developing countries want a "new international economic order." They want economic arrangements that more fairly take into account legitimate needs of poor countries and are
less weighted in favor of rich countries. The changes requested
include, among other things, more open markets from poor countries (so that the latter can increase employment and income)
and a sharp increase in development aid. The case for larger
transfers of resources to developing countries was made once
again in 1980 by a distinguished international commission under
the chairmanship of former West German chancellor, Willy
Brandt, in its report: *North-South: A Program for Survival* (Cambridge, MIT Press, 1980).

"Money is not the answer," many critics say, and they have
a point—though it is a response that I rarely hear critics apply to
themselves personally. In any case, what is at stake is not so
much the transfer of money as the extension of opportunities so
that people can work their own way out of hunger and poverty.
Because of the critical role that the United States plays in international affairs and the impact of this nation's policies on pover-

ty and hunger abroad, U.S. Christians have a special responsibility and a special opportunity to let their voices be heard in the halls of Congress and across the land on behalf of hungry people.

3
Tradition

Kristen Wenzel, O.S.U.

Tradition connotes passing and continuity. Ways of thinking and acting are passed down generation to generation so that some continuity becomes characteristic of those thought and behavior patterns.

What do we eat and how do we eat it? The "what" suggests inclusion and exclusion of elements in a traditional diet. The "how" relates to traditional ways of growing, harvesting, hunting, fishing, slaughtering, cooking and consuming food.

Where traditions are strongest, the inclusions and exclusions are most rigidly observed.[1] So also are the accompanying efficiencies or inefficiencies of the preparation process, together with an openness or foreclosure relative to mechanical, chemical and biological food-production technology.

Every culture experiences the development and decline of traditions. Not all traditions deserve to survive and thus sustain what might well be life-diminishing behavior. Some good traditions experience a lamentable decline and thus the culture loses a sustaining force for humanly progressive and life-enriching behavior. The "Fiddler on the Roof" quite rightly celebrates the beauty of tradition. On the other hand, the starving child in India wonders why there are so many sacred cows and so little milk for him or her. Because of tradition, cows are kept alive beyond their producing capacity. However, tradition is neither all good nor all bad. Unfortunately, an analysis of the causes of hunger forces us to face up to a great deal of negative impact that traditions can have on the chronically malnourished of our world.

This chapter will consider both the positive and the negative impact of tradition on (1) the production and distribution of food, (2) the consumption of food, (3) the position of women relative to food availability, (4) the acceptance of technology, and (5) necessary land reform, and a concluding consideration will be given to religious tradition and its relationship to the world hunger issue.

The Production and Distribution of Food. Needless to say, one of the oldest and most prevalent ways of dealing with this economic challenge has been tradition. It has been "a mode of social organization in which both production and distribution were based on procedures devised in the distant past, rigidified by a long process of historic trial and error, and maintained by heavy sanctions of law, custom, and belief."[2] For example, laws of inheritance have assured these societies that land, the necessary skills and the motivation to work to produce and provide adequate food for one's family would be passed along to the next generation. Consequently, societies based on tradition have been able to deal quite adequately with the production of food.

Where the majority of people in a given society are responsible for feeding themselves and their own families from the crops produced on their respective lands, the question of adequate distribution is not as serious. Even where the need for the distribution of food is more extensive, tradition has provided a functional role in regulating it. An unquestioning acceptance of traditional ways often provides the necessary motivation and perseverance to accept and confront such problems as periodic drought and crop losses from pests. Certain customs and beliefs can provide an important mechanism for holding hunger in check in selected areas of the world.

However, the means by which traditional societies "solve" the problem of food production and distribution is a static one.[3] Societies which adhere to tradition in managing food production and in regulating its distribution forego progress that could come with large-scale economic change. Internal, self-generated change in food production and distribution is very limited among traditional societies when faced with the harsh realities of chronic malnutrition and starvation. Such societies are at the mercy of external events—climate, world trade market, Westernization—for determining whether they will face fortune or misfortune in feeding their people. Certain elements of tradition can contribute but other dimensions hinder economic progress in overcoming current problems regarding available food supplies. The challenge that faces us today is to identify and work to change those beliefs and customs which seriously inhibit food production and distribution and thus cause this perpetuation of hunger in those societies influenced by such traditions. On the other hand, traditions that help certain societies to deal effectively with hunger should be highlighted, retained, and/or reinstated.

The Consumption of Food. The consumption of food is found to be influenced, if not actually determined, by all types of traditions of what is and is not acceptable for human nourishment. To outsiders of a given culture, often these proscriptions seem quite irrational when evaluated from the perspective of health and nutrition. Unfortunately, these beliefs and customs of what can and cannot be eaten are most influential in those areas of the world where hunger and malnutrition are most prevalent.

In northern Kenya, for example, stocking fish in Lake Turkana has helped to stabilize a certain number of nomadic people because it has given them a stable source of income. However, it has not changed their eating patterns. The Turkana people continue to eat camel's blood and goat's milk which keep them alive, but because of tradition they will not eat the fish and so they send it south. Now with the drought the camels and goats are dying and blood and milk are scarce. Even with all of the professional assistance, these people continue to refuse to eat the fish which would introduce protein into their diet.

In Nigeria, the goat is highly valued by the wealthy and the poor alike. It is associated with festivity, prestige, honor and winning favor. It is the goat that is killed and consumed for festive occasions and for religious ceremonies. Since the sacrificing of the goat is such an integral part of ritual, any goat that is available, whether it is healthy or diseased with brucellosis or anthrax, will be killed and eaten. These diseases are fatal if humans become infected.

We see, therefore, the strong traditional dimension associated with the consumption of food. Where the basic diet is not nu-

tritious or the eating of certain foods can be a health risk,
tradition contributes to maintaining hunger and malnutrition
and widespread sickness. Efforts to deal with the underlying
causes of hunger must take into serious consideration the extent
to which tradition is the underlying cause for the resistance to
"rational" change.

The Position of Women Relative to Food Availability. If the
situation of the hungry and undernourished peoples of the world
is to be improved, it is essential not only to increase the overall
availability of food supplies as well as their more equitable distribution, but also to ensure that this food is eaten by those who
need it most. Unfortunately, it is status that often affects not
only the quantity but also the quality of food available to people.
By status we mean the socio-economic class you are born into or
achieve on your own, whether you happen to be female or male
or twenty-five or sixty-five years of age. The more scarce food is,
the more status determines its availability. Here tradition often
functions as the preserver of the status quo. This is particularly
devastating for women throughout the world.

The low social and economic status given to women is at the
root of much of the hunger and malnutrition that exists in the
world today. As second-class citizens, they get mainly the "left-
overs" in terms of available food, wage-paying jobs, and land to
grow crops for local consumption. Not only do women get less,
but they have been "educated" to want and expect less than men
in terms of education, work opportunities and corresponding
wages and even food and diet. Better education, jobs and wages
would put women in a more effective bargaining position for decent food and a more adequate diet. That most of the world's
hungry are female has widespread implications for our efforts to
reduce world hunger.[4]

Traditionally, in American culture, women are associated
with the preparation of food. Despite the many positive influences that have been affected by the women's movement, they
are still chained to tradition in the sense that they find themselves presented with a cultural double message:

> We are to purchase and prepare food, but we are not to
> eat it—at least not too much of it! We are expected to

make food as delicious and appealing as possible, yet we are expected to maintain the slim, firm figures that are pictured in magazines, on TV, and in the movies.[5]

Consequently, many American women have developed very ambivalent feelings about food because it is fraught with conflicting cultural messages. Such ambivalence hinders women in many of the developed nations where this message prevails from taking the food issue seriously and uniting with women from underdeveloped countries to reduce widespread hunger and malnutrition among the female population of the world.

There is no doubt that tradition as it affects the status of women and prevents them from sharing equally the food that is available is a serious underlying cause for the continuation of world hunger. Traditionally, in many cultures, adult women and young girls do not begin their own meal until they are sure that the men and boys have been adequately fed, and it is expected that the women and girls will take less if there is not enough to go around. This intra-familial way of distributing food is very problematic. Even where tradition is effective in reducing hunger and malnutrition and in encouraging breast feeding babies and locally grown infant foods, tradition functions differently for boys and girls. For example, in Kashmir, as is true in many Muslim areas, girl babies will nurse for eight to ten months while a boy baby will do so for three years or perhaps longer. Consequently, malnutrition rates are considerably higher for girls than for boys in many areas of India.[6]

The following poem, written by an Indian named Appadura, concludes one of the chapters of the Report of the Presidential Commission on World Hunger:

Decide, mother,
who goes without.
Is it Rama, the strongest,
or Baca, the weakest
who may not need it much longer
or perhaps Sita?
Who may be expendable?

Decide, mother;
kill a part
of yourself
As you resolve the dilemma.

Decide, mother,
decide
and hate.[7]

This poem reflects a point made by the report that hunger and malnutrition affect female and male members of society differently. As with the girl Sita, traditionally women are viewed to be expendable when there are food shortages.

The traditional attitude toward women, even when not harshly shown, affects the world hunger situation by the force of its own inertia. Habit and fear of change provide the direction of maintaining the status quo. Equality, development and peace, the triple goals of the United Nations Decade for Women, will not be realized until major steps are taken to redirect the role and function of tradition as it adversely affects women's potential involvement in the development process[8] for reducing world hunger.

The Acceptance of Technology. What does the acceptance of technology mean to us? Computers which frustrate us in our efforts to get a bill corrected or a simple basic service performed? Increased mechanization which subjects us to labor strikes and subsequent higher prices? Disillusionment with the green revolution or farming with chemicals and their failed technological solution?[9] If this is our attitude and feeling toward the acceptance of technology, justifiably we raise the question: Then why change tradition? A culture's resistance to introducing technology can be either positive or negative in its effect and whether this will be functional or dysfunctional for a society in coping with hunger ultimately depends upon the type of technology that is introduced.

There is a type of high technology which proves to be successful in the developed societies. Often the technology is good but not appropriate for underdeveloped or developing countries, and consequently it does not have the same effect when introduced in third world countries. This is the story, for example, with the green revolution in certain regions of India, Pakistan and Mexico. Often this technology is imposed on a country without any adaptation. Western nations espouse the type of technology that will "trickle down" to the masses, whereas third world countries support the type of technology that will meet the basic human needs of the masses of people in a country through strategies directed to the particular human and natural resources, values and traditions of that country.[10]

There is an intermediate level of technology, defined as "appropriate" technology which is a technology most suitably adapted to the conditions of a given situation and which is compatible with the human, financial and material resources that affect its application.[11] This principle implies that land and other agricultural resources would be used first to produce adequate and nutritious local staples and, secondarily, industrial crops, livestock feed crops and non-essential vegetables and fruits. Here the native people are the agents of development and production.

> The choice of an appropriate technology must consider that in every culture, there is a complex interweaving of many different aspects of life, and any particular change will affect the whole. An approach which looks only at purely technical aspects would neglect the dynamic interrelationships among *the technology* in whatever form it takes, *the users* of the technology and their attitudes and values, the *resource base* of the region, and the *economic and political structures* surrounding the other factors.[12]

To speak of the users' attitudes and values and the economic and political structures is to express a sensitivity to tradition and the critical role it plays in determining the ultimate success or failure of technology in reducing world hunger.

Necessary Land Reform. The usual example of the relationship between land reform and food production tends to cite a situation of highly concentrated ownership (the very rich own most of the arable land) and a widely dispersed landless peasantry. The dominant rich prefer to produce grapes for wine, or coffee for export, instead of grain to feed the poor. Sometimes, the wealthy and powerful let vast tracts of arable land lie idle and thus open themselves to the charge of "unjust activity" leveled by Pope John Paul II at Oaxaca, Mexico in 1979, as he condemned the rich classes who often leave untilled the lands in which lay hidden the bread that families need.

Land reform, in the sense of the breaking-up of large land holdings, requires a break with traditions as well—traditional inheritance patterns and the traditional tendency in some places to absolutize the right to the possession of private property. The traditional absence of penalty for failing to put private lands to uses that serve the common good would also call for remedy.

Patterns of landholding and land use are greatly influenced by cultural beliefs, religious traditions and political ideologies as well as by climate conditions and economic forces. Cultural influence on the relationship of land to its people is significant throughout the world. In Ethiopia, land is owned communally in the Governorate General of Begemedir and Semien. The rights to the land are shared collectively based on common descent from "Akni Abat," the founding father of this area. Consequently, family land is held by members of the extended family. It may not be given as a gift or sold, only inherited by heirs.[13] In Latin American countries most of the land is held by wealthy individuals who, numerically, are a small minority. Tenant relationships are more common in Asia and the Middle East. In Africa, however, the common traditional pattern of group ownership and communal rights is being replaced by individual land ownership that continues to gain acceptance.[14]

There are many cultures and traditions the world over that contribute to the many variations in ownership and control that exist. Consequently, no general formula for land reform can be applied to the developing nations. There is no question that land reform is necessary in order to assure the masses in poor nations of adequate as well as proper food. However, when considering land reform in the context of the world hunger issue, tradition is only one of several factors that must be studied.

Religious Tradition and Its Relationship to the World Hunger Issue. An integral element of tradition is the religious beliefs that shape it. Here we are concerned not so much with the religious beliefs of the peoples suffering from hunger and malnutrition but rather with the religious norms and values of those who are in a position to do something about reducing world hunger. To be deprived of the necessities of life, such as food, is seen, in the Christian tradition, as an evil. Those who are deprived are suffering violations of their dignity. We, as Christians, are called not only to examine the ways in which we as sinners might be inflicting or at least contributing to such deprivation, but also how we must deal with and try to reduce this evil in the world.

Traditionally, the working to overcome hunger has been a matter of charity. Here, as Christians, we are called to take and give from our abundance. Where our response to world hunger is one of charity, we are acting out of a tradition that must be seriously re-examined and challenged. We propose that working to overcome hunger, to get at its underlying causes, presupposes that we loosen ourselves from this bond of tradition and see that, as Christians, hunger is no longer a matter of charity, but rather an issue of justice.[15] No longer do we have the option but rather the duty, in the spirit of justice, to work to overcome this injustice, this evil in today's world.

The next chapter deals with "theological underdevelopment" as a cause of world hunger. It develops more fully my final point and invites contemporary Christians to move their tradition forward to touch the hunger issue directly and effectively. Beliefs become a part of the very traditions they maintain. But beliefs can also move traditions forward. The Christian faith, developed theologically and applied courageously, thus holds out hope for the hungry poor. However, the Christian tradition will not reach the heart of the hunger problem unless an authentically Christian understanding of justice reaches the minds and hearts of Christians.

NOTES

1. For a comprehensive and systematic analysis of tradition see Edward Shils, *Tradition,* Chicago: University of Chicago Press, 1981.

2. Robert L. Heilbroner, *The Making of Economic Society,* Englewood Cliffs, New Jersey: Prentice-Hall, Inc., 1962, pp. 9–10.

3. *Ibid.,* p. 12.

4. Barbara Howell, "Women in Development," Background Paper #29 published by Bread for the World, November 1978, p. 1.

5. Jane Rachel Kaplan, *A Woman's Conflict: The Special Relationship Between Women and Food,* Englewood Cliffs, New Jersey: Prentice Hall, Inc., 1980, p. 2

6. Mary Roodkowsky, "Underdevelopment Means Double Jeopardy for Women," *Food Monitor* (September/October 1979), p. 9.

7. "Overcoming World Hunger: The Challenge Ahead," Report of the Presidential Commission on World Hunger. Published by the Presidential Commission on World Hunger, Washington, D.C., March 1980, p. 18.

8. For a good resource on women's participation in the development process see *Women in a Hungry World* Study/Action Kit, World Hunger/Global Development Project. Published by the American Friends Service Committee, New York, 1979.

9. Rene Dumont and Nicholas Cohen, *The Growth of Hunger,* Salem, New Hampshire: Marion Boyars, Inc., 1980, pp. 166–184.

10. James B. McGinnis, *Bread and Justice: Toward a New International Economic Order,* New York: Paulist Press, 1980, pp. 257–261.

11. *A Handbook on Appropriate Technology,* Ottawa, Ontario: Canadian Hunger Foundation, 1979, p. A1.

12. *Ibid.,* pp. A2 and A3.

13. Douglas Ensminger and Paul Bomani, *Conquest of World Hunger and Poverty,* Ames, Iowa: The Iowa State University Press, 1980, pp. 75–76.

14. *Ibid.,* p. 77.

15. McGinnis, *op. cit.,* pp. 21–26.

4
Theological Underdevelopment and Ethical Insensitivity

Edward J. Brady, S.J.

"When I touch the body of the poor, I touch the body of Christ." Mother Teresa of Calcutta said that. She also believes it! It is a theological statement inviting assent from believers throughout the world. When that worldwide assent of faith comes, the problem of hunger will be no more!

Regrettably, however, most of the world's Christians see hunger as a secular problem only. They fail to see, with the eye of faith, Christ present and suffering in the hungry poor. Those Christians are underdeveloped theologically; they are also ethically insensitive.

They recognize the importance of charity. And it is somehow etched in their minds that "charity begins at home." But they do not understand Dom Helder Camara, the archbishop of Recife, Brazil, when he says that "the great charity of our times consists in helping promote justice." For most Christians, hunger is a "charity" issue, not a question of justice. Their theological understanding needs broadening and deepening. By theology, I mean an exercise of understanding and reflection on Sacred Scripture, particularly those passages that touch our daily lives. We read: "Lord, when did we see you hungry?" in St. Matthew's Gospel (25:37). Assimilation of that text and its application to daily life is what I mean by theology.

Is hunger a charity issue only? No, it belongs in the area of justice—justice understood in the biblical sense of fidelity to Yahweh, to community, to self. The word "charity" in the Bible, particularly in the New Testament, is in most instances synonymous with "love." But this meaning is not carried over to the remark that "hunger is a charity issue," where charity means giving, if so inclined, from abundance, from whatever may be left over after personal needs and preferences are attended to. The once beautiful word "charity" is debased to a level of meaning synonymous with "dole."

Of course, emergency food assistance, relief shipments and similar donations are critically important in times of famine, flood, earthquake and similar disasters. But the deeper problem of chronic hunger which reduces the life chances of millions—probably five hundred million suffering people in the world today—is not touched by emergency relief efforts. Arthur Simon's chapter in this book shows that poverty is the basic cause of the sustained undernutrition suffered by hungry people throughout the developing world and even in pockets of deprivation in the economically advanced nations. Food aid will not get at this basic cause of hunger. More equitable economic and political relationships are needed in order to get at poverty, the basic cause of our problem. These relationships must be seen and spoken of in terms of justice. Christians face a moral obligation to do all they can to set these relationships straight. This obligation will not be felt in the absence of reflection on the biblical roots of this idea.

The Old Testament presents care for the poor and oppressed in terms of justice. In Isaiah 58:1–10, the prophet is to "declare to my people their transgressions," for "they ask me for righteous judgments. . . . Behold, in the day of your fast you . . . oppress all your workers. . . . Is not this the fast I choose . . . to let the oppressed go free and to break every yoke? Is it not to share your bread with the hungry?"

The Old Testament writers did not speculate about the nature of justice. They recorded concrete instances of justice and injustice in the lives of people. Modern scholarship locates justice as a central theme of Scripture but recognizes its relatedness to other themes like truth, loving mercy and fidelity to the covenant. The Bible, it should be noted, invites a living response to

Yahweh; it does not encourage philosophical speculation. In Old Testament usage, the word *sedaquah,* "justice," means "fidelity to the demands of a relationship."

> In contrast to modern individualism the Israelite is in a world where "to live" is to be united with others in a social context either by bonds of family or by covenant relationships. This web of relationships—king with people, judge with complainants, family with tribe and kinfolk, the community with the resident alien and suffering in their midst and all with the covenant God—constitutes the world in which life is played out. The demands of the differing relationships cannot be specified a priori but must be seen in the different settings of Israel's history.[1]

The just person of the Old Testament is depicted often in the Psalms, in Proverbs and the Book of Job. In the Psalms we see that Yahweh rewards according to justice (Ps 18:20). The justice of the individual is depicted in Psalm 112. In Proverbs and Job, the just one is a good steward of land and work animals (Jb 31:13) and particularly one who cares for the poor, the fatherless and the widow (Prov 29:7; Jb 29:12–15).

The justice of God is his fidelity to his role as Lord of the covenant (Ps 7:9; 71:2; 103:17). "But the steadfast love of the Lord is from everlasting to everlasting upon those who fear him, and his righteousness to children's children, to those who keep his covenant and remember to do his commandments" (Ps 103:17).

Both Jeremiah (22:1–3, 13, 15–16) and Isaiah (58:6–7) are quite clear that doing justice means being faithful to one's relationships to the poor, the needy, and the alien. In fact, the marginals of society are the scale on which the justice of the whole society is judged. When the poor and oppressed are exploited, then the whole society has no true relationship with Yahweh. "I take no delight in your solemn assemblies. . . . But let justice roll down like waters, and righteousness like an everflowing stream." These are the words Yahweh spoke through Amos, urging his people to live justly so that their worship would be pleasing to him (Am 5:21–24).

In the several hundred years before the time of Christ, the

notion of justice took on a more individualistic meaning as opposed to the communitarian meaning of the earlier centuries. Also, the word *sedaquah* shifted to embrace "almsgiving," which is seen as a "proper relationship" to the poor and needy. Further, the situation of exile and foreign domination brought with it the expectation that true justice is only to be expected at the end time. These notions are important, since they contributed to the body of meaning of the word "justice" in the time of Jesus and his first followers.

Turning now to the New Testament, the main point to note about justice is its personification in Jesus Christ, "the just one" (Acts 3:14; 7:52). The works of Jesus are seen as works of justice (Mt 18:23–24). Particular attention is to be paid to Matthew's last judgment scene, in that the "unjust" are condemned not because they did not know what justice demanded, but because they did not know to whom they should do the works of justice, namely to the marginals and oppressed of society, to the hungry and those in prison. In the New Testament as the Old, caring for the marginals of society is a matter of justice.

For Paul, justification is a key theme that flows from the suffering, death and resurrection of Christ. Justification is a free gift to the individual who believes; such justification is not without its social dimension. The "Second Adam" theme in Romans 5 and 1 Corinthians 15 shows that the result of justification has to do with more than the individual. Justification means incorporation into a new social structure, the body of Christ (1 Cor 12; Rom 12:1–8) and the household of the faith (Gal 6:10).

> The faith that justifies is the faith which leads to knowledge of Jesus Christ—a knowledge which involves persons sharing in the life and death of Jesus. The life and death of Jesus is his emptying (Phil 2:5–11), his renunciation of grasping and the giving of his life for others. Therefore, the justice of God which comes from faith in Jesus is fidelity to the demands of a relationship—the relationship that the Christian is to have with Christ by being "in Christ" (over 165 times in Paul) and putting on Christ and the mind of Christ. Kasemann describes well this Christological aspect of justifying faith: "Justification is the stigmatization of our worldly existence

through the crucified Christ. Through us and in us he simultaneously reaches out toward the world to which we
belong."[2]

In both his Gospel and Acts, Luke intended to present to early Christians a paradigm for living in their everyday environments. Of all the evangelists, Luke has Jesus sounding most like
an Old Testament prophet in his condemnation of the rich (Lk
6:20) and wealth itself (Lk 12:16; 14:33). In fact, Luke is seen as
the evangelist most interested in what today is called "social justice."

John R. Donahue has been my guide in this biblical reflection, and I turn to him for a summary:

The cause of the poor, the hungry and the oppressed is
now the cause of Jesus. He is the Son of Man, present in
the least of his brethren. Christians are called on to bear
one another's burdens. This is to fulfill the law of Christ,
to be a just people.

Engagement in the quest of justice is no more "secular"
than the engagement of Yahweh in the history of his
people or the incarnation of Jesus into the world of human suffering. The Bible gives a mandate and a testament to Christians that, in their quest for justice, they
are recovering the roots of the biblical tradition and are
seeking to create a dwelling place for the word of God in
human history.[3]

Discussion, prayer, reflection and theological development
along these lines must happen in the contemporary Christian
community if hunger is to be overcome. We have a mandate,
nothing less, to eliminate this scourge from the face of the earth.

Scriptural scholarship suggests that the biblical notion of
justice involves fidelity to the demands of a relationship between
persons, groups and their God. How are these relationships to become real and concrete in our lives? This is the role of Christian
ethics.

In general, ethics deals with the human dimensions of the
given situation, what is "good" or "bad" in terms of what is the

human thing to do. Several different ethical systems are at work in the U.S. today. They stress in varying degrees the value components of self-interest (dignity of the self), social responsibility (responsibility for others), and social vision (the way the future of society is cared for). These various systems differ one from the other according to what each holds as most important of these three major values. For example, the ethic which underlies our present-day competitive economic system holds personal self-interest as the major "good" to be achieved. In such a system, striving for one's own self-interest will provide for the "good" of society. The experience of several hundred years of industrialization shows the shortcomings of this system, yet the self-interest theory in one or another form affects the lives of many in our society.[4]

Among such value systems, the unique contribution of Christian ethics is "the identification of the moral ideal with an historical person, the transformation of ethical theory into concrete terms in a real human life. . . ."[5] Christ, his person and his actions are the norm, the model for Christian ethical thought and action.

As there are various ethical systems present in our culture, so too are there various meanings of the term "justice." Taking the classical notion that justice means "to each his own" (*suum cuique*), we find that different philosophers interpreted these words according to circumstances of time and place. For Plato, the phrase called for persons within a particular society to respect the structured system of roles, offices and powers in society. For Aristotle, "to each his own" was a call to respect some form of excellence, achievement or merit. For John Locke, justice meant a call to respect what belongs to each person, namely, property. A contemporary North American, John Rawls, sees the term meaning a demand for equal liberty and opportunity. All of these meanings influence how we, as Americans, understand the notion of justice.

So when Christians say concern for the hungry is a matter of justice, care is needed that biblical language not be used to make an absolute of one's own way of defining justice from one's own cultural preferences. A major task for Christian ethics is developing and refining the notion of justice from a Christian perspective.

When we say that we as Christians are obliged to act justly in our relationships with the poor and needy of the world, what sort of "right relationships" are we talking about?

We know we are not speaking about the individual relationships of the marketplace—for example, purchasing a new coat. We are obliged in justice to pay for the coat. In this situation, we say that between us and the person selling the coat there is a relationship in justice.

As citizens, we pay taxes so that community services which we as individuals cannot perform, or perform only with great difficulty, are done by civic authorities. Such is the rationale for public fire and police protection, mail service, libraries and the like. The authorities are bound to see that these services are performed; we are bound to pay taxes to support them. It is *not* this type of relationship I have in mind in this essay.

The type of justice the Bible speaks of in dealing with the poor and oppressed is that which deals with relationships of individuals and groups within the larger community. Some scholars call this "social justice." The Bible is clear that the right relationships of the community extend to the widow, the orphan, the poor, the stranger, the oppressed (Jer 22:1–2). Of particular interest is the reference to the "stranger." Today's "stranger" to many of us American Christians can well be the millions on the planet who are severely undernourished.

The last judgment scene in Matthew 25 speaks of the hungry and imprisoned without community or racial distinction.

Further, the obligation to help the needy and hungry of the earth when based on the value of human solidarity—our common origins, common habitat and destiny[6]—can readily be integrated with the biblical tradition of humanity's common origin in God (Gen 1–2) and common destiny in Christ (1 Tim 2:4: "God wills the salvation of all").

The Bible speaks of helping the poor and needy in terms of justice. Justice deals with obligation and responsibility. How responsible are individual Christians for the massive under-nutrition on the globe? How responsible are Christian communities, denominations, groups acting ecumenically across denominational lines for the poverty and oppression that are basic to the hunger problem?

This question deserves to be faced as truthfully as possible.

To say one is responsible is not to concede that one is necessarily guilty. Set all guilt aside and the question remains: Just how responsible are we? How responsive can we be?

Obviously, no answer can be given to such a question until it is fleshed out in the particular terms of who is in need, where, and in what condition of need. I do think that one important key to the answer is found in the very word "responsibility." "Responsibility" is a combination of "ability" and "response." One of its root meanings is "the ability to respond." The question then becomes how I (or we) can respond to this particular need, to this particular situation.

There are many instances when I can respond, and thus am responsible. To the person in my neighborhood or town who needs immediate food assistance, I can give food. To persons on fixed income who need more state or federal assistance to help them make ends meet, I can join with others to lobby for better legislation. To undernourished persons in low income countries, I can respond by identifying private voluntary groups which are effective and support them, and I can become a citizen advocate for better federal programs and projects to attack the root causes of such under-nutrition. These are some of the types of responses that can and are being given to help eradicate the problem of hunger.

My responsibility lies in my ability to respond to the specific situation. My response must take into consideration my other responsibilities and admit of priorities to those who have greater claims on me, by reason of the same web of relationships that bind me to my "neighbor" up the street or across the globe.

At times, the truth of the situation is that I am effectively unable to respond. Recall Kampuchea (Cambodia) in the fall of 1979, when the American public became aware that hundreds of thousands of Cambodians were severely undernourished and that thousands were literally starving. Food stuffs were available on the Thai borders; some trickle of food was being allowed into the country. The political reality of the world was such that the food was not being allowed to reach those who were starving. How responsible for that were you? How effectively could you respond to those starving people at that time in Kampuchea? We as Christians may be able to name a reality as an unjust structure, a sinful situation. But the naming of the reality does not take away the fact that we were, for all practical purposes, powerless to do anything to help all those starving and undernourished people. Steps were possible to help some of the starving but not all. That was the tragic reality of the situation.

Our inability to respond to a given situation touches upon the reality of powerlessness and sinfulness in our world and in our individual lives. It also forces us to hope in Christ, who died, was raised from the dead and is at the right hand of the Father, interceding for us (Rom 8:34). Confounded by the mystery of Christ suffering in our world and by my own powerlessness and sinfulness, I also look to the Christ of the resurrection. I then know that this state of pilgrimage, with its ambiguities, injustices and sinfulness, leads in faith to that state when "the first earth had passed away. . . . He (Yahweh) will dwell with them, and they shall be his people; he will wipe away every tear from their eyes, and death shall be no more, neither shall there be mourning nor crying nor pain anymore" (Rev 21:1–4).

I am humbled by my own limitations and that of my fellows. Yet, in Christ, I am empowered to be and to do. Addressing the question of human limitations and cooperation with God, Augustine said, "God does not command the impossible, but in command advises one to do what one is able, to pray for what one is not able, and he will assist one to do what one should."[7]

Not only does faith tell me that Christ is in those who suffer. Hope tells me that Christ is in all of us who strive to work out the Lord's redemption in our lives and in our world.

If it takes faith to see Christ in the hungry, and hope to avoid despair at times over our inability to touch him there, it will take a new understanding of the link between faith and justice to provide a strong moral mandate to work for the elimination of hunger in our world.

Christian ethicians of various denominations are currently trying to clarify how justice and faith interact in our world. Summarizing the Roman Catholic tradition of Christian ethics, David Hollenbach writes:

> In all the documents of the tradition, then, the theory of justice is rooted in a philosophical view of the nature of the person as essentially social, and simultaneously in any explicitly Christian notion of love as mutuality and

as a response to persons in the concrete, especially those in need. . . .

> What is just, that is, what is *due* to a person or group, is to be determined by the kinds of relationships which shape and influence the life and action of that person or group. Human dignity—the fact that human beings are not things or mere means—always exists within these various concrete relationships. The justice or injustice of these relationships is to be judged in terms of the way they promote human dignity by enhancing mutuality and genuine participation in community or, put negatively, by the way they abuse human dignity by reifying persons and excluding or marginalizing them from the relationships without which humanity withers.[8]

Scholars of Christian ethics note the need for a developing sensitivity and better understanding of how Christian principles are applied, "lest the imitation of Christ . . . descend to a mere antiquarian hero worship, disguising a moral retrogression from modern life and duty into a profitless nostalgia for a lost age." This continuous development is found in "the dynamic presence of the Spirit . . . the on-going source of Christian morality and the form of the contemporary Christ in the experience of believers."[9]

We have already looked to scriptural scholarship for development of the notion that hunger is a justice issue. Now we look to the "contemporary Christ in the experience of believers." We look in particular to those Christians who, as individuals or groups, foster "right relationships" between themselves, their community and their God by acting in faith and acting for justice.

I began this chapter by recalling the words of Mother Teresa, "When I touch the body of the poor, I touch the body of Christ." These words point to the faith experience of countless Christians across the denominational spectrum who are active in one or other aspect of combating the hunger problem. For the Christian, hunger is about the person of Christ, who suffers in the hungry. "Whenever you did it to one of these . . ." (Mt 25).

This person-focus is not just a matter of a faith preference. The hunger problem is a people problem that not only touches the lives of the millions of severely undernourished living today, but also reaches into the lives of generations to come. The poverty cycle is a "people" cycle. Persons with years of field experience point to this "people" focus as a necessary criterion by which to judge the feasibility and practicality of various development theories of aid and trade. It is too easy to discuss food aid, its good and bad points, in the sterile atmosphere of statistical analysis and cost benefits. Such an atmosphere also allows the "specialists" to plan in isolation from the people involved how such aid should—or should not—be used. More and more, persons in food deficit countries are demanding to plan their own initiatives.[10] They, the people, are not mere objects of statistical analysis or of planned socio-political programs of development. They are demanding their right to be the subjects and planners of their own future. A "people first" approach to questions of aid and trade is a perspective that the food deficit nations are increasingly and rightly demanding.

Although there is a growing awareness among American Christians that we as individuals and as groups should "act justly" in our relationships with the poor and oppressed on our planet, the question can be asked: Why has such thinking and acting not taken place sooner and is not more widespread? John Haughey, editor of *The Faith That Does Justice,* asks that question and responds by saying that Christians have not, by and large, made the connection between the person of Jesus and the justice issue. For many, being a good individual Christian involves many things, but it does not involve matters of social justice related to persons in our inner cities or halfway around the globe.

In order that our awareness of the justice aspects of our Christian living be made more vital in our lives, Haughey suggests that we as individuals and as Christian communities need to "re-image" Jesus, that is, we need to realize anew how Jesus related to the needs of his times. He adds that in addition to studying the Christ of the Scriptures, we need to discover "that which is true about the risen Lord as he reveals himself to the contemporary community of believers united to him in the Spirit. What is being re-imaged, in other words, is not only the Christ who was but who is now."[11]

So now we look to the activities of Christians confronting the hunger problem to learn something of the "Christ who is now." From such a study we hope to get at least some initial outlines of how Christian individuals and groups are being forged into the fullness of Jesus, the justice of God.

In areas of domestic under-nutrition, church groups, along with others, are fostering emergency feeding programs and the "right relationships" that can change food delivery systems. By and large, persons are undernourished in the U.S. because they can't buy the food they need. Therefore, arrangements like food co-ops and producer-consumer "tail-gate" marketing are becoming common. In many large urban areas, church groups are prominent among those who are attempting to change legislation to benefit those on low fixed income and welfare.

Turning to the international scene, many Christian denominations have personnel working directly with local communities in food-related projects. Research into the effectiveness of people-centered development efforts indicates that the smaller, private groups, many of which are Church-related, can expect a higher rate of success in meeting local community needs than can the larger, government-sponsored efforts.

The majority of U.S. Christians relate to the globe's undernourished through the various hunger appeals, many of which are sponsored by the various Christian denominations. But there are other actions that groups of U.S. Christians are doing that aim at fostering "right relationships" on behalf of the hungry. Two initiatives come readily to mind—that of the Interfaith Center for Corporate Responsibility (ICCR) and of Bread for the World (BFW). The ICCR fosters ethical business practices among large corporations which impact upon the lives of the poor both in the U.S. and abroad. Among its initiatives is one that seeks, in cooperation with other like-minded groups, to effect some needed changes in infant formula marketing practices in Africa and Latin America. While the concern still continues, a relatively small group of Christians, joined with others, has been able to effect some change for the better. Perhaps more importantly, their efforts have helped show to all of us some points of linkage between the American consumer and multi-national practices abroad.

Bread for the World invites U.S. Christians to use their citizenship to affect federal policies and practices aimed at helping the hungry, both in the U.S. and overseas. The strategy of BFW is that U.S. Christians become "citizen advocates for the hungry" by becoming grass-roots lobbyists on specific pieces of federal legislation. The members, now numbering over 40,000, are kept informed through monthly newsletters and urged to form local networks to contact their elected representatives on specific pieces of legislation. This system of grass-roots lobbying has shown itself to be effective. Pieces of legislation such as the "Right to Food" resolution bear the direct imprint of BFW membership. In the summer of 1980, the supplemental allocations of federal funds for food and development projects for Kampuchea and West Africa were influenced, in part at least, by BFW members.

The ICCR and BFW are not unique. The Interreligious Task Force and a number of research groups that have denominational funding could also be described. From all such initiatives, one can notice that U.S. Christians are joining forces across denominational lines to help foster "right relationships" among U.S. Christians and the poor and oppressed, both domestic and overseas. We can speak of these movements as part of the new "image" of the risen Christ, "revealing himself to the contemporary community of believers."

However the new image of the risen Christ is being revealed, Christians know that shared actions among themselves will be rooted in a shared Christian identity. The enduring symbol of that identity is found in an action of Christ and the early Christian communities which has served both as a norm and an inspiration for Christians down the centuries. It can serve as a basis for actions for justice in this age of massive undernutrition. I would like to propose now in some detail the various meal ministries of the Lord Jesus as a rich source of reflection for us as individual Christians. My hope, too, is that they will provide a basis for building common Christian actions, both within specific denominations as well as in ecumenical settings such as Bread for the World.

It was while sharing a meal that the Lord performed many of his miracles, multiplying the loaves and fishes, healing, and driving out devils. It was at the supper the night before he died that the Lord washed the feet of his disciples; it was there at table that he broke the bread and shared the cup of the new covenant. And it was in the same meal setting after the resurrection that the apostles and disciples came to know the risen Lord. These are high points in the Lord's life of care and concern.

Around Christ's table, and that of the early Christian communities, there were no distinctions of rich or poor, slave or free (1 Cor 10). All, sinners and faithful followers alike, were treated with the respect due God's people.

We also note that the meal itself is an act of community, a mutual sharing at which all are welcome because all are related in some way to Christ.

These two characteristics, human dignity and mutual participation in building the community, are prominent in Jesus' meal ministry. These two points Christian ethicians hold up as the mainstays of a just relationship, i.e., respect for human dignity and the building of community.[12] Thus the meal fellowship of Jesus, in fostering such values, can be held up as a model of the type of relationships we Chirstians must foster in acting for justice.

The setting for the Lord's supper the night before his final passion was the Jewish Passover meal, the remembrance of the Jewish community's deliverance from slavery into freedom. The first Passover initiated the process through which the Jews were to be formed into a people, God's people. The process entailed years of nomadic life, times of trial, yet all done under the special protection of Yahweh, who provided them with continuous guidance as well as with daily food for the journey. The giving of the commandments and the people's being invited into a covenant with Yahweh were all part of this journey.

This was the setting that Jesus chose on the night before he suffered. Bread breaking had been for centuries the sign of friendship and concern. Jesus took this sign and made it into the symbol of his friendship and concern for his disciples. The early Christian communities focused much of their attention on the "meal appearances" of Jesus—the upper room, the disciples on the road to Emmaus, the seashore on the lake of Tiberias.

The passage about the disciples on the road to Emmaus begins with the disciples discouraged and disoriented, disappointed that the Jesus in whom they "had hoped" had, in fact, suffered and died. Their expectations for the Messiah apparently did not include the suffering and death of the Lamb of God, the one who would set Israel free.

We are familiar with the story—how Jesus explained to them what the Scriptures said of him and how "he appeared to be going farther" (Lk 24:28). The two disciples welcomed the stranger to their table, and they came to know him "in the breaking of the bread" (Lk 24:35).

This scene from the risen life of the Lord, selected to be recorded from among the many appearances of the risen Christ (Jn 20:30), was treasured by the first Christians. In fact, when describing who they were and what they did, they significantly mentioned the "breaking of the bread" as one of the community actions that identified them as followers of Christ (Acts 2:42, 46).

Several centuries later, the breaking of bread in the assembly was so central to the Christian community that Augustine could hold it up as a norm of Christian living. "Be what you see" was his advice to those communities with whom he broke bread in remembrance of Jesus.[13]

In all this discussion, I have prescinded from the different Christian theologies regarding the "breaking of the bread." I have done so with a purpose. No matter what one's theological understanding of Jesus' bread breaking, I suggest that today we Christians can find a model, an ideal norm for our actions in this age of under-nutrition, in the breaking of the bread.

If we are faithful to the meaning of Christ's life, we, too, are to live lives of sharing; we, too, are to share ourselves, our resources, insofar as we can, with our neighbor in need. We too are invited to come to know him "in the breaking of the bread" where St. John Chrysostom's remark may quite properly rise to haunt us: "What is the use of loading Christ's table with cups of gold, if he himself is perishing from hunger?"[14] In another place, Chrysostom has Christ speak to us about the *then* of his cross and the *now* of his crucifixion in these words: "I fasted for you then, and I suffer hunger for you now; I was thirsty when I hung on the cross, and I thirst still in the poor, in both ways to draw you to myself and make you humane for your own salvation."[15]

By way of summary, this chapter has focused on hunger as a justice issue. Biblical scholarship shows justice to mean fidelity to a relationship—fidelity to Yahweh, to the community and to oneself as part of the covenant people. In particular, the Old Testament speaks of the just person's relationship to the poor and needy in terms of justice. In the New Testament, the life and ministry of Jesus give us the ideal example of how one is to act in fidelity to the Father, the community and oneself. Jesus, the justice of God (Acts 3:14), becomes both norm and ideal for Christians acting for justice. We then considered how Christian ethics is now trying to apply Jesus' example to the conditions of our world with its massive poverty and undernourishment. We looked to the Spirit of Christ working today in the Christian community. We also considered persons and groups "acting in faith" and "acting for justice." In closing, I proposed Jesus' ministry of bread breaking as model and norm for our Christian actions for justice in a hungry world.

If the ideas presented here are accepted by the reader as material for reflection, study and prayer, they will have served their purpose of challenging both our "theological underdevelopment" and our "ethical insensitivity." If left unattended, both of these deficiencies will continue to serve as causal contributors to the problem of hunger in the world.

NOTES

1. John R. Donahue, "Biblical Perspectives on Justice," in John C. Haughey (ed.), *The Faith That Does Justice* (New York: Paulist Press, 1977), p. 68.

2. *Ibid.,* p. 99.

3. *Ibid.,* p. 109.

4. See *Ethics for a Crowded World* (Berkeley, California: Graduate Theological Union, Center for Ethics and Social Policy, 1979), pp. 2–6.

5. R.E.O. White, *Biblical Ethics* (Atlanta: John Knox Press, 1979), p. 231.

6. Denis Goulet, "World Hunger: Putting Development Ethics to the Test," *Christianity and Crisis* (May 26, 1975), pp. 125–132.

7. *De Natura et Gratia,* c. 43, #50, *PL* 44, 271.

8. "Modern Catholic Teachings Concerning Justice," in *The Faith That Does Justice, op. cit.,* p. 213.

9. R.E.O. White, *op. cit.,* p. 233.

10. Recent examples of this are the Asian Partnership for Human Development, energized by Bishop Labayan of the Philippines, and the Socio-Economic Development Center of Sri Lanka.

54 EDWARD J. BRADY

11. "Jesus as the Justice of God," *The Faith That Does Justice, op. cit.,* p. 288.

12. See David Hollenbach, *op. cit.,* p. 213.

13. Sermon 272, *Collected Writings,* Migne.

14. Hom. in Matt. 88, 3 (*PG* 58:778).

15. Hom. in Rom. 15, 6 (*PG* 60:547–48).

5
The Complexities and Consequent Neglect of Agricultural Development

Douglas Ensminger

My time frame for discussing the complexities in agricultural development in the developing countries is roughly the past thirty years. Hence, I begin with the decline of the colonial empires and the emergence of new, independent countries which have become known as the developing countries. Permit me to post three questions at the outset:

1. If most of these developing countries do, in fact, have the potential to produce enough food to feed their own people, why does the food gap, which in 1980 exceeded eighty million tons of cereals, continue to widen?

2. If increasing agricultural production is a necessity for political stability and a viable economy, will the small-sized farming units forever be an inhibiting factor in increasing agricultural production in the developing countries?

3. With all that is known about agricultural production in the U.S., why is the U.S. experience not being widely accepted as the way to increase agriculture production in the third world countries?

My answers to these questions, documented by the past three decades of development experience, suggest that U.S. farming "know how" has limited applicability when transferred to the third world countries. The past three decades of development experience also prove that in following the development model of industrialized nations, the third world countries chose the wrong route.

The basic and persistent question being asked by both the developed and third world countries is: Why, after three decades of development experience, are the small, food crop farmers in the developing countries still following traditional ways? What are the major constraints to progress?

Only as we understand the constraints can we begin to comprehend the complexities in transforming traditional societies. We also need to understand that small farm, food crop agriculture in the developing countries, unlike U.S. agriculture which is both occupation and business, is an integral part of the rural culture and greatly influenced by cultural values.

Two technical questions related to increasing agricultural production in the developing countries are: (1) What annual rate of production is generally accepted as necessary in the developing countries to provide enough food to meet the nutritional requirements of the present and projected growth in populations? (2) What is the present and historical annual rate of growth in agriculture in the developing countries?

As early as the middle 1960's, the Food and Agriculture Organization of the United Nations began assisting the developing countries in the preparation of plans to increase agricultural production up to four percent per annum. The four percent annual growth rate in agriculture was then, and will continue to be so in the future, considered to be the necessary annual agricultural growth rate essential to meeting basic food needs of a world population moving toward eight billion people early in the next century.

When one examines the agriculture production trend line, using 1951–52 as the base year and extending this trend to 1980, one finds that the annual rate of growth remains as it was in 1951–52—2.6 percent per annum. Given the unchanging annual growth rate in agriculture and the geometric growth in population, there is little wonder that the developing countries had a food deficit of eighty million tons in 1980, with every prospect for that deficit to grow over the next two decades.

In view of all this, three additional questions appear obvious:

1. If increasing agricultural production is a necessity for political stability and a viable economy, why do the political lead-

ers in the developing countries *not* make the urgently needed commitments to give priority, both political and financial, to the development of small farm agriculture?

2. If it is in the economic and political interest of the U.S. that the developing countries succeed in increasing their agricultural production enough to assure an adequate nutritional diet for all the people, then why does not U.S. foreign policy express these U.S. interests by encouraging the developing countries to emphasize economically sound and viable small-farm, food-crop agriculture?

3. If world hunger has its roots in poverty, why isn't the U.S. international assistance program sharply focused on assisting the developing countries that are committed to carrying out land and institutional reform? Why do we not help them more in developing programs and strategies to provide opportunities for the poor people to work their way out of poverty?

Let me identify now the interrelated issues which have an impact on small-farm, food-crop agriculture. Taken together, these issues may appropriately be called "the complexities" involved in changing the annual growth in agricultural production from the historical trend of 2.6 percent per annum to 4 percent per annum. If one prefers, these issues might be called "the complicating factors" in transforming traditional and self-sufficient small-farm, food-crop agriculture in the third world countries. These complicating factors are:

1. *A low socio-economic and political status is assigned to agriculture by all the developing countries.* This low status assigned to agriculture is deeply rooted, dating back to the colonial era. It manifests itself in many ways.

Farm families want to educate their children for a government job or work in the cities. They do not want them to do the drudgery work of farming. Government workers look down on rural people as being incompetent to make decisions. Young people seeking entrance to a university will go to an agriculture college as a last resort. In government cabinets it is the exception rather than the rule that the minister of agriculture has enough political clout to influence political decisions, let alone political commitment.

2. *Small farmers mistrust government and institutions which serve agriculture.* Most of the institutions serving agricul-

ture in the third world countries were created during the colonial rule to serve plantation farming and export cropping. These same institutions are still in place and they continue to serve the larger-sized farms. The small farms subsist outside government policies and outside the institutions created to serve export, large-farm agriculture. The small farmers know they cannot trust the institutions dominated by larger farmers. Their mistrust of government is deep and long-standing.

3. *The way agriculture is now organized favors the larger farmers.* The present tenure arrangements are a complicating factor in increasing agricultural production; most of the land is controlled by a few and rented on terms favorable to the landlord.

Conversely, since World War II, which also dates the decline of the colonial empires and the emergence of the new, independent, self-governed developing countries, only three countries—Japan, South Korea, and Formosa—have carried out far-reaching land and institutional reforms. In all three of these countries, small farms have developed into economically viable units. Production is market-oriented, with guaranteed floor prices and agriculture price policies that are farmer-oriented. Trustworthy, improved agriculture technology has replaced traditional methods. Institutions have been created to serve the needs of small farmers; the farmers relate to these institutions with trust. In addition, the farm families enjoy a very good level of living with a sense of security.

4. *Agricultural price policies have persistently been oriented to providing cheap food for the urban population.* There is little likelihood that the small, food-crop farmers will accept the risk and borrow money to invest in the new and expensive agricultural inputs until their governments' agricultural price policies provide an incentive to the producer and assure the farmer a guaranteed floor price when he sells it. Since governments have followed the urban, consumer-oriented agricultural price policy for the past three decades, it will be difficult now to switch to a farmer/producer-oriented agricultural price policy. The dilemma governments now face is either to subsidize food prices for the urban population, or to subsidize the farmer/producer, or both.

5. *The educational emphasis of institutions serving agriculture is male-oriented, even though women are directly involved in*

caring for the livestock and poultry as well as the production of the basic food groups. This reflects a culture that dictates the supremacy of the male as the head of the family. Even though women play a major role in food-crop agriculture, agricultural workers are generally male, and they, in turn, work with men when they are recommending new and improved agricultural methods. Women in agriculture are seen as part of the labor force and not as decision-makers or potential motivators for the acceptance of change.

6. *Small farmers and landless laborers live under conditions which deny them access to agricultural production resources.* Since world emphasis is on a crisis of food, it is difficult to break through the communications barrier and gain acceptance for the fact that hunger has its roots in poverty. People are in poverty because they lack access to production resources such as land and water, and because they lack opportunities to work and earn enough to pay for basic human needs. Chief among these basic human needs is a minimum nutritional diet. Living under conditions of extreme and absolute poverty are the rural artisans, the landless laborers, tenants and sharecroppers, and the farmers who have very small acreages.

It is all too clear that countries in need of food can procure food if they have the foreign exchange to pay for it. The formula is very simple: those who can afford to pay for food will not be hungry, and those who cannot afford to pay will not only go hungry, but they will experience varying degrees of malnutrition.

7. *In the developing countries, poor, hungry, illiterate, malnourished, unemployed, and partially employed people are accepted as being inevitable.* While the state of poverty in the developing countries was always prevalent in the colonial era, it has become more prominent following the transition from colonies to self-governed nations. The development policies and strategies followed for the past three decades have contributed to the institutionalization of an elite minority and a poor majority.

8. *There is little technology oriented to the limited resources and managerial capabilities of the small, food-crop farmer.* The technology that fed the green revolution featured high-yielding varieties, fertilizer and water. These technological developments have limited application for small-farm agriculture in the rainfed, high-risk agriculture areas of the world.

Needed is research addressed to the question: What kind of farming (choose from livestock, poultry, fisheries and cropping systems) offers promise of returning the greatest profit and providing the family the greatest security? Such farms make up eighty-five percent of the world's agriculture.

9. *The organizations and institutions that serve agriculture, such as cooperatives that provide credit, stock fertilizer and pesticides, and groups that educate the farmer about improved and new technology, give priority to the large farmers who produce for export markets as well as food crops for domestic markets.*

It is the same story, whether one is talking about small-farm, food-crop agriculture in Asia, Africa, the Middle East or Central and South America. The organizations and institutions that serve agriculture are dominated by the large farmers. These organizations and institutions accept their primary function as that of serving the large farmers.

In a sense, this means that small-farm, subsistence agriculture exists outside government policies and functions independently of the organizations and institutions that exist and were created to serve agriculture.

10. *In placing the emphasis on developing a modernized, small-farm agriculture through application of improved technological inputs and farming systems, little attention has been given to reducing field losses due to (a) rodents, insects, and plant diseases, and (b) poor methods of harvesting, threshing, and storage.* Estimates of post-harvest, harvest, and storage losses range from fifteen to twenty-six percent.

Since the practices and attitudes related to losses are, like production practices, deeply imbedded in the culture, changes will come slowly. Like changes in production practices, a prerequisite to cutting down on post-harvest and storage losses is a decision on the part of the topmost political leaders to make reduction of losses a national priority. While a great deal can be accomplished through a well-planned and continuous education program with existing resources and knowledge, one must understand the need for research in order to provide technology and to get the technology applied.

In essence, meeting present and projected food needs will require a dual approach: (1) research and strategies for increasing production, and (2) research and strategies to cut down on losses.

For the past three decades, the methods for dealing with world hunger were limited to the development of policies and implementation of strategies for increasing agricultural production. The evidence, however, is overwhelming that hunger has its roots in poverty. Poverty is caused by people either being denied access to production resources such as land and water, or lacking opportunities to work and earn enough to meet basic needs. The evidence is also conclusive that the tillers of small farms, be they owner, tenant, or sharecropper, are a part of the rural population classified as living in poverty.

The conclusion is inescapable. If people in the developing countries are to be freed from malnutrition and the fear of hunger, a strong, unwavering commitment must be made in the developing countries themselves to: (a) carry out revolutionary land and institutional reforms, (b) provide conditions for all the people to work and earn enough to pay for a minimum, nutritionally adequate diet, and (c) give priority to the development of small-farm agriculture within a strategy of integrated rural development.

In brief, I am saying that the solution to the food and hunger crisis will require a dual approach of policies and programs to alleviate the conditions that create poverty, as well as policies and programs to increase agricultural production on the small farm within a strategy of integrated rural development.

The more one understands the hunger, poverty and population issues, the more one comes to understand its complexity. While this chapter is focused on the complexities of agricultural development, the analysis would be faulty if it didn't recognize that unchecked population growth will make it difficult, if not impossible, to increase agriculture production enough to feed the world's people. J. Bryan Hehir addresses the population issue elsewhere in this book.

If this chapter concludes here, the reader will be justified in asking two questions: (1) What benefit, if any, have the past three decades of providing and receiving assistance been to the developing countries? (2) Given the complexities, is it really possible to increase agriculture production from the present and historical trend of 2.6 percent per annum to the 4 percent per annum needed?

Following three decades of development, all the developing

countries are trending toward becoming dual societies—a culture of the elite and a culture of the poor. The rich have become richer and the poor have become more destitute. Without question, development policies and strategies have contributed to the further institutionalization of an elite minority and a poor majority.

During the past thirty years, the U.S. has justified its food and economic aid to the developing countries largely on humanitarian grounds. So long as the U.S. had huge surpluses of food grains, there was a feeling that the U.S. could be counted on to meet the world's food needs. Also during this period, the developing countries had a false sense of food security, feeling that they could always count on the U.S. surpluses to meet their food deficits. The availability of U.S. food aid made some leaders in less developed countries complacent. Neglect of the agricultural sector was not always a conscious choice for them; our policies encouraged it.

The 1974 U.N. World Food Conference highlighted the growing food deficits that the developing countries would face as they moved into the decades of the 1980's and 1990's. In the future, the developing countries must look inwardly to meeting their food needs instead of looking to the U.S., Canada, and Australia as they have in the past three decades. Thus, we enter the 1980's with a greatly different orientation to agricultural development in the third world countries than was the case three decades ago.

There is now emerging an increasing awareness that it is in the economic and political interest of the U.S. to assist the developing countries in all phases of development, giving priority to agriculture. During the decades of the 1950's and 1960's, the U.S. assistance in agriculture was always tempered by not wanting its assistance to contribute toward increasing agricultural production in the areas where the U.S. had surpluses. The U.S. was more interested in maintaining market outlets for its surpluses than in helping the countries become self-sufficient in food. It would not be wrong to conclude that the role played by U.S. agricultural surpluses has been one of the more important complicating factors having a negative effect on overseas agricultural development.

While not yet widely understood, there is a growing awareness within the developing countries that their economic and political future will be determined by their success in meeting food needs. Within the U.S., there is a growing realization that as the developing countries strengthen their economies, they will increasingly become more important markets for U.S. agricultural exports.

The third world countries represent the only remaining frontiers for development, not simply burdens the developed countries must help to bear. What happens in the developing countries in the 1980's will have far-reaching implications throughout the world—economically, socially, and politically.

Taking the long-term perspective and allowing, as we must, for both the complexities and the time involved in transforming traditional societies, we must view the past three decades as positive. There should be no hesitation in admitting that neither the developed nor the developing countries were prepared for the social, economic and political complexities that emerged following the decline of the colonial empires.

There is abundant evidence that most of the developing countries have the resource potential to increase their agricultural growth-rate up to four percent per annum. Needed on the part of the developing countries is the political will to legislate and implement land and institutional reforms. Also needed is an unwavering commitment on the part of the U.S. and all developed countries to assist with the complex and time-consuming task of developing a viable, small-farm, food-crop agriculture. Needed is a time frame of several decades, if not several generations. An investment in human resources and the application of funds to assist the developing countries increase their agricultural production should be viewed as a contribution toward achieving the conditions of world peace and political stability.

6
The Colonial Legacy: From Guilt to Responsibility

Richard John Neuhaus

It is no secret that many Americans are disillusioned with almost everything that goes under the label of foreign aid. James Cogswell devotes an entire chapter to that topic in this book and labels such disillusionment as still another cause of hunger. U.S. citizens have been told that foreign aid is a form of global welfarism that is wasteful and dependency-producing. Voices on the political right and on the left have told them that foreign aid is ineffectual and may actually do more harm than good. And, perhaps most damaging, most likely to generate resentment, Westerners have been told that foreign aid is a form of reparations for the crimes they have committed in the past. All these arguments have reduced U.S. economic assistance to poor countries to less than two-tenths of one percent of our GNP. It is the purpose of this essay to address that last and most damaging argument, namely, aid as reparations for colonial excesses. Specifically, we want to examine those "crimes" that are bundled together in the frequent charges about Western "colonialism."

One would not be too far afield in viewing this essay as a development of the thesis set out by Willy Brandt in the much and justly praised Brandt Report ("North-South: A Program for Survival," the report of the Independent Commission on International Development). In his introductory chapter, Brandt writes: "The dangers of 'cultural imperialism' should not be overlooked. . . . Nonetheless, a technologically based world civilization may require a common social and work ethos. . . . Focusing on questions of historical guilt will not provide answers to the crucial problem of self-responsibility on which alone mutual respect can build. Self-righteousness will neither create jobs nor feed hungry mouths."

This is not to suggest that there are not causal connections between past behavior and present sorrow. There are. For instance, colonial powers frequently failed to encourage, and often actively discouraged, the development of native leadership, and this was also true in the area of agriculture. Then, too, some of the well-intended efforts to introduce "modern" agricultural techniques undermined traditional agriculture which had at least warded off starvation. The above statement from the Brandt Report does not mean that nobody is at fault. It does mean that the more we focus on "historical guilts" the more we become embroiled in the ambiguities of cause-effect relationships, and the more we are distracted from what can and should be done now.

Economic assistance—the adjustment of development, trade, and resource policies to accommodate the material aspirations and enhance the self-dependency of the world's poor—is important for many reasons. The argument is made that it is essential to diffusing revolutionary unrest and turning countries away from the seductions of communism. Or it is said that in the long run it is in U.S. and Western interests to secure world stability and enlarged markets and trade opportunities for the industrialized nations. These and other arguments may have some merit. But for Christians there is one inescapably compelling argument for economic assistance which needs to be lifted up, and for all Americans there is one lamentably confusing argument which needs to be deflated. The compelling argument is that Matthew 25, for instance, is not mere poetry but the revealed statement of simple fact: the hungry and deprived of the world are our sisters and brothers for whom we are ultimately accountable before one another and, most ominously, before God. The confusing argument that sometimes gets in the way of people acting upon that responsibility is that economic assistance is a payment we owe to the poor in order to assuage our guilt for sins past and present.

The term "colonialism" once had a fairly straightforward

meaning. It means a larger power taking over and controlling another territory or people as a colony. The controlling power was called "imperial" and it usually exercised its control through an aggregate of economic, political, social, and military policies. Most characteristically, the colonized subject was denied political sovereignty and independence. In today's world, the control exercised by Moscow over the nations in its bloc is the clearest and most precise instance of colonialism. But, for many reasons which need not preoccupy us here, talk about colonialism today is not so clear; indeed it usually obscures more than it illumines the relationships between powers and peoples. Today, formal Western colonialism has been ended, the great colonial empires having been dismantled beginning thirty years ago. The Portuguese in southern Africa were the last to go, in the mid-1970's, leaving a few pockets such as prosperous Hong Kong, still under British control, and Puerto Rico under U.S. control, although the Puerto Rican people consistently reject the claim that they are a colony.

With the ending of the colonial empires, the term "neo-colonialism" came into vogue. The concept was designed to describe new and residual influences by which the old imperial powers or other rich nations continued to oppress and exploit previously colonized peoples. More recently, the term "internal colonialism" has been used to describe exploitative relationships within countries where the government and other elites, in collusion with rich nations, oppress the masses. In short, "colonialism" and its variants are today employed to describe almost any relationship of perceived oppression between rich and poor, between gradations of privilege and power. The result is that "colonialism" is almost emptied of meaning, a vague synonym for injustice of any sort. The further and paralyzing result is that charges and counter-charges multiply, polarizing public opinion in the developed countries. Those who take the charges seriously feel impotently guilty, while others, probably a majority, are angry and hostile because they believe that they have been accused unjustly. If Americans are to respond more imaginatively and generously to the sufferings of the world's poor, we must try to work our way out of this morass. We will not, however, help matters by denying that the colonial period left a legacy that cannot be ignored today as we try to understand the causes of world hunger. The present-day boundaries of African states, for example, are part of the colonial legacy. Those boundaries aggravate the hunger problems of refugees discussed by Eileen Egan elsewhere in this volume. Other examples could be cited, but let me simply offer two quotations that frame the confusion that confronts us.

These two statements about colonialism may be viewed as polar opposites. Kwame Nkrumah, president of Ghana and one of the most influential African politicians in recent decades, declares in *Africa Must Unite*: "Thus all the imperialists, without exception, evolved the means, their colonial policies, to satisfy the ends, the exploitation of the subject territories, for the aggrandizement of the metropolitan countries. . . . They were all rapacious; they took our lands, our lives, our resources and our dignity. Without exception, they left us nothing but our resentment." The second statement is by P.T. Bauer, the distinguished professor at the London School of Economics: "So far from the West having caused the poverty of the third world, contact with the West has been the principal agent of material progress there."

Who is right? Or who is right in what respects? Fortunately, we need not have an exhaustive and definitive answer to these questions before moving on to the pressing agenda of economic assistance. We do, however, need to clear away a few of the ambiguities if our concern for the poor is to be rescued from the quicksand of guilt and reconstructed on the firmer ground of moral responsibility.

Almost nobody today would offer an apologia for colonialism, claiming that it was entirely meritorious in intent and consequence. A modest respect for truth, however, compels us to acknowledge that there were various forms of colonialism, and most of them were, in intent and consequences, a mixed bag. We today are not so enlightened or self-evidently morally superior that we can afford to despise without reservation the era of "the white man's burden" and Rudyard Kipling's moral romance. However misconceived and miscarried, it would be churlish to deny that many of the agents of imperialism, especially the churches and their missionary endeavors, were inspired by the noblest human concern for the poor. Today most of us do not find believable, to say the least, the convergence between economic, social, military and missionary interests that seemed self-evident to our forebears. But we should be humbled by the awareness that the self-evident morality of one generation is not necessarily an advance over the morality that was self-evident in a prior time. And it approaches blasphemy for Christians to scorn as deluded, if not self-serving, the many thousands of heroines and heroes who gave their lives in the missionary enterprise of centuries past. That too was part of colonialism. And from it there emerges today, for example in Africa, a burgeoning of the most vital and rapidly growing Christianity on the earth. Although much of that Christianity may be directed against colonialism, it is inexplicable without colonialism. As it is said, God works in mysterious ways.

On the material level our judgment of colonialism must also be mixed. Almost every facet of modern social and economic life that is to be found in Africa today was brought there by Westerners, usually during the colonial period. There is a scholarly consensus, for instance, that sub-Sahara Africa had never invented the wheel. The control of epidemic diseases, mechanized power replacing human muscle, systems of law and order, monetary exchange, railways and roads—these too are all part of the detested colonialism. It might be objected that "modernity" is precisely the problem, that modern techniques and goods have "spoiled" third world peoples and bound them in dependency upon the West. That may be. Modernity is not all it is cracked up to be. But if one makes that argument, he is setting himself *against* almost all the third world leaders and advocates who today call for some form of a new economic order. With few exceptions, such as the Khomeini regime in Iran, the third world is clamoring for *more*, not for the repeal of modernity.

To be sure, countries understandably want modernity on their own terms. It is worth remembering that wherever people have been free to express a choice, they have made clear their desire to emulate the "American way of life," on which many Americans have soured. Of course their view of the American way is grossly distorted (or is it?) through Hollywood films, and of course the leaders and intellectuals of third world countries, as distinct from the populace, insist that they want to find their own way to modernity, not to repeat the mistakes of the developed nations. But, finally, they are not rejecting but eagerly embracing the ingredients of modernity, however they might plan to put those ingredients together. And those ingredients were first introduced by colonialism. It is a moot question to ask whether those ingredients could not have been introduced in a more humane way.

It is interesting to speculate what the alternatives might have been. What if vast areas of the third world had remained untouched by colonialism, left to their own resources, perhaps as great "human wilderness" tracts unexplored by the Western world? But we do not have to speculate about that, for in fact there were large areas that were not colonized. One might think that, because they escaped the alleged deprivations of colonialism, these areas achieved more in terms of progress and prosperity. Unfortunately, that is not the case. Some of the most desperately poor areas in the world were never colonies. One thinks of Afghanistan (only now "colonized" by Russia), Tibet ("colonized" by China after the revolution), Nepal, and Ethiopia (for six brief and ineffectual years a colony of Italy). Similarly, many of the nomadic peoples of, for instance, northern Africa were in territories included on Europe's imperial maps but were in fact relatively untouched by colonial influences as they continued ways of life centuries and even millennia old. At the same time, there are former colonies, such as North America, Australia and Singapore, that are exceedingly prosperous. In Africa one notes that one of the last remnants of the colonial pattern, Zimbabwe (formerly Rhodesia), is among the most prosperous of African countries, although its natural resources are not superior to some of its impoverished neighbors. In brief, one must conclude that, as a generalization, the colonial heritage is not the chief cause of poor countries being poor.

No one can deny that colonialism was accompanied by unspeakable horrors. Joseph Conrad's *Heart of Darkness* remains as the most classic literary indictment of the colonial enterprise. Then, closely related to colonialism, there was African slavery. While historians can observe that slave trade preceded and outlived the European involvement, and that west African countries, where slavery was most active, have in general done better economically than some parts of Africa untouched by slaving— the moral and human horror of slavery cannot be tempered. The ugly aspects of colonialism are characteristic of most relationships between the weak and the strong, even when the strong try to be benevolent. The special ugliness of colonialism, however, was the potent ingredient of assumptions about racial and cultural superiority. These assumptions, still alive and often flaunted today, have severely and understandably scarred the consciousness of formerly colonized peoples. The costs in the loss of human dignity and self-esteem cannot be measured in dollars and cents but are painfully real nonetheless.

Much loose talk about colonialism only continues to obscure the issues and heighten mutual resentments, thus bringing about a stand-off in which recriminations are exchanged while changes that are necessary and possible are neglected. The desperate effort to apportion blame and exact compensation for the alleged crimes of the past is an exercise in scapegoating, and scapegoating is dead-ended. Because they resent what they feel are false and unjust accusations by some third world leaderships, many Americans and other Westerners think they are compelled to defend themselves, even to the point of defending the colonial enterprise. They point out, for example, that the fifty independent black-ruled nations of Africa are, with very few exceptions, oppressed by brutal one-man, one-party dictatorships. It is claimed that the lot of most Africans today is worse than it was under colonialism. Such a claim is made plausible by reference to Idi Amin, the genocidal conflicts in Rwanda and Burundi, the atrocities in the Central African Republic, and a host of other horrors. In terms of terror against the person, civil strife, and brutal hunger, post-colonial history has not been a happy one. Some countries are undoubtedly poorer in almost every respect than they were when they were colonies. And it is futile to deny that in some instances the responsibility for this sad disappointment of liberation hopes lies with indigenous political leadership. Zaire, the previously wealthy Belgian Congo, is frequently cited in this connection. But all this is beside the central point for people who want to act on world poverty and hunger. It is the counter-scapegoating in reaction to propagandistic talk about the crimes of colonialism. Groups of concern, such as Bread for the World, dare not permit themselves to become bogged down in these sterile recriminations.

Christian thinkers such as Reinhold Niebuhr and John Courtney Murray have always had the keenest appreciation of the ironies of history. They did not, and we should not, operate

under the delusion that history is a mechanism in which all the
parts have a rational reason, if we are only rational enough to
discover them. In that sense, history does not "make sense." We
Christians, who believe that creation's redemption was effected
in the criminal execution of an itinerant rabbi on the killing
grounds outside a medium-sized city in the boondocks, should not
have to be reminded that history is not a series of rational causes
and consequences but a very mixed story of tragedy and happy
surprise. It is ludicrous, for example, for those of us who are descended from the barbarian cave-dwellers of Europe to claim racial superiority to the peoples of color in the third world. The
historical fact, for which we cannot take credit, is that we and
not they received the Jewish Scriptures, the Christian faith, the
intellectual heritage of Greece and the legal achievements of
Rome. Nor are these cultural factors necessarily "superior" to
the achievements of other cultures. They happen, however, to
constitute the motor force of modernity which, for better and
worse, is coveted by the rest of the world. Colonialism was the
historical means by which others were brought into contact with
the European matrix. One cannot help but believe that it was far
from the best of means, but even if we can speculate about what
a better means might have been, we cannot rewrite history. The
urgent task now is to recognize and help others to recognize that,
however it came about, we do live in an inter-dependent world in
which we must exercise a greater measure of responsibility for
every member of the human community.

In considering the colonial legacy and our present responsibilities, we might keep in mind the words of Reinhold Niebuhr:
"Nothing that is worth doing can be achieved in our lifetime;
therefore we must be saved by hope. Nothing which is true or
beautiful or good makes complete sense in any immediate context of history; therefore we must be saved by faith. Nothing we
do, however virtuous, can be accomplished alone; therefore we
are saved by love. No virtuous act is quite as virtuous from the
standpoint of our friend or foe as it is from our standpoint.
Therefore we must be saved by the final form of love which is for-
giveness."

So far we have discussed colonialism as an historical phenomenon. As was mentioned at the start, however, much of today's talk about colonialism is about residual or new forms of

exploitation by which poor countries are kept poor and dependent. It is said, for example, that the international monetary system is biased against poor countries, that rich countries have restrained and actually decreased the third world's share of global trade, that the "demonstration effect" of Western consumerism distracts poor countries from real development, and that multi-national corporations "colonize" the countries in which they operate. There is not space or need to discuss here all these charges and others that are lodged in the name of anti-colonialism. In fairness, one must note that the charges do not go unanswered.

With respect to the monetary system, it is answered that soft loans and grants in the many billions of dollars are desired by the third world leaderships, that some countries have done relatively well with little such assistance, while others, such as Zaire and Jamaica, have received massive assistance on the most favorable terms and have only their own mismanagement to blame for their ever deeper slide into economic disaster. It is answered that the question of the share of global trade is misleading or irrelevant; because other countries are doing better, one country's *share* may decline while in fact its absolute export increases. As to the complaint about "demonstration effect," it is answered that "consumerism," whether or not we approve of what people want to consume, is in fact what development means. In any case, presumably governments can exercise greater control over what is imported. On control by multi-nationals, the rebuttal is that even the smallest sovereign state can kick out the largest multi-national corporation. And so the litany of charges and rebuttals goes on and on.

It is important to note that in many of these issues the crucial responsibility lies with the governing elite of the under-developed country. It is not simply a question of the third world being the "victim" and the rich countries the "oppressor." Again and again throughout the world we witness peoples being oppressed by their own leaderships. It matters little whether a country calls itself socialist or capitalist or something else. The outrageous gap between people and governing elites is one of the most pervasive characteristics of the third world. Thus it may actually be in a country's interest to eject a multi-national corporation, but there may also be an indigenous elite that puts its own interests ahead of the country's. On the one hand, the multi-national is taking advantage of (exploiting) that situation, but, on the other, unless we condescendingly treat the people of that country as children devoid of moral responsibility, those who are served by the arrangement are not simply "victims." In thinking about how elites can be held accountable to the people, we discover, incidentally, one of the many connections between democratic political processes and economic development. And, of course, many scholars would insist that, on balance, the activities of multi-national corporations advance the economic well-being of both elites and the general populace.

Here again we run into a mare's nest of questions that cannot be readily resolved. The gravamen of this essay is that it is not helpful to describe these problems under the rubric of colonialism, neo-colonialism, internal colonialism, or whatever. They are economic, political, and moral problems that arise universally in relationships between those who have more and those who have less. The comedian who commented that he had been poor and he had been rich and it is better to be rich was making a commonsensical observation that is sometimes forgotten in discussions of world poverty. As a general rule, in transactions between the rich and the poor, the rich have a distinct advantage. In many transactions, whether between persons or nations, the result is to the mutual advantage of both parties. That is the basis of trade itself, whether at the level of barter between neighbors or of international finance. To take advantage of an advantage is to "exploit" an opportunity; it only becomes "exploitation" of others in the morally negative sense when one takes unfair advantage.

But that, of course, is the rub. What is fair? John F. Kennedy is often quoted to the effect that "life is unfair." We are understandably offended by the statement when it is used to dismiss callously the plight of the less fortunate. And yet, as we noticed in connection with how the cultural "superiority" of the West came about, it is true beyond doubt that life *is* unfair. The question for us is how, and to what extent, we can take measures to moderate that unfairness. The extent to which we think remedy is possible depends, in turn, upon what we include in the category of unfairness. If every differentiation between people, every uneven distribution of benefit, is "unfair," then we are morally bound to pursue a course of absolute egalitarianism. Although many people sometimes talk as though absolute equality is the moral goal, almost nobody seriously advocates it.

Our conscience is uneasy because we have so much while others have so little. We know that we don't "deserve" to have so much. Our advantage is in large part a matter of historical accident, perhaps just being born into a middle-class family in North America. But it is also a matter of effort and productivity, by ourselves and others. While the disparity of advantage makes us uneasy in conscience, ignoring the effort that contributed to that advantage would violate our sense of justice. If one person practices hard for years to run the mile and does it in four minutes, while another goofs off and does it in seven minutes, we would be outraged if they were declared equal winners. As Lyndon Johnson emphasized in his famous speech on racial justice at Howard University, however, it is quite a different case if one racer is given a quarter-mile head start and the other, as an additional penalty, must run in chains. We have argued that, on balance, colonialism is not the handicap imposed upon the third world runner. But there is no doubt that, in terms of everything meant by modernity, development, and economic advance, we in the industrialized world have an enormous head start. Contra some conservative critics, our effort to increase the opportunity of the second runner is not aimed at undercutting the nature of a race but rather at making the race a meaningful competition.

The racing metaphor should not be pushed too far. Obviously, the lead runner could "help" the second runner simply by slowing down. There are in fact some who propose that greater global equality could be achieved if we in the rich nations became poorer. One reason it is impossible to sell this proposition to the better-off (aside from the obvious one of self-interest) is that they are unconvinced that their becoming poorer would make others richer. It is hard to see how the economic decline or collapse of the United States would benefit the people of Zambia. Economic progress comes not by impoverishing the rich but by including the poor, as much as possible on their own terms, in the process by which people become rich. Colonialism must be judged by reference to how it included or excluded others in relation to that process.

Some critics lament that the third world has not been included adequately into the processes of Western economic advance. Others take the opposite tack, claiming that the third world has been included altogether too much, thus binding it to a pattern of exploitation and dependency. As an alternative to "neo-colonialism," some propose a course of autarky, of absolute self-sufficiency and independence from global systems of trade and commerce. That is not a course that many nations find attractive or deem possible. And if one surveys the less developed countries of the world, it would seem that those that have the greatest external economic relations with the world economic system are generally better off—better off both in terms of measures such as gross national product and in terms of the actual welfare of their people. That at least is the conclusion reached by the leadership of China after Mao's death and following almost three decades of history's most monumental experiment in autarky.

Inclusion need not be exploitative, in the negative sense of that word; it need not be an instance of neo-colonialism. As we have noted, a sustained economic relationship, whether between nations or at the corner butchershop, depends upon mutual advantage and necessity. It might be objected that a landless peasant working at subsistence wages for a wealthy landlord is an economic relationship based upon the advantage of one and the necessity of the other. In truth, considering the alternative of starving to death or being beaten, the relationship is also to the "advantage" of the peasant. We need not deny that obvious fact in order to insist that his work should be of *greater* advantage to the peasant. Perhaps, but not necessarily, it would then be of less advantage to both since the peasant might then be a happier and more productive worker. That is the way it has turned out— against all the conflictual theories and revolutionary predictions—with most workers in industrialized societies.

That illustration assumes something that cannot be lightly assumed today. It assumes an agreement that economic advance is not a zero-sum game. It assumes that one party's benefit is not necessarily at the expense of another party's loss. It is not true that there is just so much wealth in the world and it must therefore be divided up into equal shares. It is true in one sense that wealth may be discovered or literally found in the ground. But the oil wealth of OPEC was just slime under the earth until it *became* wealth by virtue of Western technology and the consequent need for oil. In short, while resources or potential resources may be a given of nature, wealth is *produced* by the ingenuity and efforts of people.

Supply-side economists may be wrong in implying that production is the whole of the matter, but production is unquestionably a key to the matter. For example, Americans are criticized for eating so much food in a hungry world, and they probably do eat more than is good for them. But talk about the "injustice" of the disparity between what Americans eat and what others eat must take into account that Americans *produce* considerably more food than they consume. It may be a medical good, but it is not a moral good, in itself, for Americans to eat less. Except for relief purposes in famines and other emergencies, the long-term goal is not that the U.S. "share" more of its food with the poor of the world, but that policies be adopted that will encourage and enable the poor of the world to produce their own food. Meanwhile, increased food aid and reserve systems are essential. Nor are they morally unacceptable because even aid programs redound to the benefit of the American farmer-producer. It would be difficult, if not impossible, to sustain production if that were not the case—as "collective" agricultural experiments that are devoid of individual economic incentive have amply demonstrated in the Soviet Union, China, Cuba, and elsewhere.

Economic relationships between nations that are based upon mutual advantage and necessity are not an instance of colonialism in any of its forms. That, at least, is our thesis. Almost all relationships between poor and rich nations are affected by the history of colonialism—for better and for worse. The present state of those relationships is unsatisfactory in the extreme—for all parties concerned, but most particularly for the poor. In all the countries involved we must strive for new analyses and new policies *that combine morality and self-interest.* That is the combination that is essential if we are fundamentally to change American attitudes toward the economic aspirations of poor peoples. This is not to say that self-interest is immoral, only that it is woefully insufficient. Morality that ignores self-interest, however, is moralism, an irresponsibility that parades under the banner of "idealism." Economic proposals that require people to be moral heroes and heroines are less than helpful. An economy designed for a global, or even a national, society of saints is not among our options.

We also have too high an estimate of ourselves if we think that everything that is wrong is somehow our fault. Some things are our fault, but most of what's wrong with the world is beyond our doing or undoing. In the last century Americans thought of themselves as the source of the world's hope; now some Americans think that we are the chief, if not sole, source of its wretchedness. It is the second view that leads to such eager confession of the crimes included in the charge of colonialism. Both views reflect a prideful exaggeration of our importance, as though everything depends upon us, as though we are the only real actors on the world scene and everyone else is either an incompetent child or a victim of our actions. Such an attitude is not only prideful, it is condescending and contemptuous of the poor.

During the Vietnam war years, the late Abraham Joshua Heschel frequently declared, "Some are guilty; all are responsible." It is a critically important distinction. The colonial governor is guilty who compelled people to forced labor. The soldier who raped a native woman is guilty. The corporate executive who pays terrorists to intimidate workers demanding their rights is guilty. The African president who siphons off scarce revenue and foreign aid to buy a fleet of limousines and live a life of personal luxury is guilty. The Asian politician who votes for Palestinian liberation at the U.N. while approving the torture of political prisoners in his own country is guilty. Most of us are not guilty of these or similar crimes. Of course the guilty, and we with them, are part of a system that is wrong. But upon examination the system turns out to be a confused amalgam of systems and non-systems, of individual and corporate prides and hates and fears of conflicting visions of the common good. To say that we are guilty of the ways of a world that inflicts wrongs and fails to pursue the right is to rob guilt of its meaning.

We are responsible—responsible to do what we can to alleviate the hurt and advance better ways. Those in the poor countries who attribute their poverty to colonialism are playing with the language of guilt—our guilt—and excusing themselves from responsibility. Americans who use the same language end up polarizing their fellow-Americans and paralyzing the will of even the well-intended public. In mobilizing people for action, guilt is a forced and fetid thing; response-ability is free and open-ended. True, if we fail to respond—in caring, in praying, in appropriate action—we may finally be found guilty. We will be found guilty not of having caused the problem, not even of having failed to solve it (who knows whether we are able?), but simply of having not responded, of having not lived out the love of Christ for us and in us.

We should no doubt show a degree of toleration and understanding for people who will continue to accuse us of the crimes of colonialism, and worse. But in our own thinking and for purposes of persuading others to concern and action, we should move from guilt to responsibility. That the U.S. does so much less than it could in the area of foreign aid and does not change policies that would benefit the poor and not injure, perhaps even benefit, us—all this is a great shame. The moral philosopher Herbert Morris makes the suggestive proposal that we should in many areas shift from a "guilt morality" to a "shame morality." His proposal can be of some help in our thinking about relationships between rich and poor.

The concept of shame suggests that there is an ideal or a model, and we have fallen short of it. "You don't find your bigger brother doing that!" a parent might say. It is not that we are guilty for the world being hungry, it is that we have fallen so far short of being the caringly responsive people we would like to think ourselves to be. John and Robert Kennedy both understood this appeal. They would allude to some failing in American society and then exclaim, "We can do better than that!" That assumes that we have a rather positive view of what kind of people "we" are morally. Similarly, Martin Luther King, Jr., was calling America's bluff, as it were, when, in his August 28, 1963 "I have a dream" speech, he reminded Americans of what most of them wanted to believe is the American dream. Hosea, Jeremiah, Amos and other prophets could scathingly denounce the people precisely because they made clear that they had a higher estimate of the people and their destiny than did the people themselves. Their failure to live up to that estimate was their shame.

Shame is a "scale morality" while guilt is a "threshold morality." That is, with guilt you have either violated the rule or you haven't; it is a static concept not admitting of degrees of actualization. Shame implies a good toward which we may have traveled some distance, but we have a long way to go. Shame points to some maximum, whereas with guilt it is a minimum demand that has not been met. Two-tenths of one percent of the GNP for foreign aid is a great shame, but it is not a crime. If it is viewed as a crime which brings guilt upon us, when would it not be criminal, when would it not be in violation of the rule—at one percent? at ten percent? Obviously, there is no rule; our responsiveness should be open-ended. Then, too, guilt has to do with fault and blame for not having observed a rule which everyone has accepted as an obligation. Shame may arise from failure to do the extraordinary, failure to do more than others do, failure to act in a way appropriate to our own self-understanding. Does the Soviet Union do almost nothing for economic assistance to poor nations? So what? What does that have to do with us as Americans? Guilt in connection with third world development tends to take an anti-American tone; shame can draw on the positive, even patriotic, feelings of Americans.

Finally, such a change in moral concepts and rhetoric could create a climate in which Americans begin to feel good again about doing good. Of course, there are those who think that would be bad. How do we know we're doing good unless we feel bad about it? But, in truth, the response to world hunger should not be grudging, hostile, coerced, because we have to make up for sins we have allegedly committed. Even if it were true, it is psychologically intolerable to believe that one is collaborating in and is morally guilty of the death by starvation of millions of people. In such a case, simply in order to maintain one's sanity, one must turn away from the ubiquitous pictures of the hunger-bloated children.

A revived responsiveness to the needs of poor people and poor nations requires a new appeal that combines self-interest and altruism, with the emphasis on altruism. Perhaps we should care because economic assistance is insurance against the spread of communism, or because it will ward off revolutionary instability, or because it will secure new markets for American goods. But the assertion here is that we should care because these are brothers and sisters in a common human family; we should care because we are a caring people. The term is probably beyond rehabilitation, but it is among the great losses of our culture that "charity" has become a dirty word. Many of the noblest deeds and most humanizing institutions of the modern world were created by people who were motivated by charity, by philanthropy, by a moral conviction that, since they had been given much, much was required of them. Today we are insistently told that charity is condescending and outdated, that the problems are "systemic" and susceptible only to "scientific analysis." Very few people, however, can either conceive or act upon supposedly systemic solutions to systemic problems. And those who claim to have such systemic solutions are, with reason, not generally trusted. The end result is that most people do nothing, while a small minority excites itself with "radical" answers that have no chance of being implemented.

The burden of this essay is that most talk about colonialism in connection with world poverty is aimed at inducing feelings of guilt, coercing change, and obscuring the real causes of human misery. In assessing the colonial legacy, we have considered two aspects of the question, the substantive and the strategic. Substantively, is it true that colonialism is the cause or a chief cause of global poverty? Strategically, to the extent it may be true, is it a useful argument to press? The answer suggested here is that—in general, and on balance—the charge is not true. Colonialism is a cause, but not the chief cause. Pressing whatever element of truth there may be in the charges of colonial crimes is not a useful basis for an appeal for public support in trying to devise policies responsive to the poor. It can only continue to provoke, as it has in the past, reactions of resentment, counter-charges, and evasion. Of course the strategic should flow from the substantive. That is, Christians should not have to be reminded that it is wrong to make even the most well-intended appeal on the basis of untruths and half-truths.

Dwelling on the past has a limited usefulness. But a new constituency of concern for world poverty can be built only if we move away from the rhetorics of guilt, reparation and appeasement and appeal to the capacities of many, if not most, Americans to come somewhat nearer to being the responsively caring people they want to believe they want to be.

7
Geography and Climate

Warren P. Henegar

My purpose in this chapter is to discuss some of the effects that soil and weather have on world food production. Geography and climate are not destiny; they do, however, lay a heavy hand on the diet of men, women and children everywhere.

Adverse geography and climate can, often but not always, be overcome. Despite handicaps in this regard, many countries succeed in feeding and clothing themselves sufficiently, even abundantly. Some countries highly favored by geography and climate suffer occasional food shortages. But, as a general rule, those countries with favorable geography and climate eat often and well, while those countries not so favored are in constant jeopardy unless they can generate the economic and military power to command food and fiber from other places, often countries lacking equal power.

Americans, especially American farmers, would like to think that the reason we are the dominant food and fiber exporter in the world is our superior knowledge and our traditional work ethic. The American commercial farmer today is certainly expert and works as long and hard as anybody in the world. But the main reason for our abundance is our incredible geographically and climatically blessed land. The American midwest corn belt is the best example of this good fortune. It is an area that stretches a thousand miles east to west, from Ohio to Nebraska, and runs approximately five hundred miles north to south, from Minnesota to Missouri, encompassing a complex of soils, rainfalls, temperatures, and topography unequaled in the world of food production.

It would take a very thick book to cover even the basic geographical and climatical aspects of world food production. What I hope to do is to give a few insights into the natural complexities of food and agricultural production, and, perhaps, stimulate the reader's appetite for further study.

We are all aware that increased food production does not necessarily benefit hungry people. No matter how well meaning and efficient a politico-economic system is, people cannot be fed without sustained, dependable, and adequate agricultural production. Geography and climate are the chief determinants of such activity.

The four main geographical and climatical factors that affect food production are soil, water, temperature, and topography.

There are many definitions of soil. An engineer, agronomist, or gardener would each define it differently. I define soil as that part of the earth's surface which can be dug or plowed and in which plants grow. It may be shallow or deep, light or dark. It can be predominantly clay, silt, or sand. Any soil consists of mineral and organic matter, water, and air. Even though the proportions vary, the major components remain the same.

So far as production is concerned, the four main soil factors are: (1) depth; (2) "extent," or how much there is; (3) fertility; and (4) "aspect," or how it lies ("the lay of the land").

Depth is important because it is closely related to how much water and nutrients the soil can hold for plant use. Depth is not so important in controlled environments as, for example, in a greenhouse where water and nutrition are applied as needed. But under most field conditions the water-holding capacity of a soil is critical for dependable production. Soil depth is effectively measured by the distance from the surface to the first impediment to root penetration.

The extent of soil is the most important factor. It is the least easily manipulated by the farmer. Every other soil factor is open to human influence. For all practical purposes, soil formation is a very slow process. It can be moved short distances, it can be shaped, and its texture and structure can even be altered, but you cannot make any more of it.

Soil productivity is dependent on many factors, but the most critical, second to water, is the availability of plant nutrients. Plants obtain carbon, hydrogen, and oxygen from air and water, but the other thirteen or more essential elements must be present in the soil, either occurring naturally or artificially applied. For sustained, adequate production, one or more of these essential elements must be regularly applied by the human factor.

How soil lies, its "aspect" or slope, determines how a soil can be managed. Steep land can produce timber, rolling land can produce forage, but the most intensively cropped land needs gently rolling to level surfaces.

The aspect of large areas of the earth has been altered by earth's human inhabitants; substantial parts of China and Europe have had their topography changed. The arable soils in parts of these regions are more extensive and productive now than they were two thousand years ago. This is an encouraging reminder that humans can change the face of the earth for good as well as for ill.

Just as it matters little to the plant rootlets whether the fertilizing elements are from natural or synthetic sources, neither does it matter whether water is from rain, snow, irrigation, or some other source. What counts is that water is present where it is needed. Moreover, water can come from this year's precipitation, or from previous years' rain and snows available from streams, lakes, reservoirs, and underground aquifers.

Agriculture's dependency on rainfall looks not only to the total annual amount but also its seasonal distribution. In the central midwestern temperature zone, the soil, at the beginning of the growing season, should be at field capacity. This means that the amount of water in the soil is just enough for plant growth; any excess is detrimental. The soil should then receive about one inch of rain a week until maturity, then no rain until crops are gathered. That is the ideal. As much as two inches a week might be beneficial in the middle of the growing season when the temperature is high and the plant demand is the greatest.

This precipitation schedule, however, does not often occur, even in the eastern United States corn belt. In eastern China, over twenty inches of its total of twenty-five inches of rain fall from June to October. Peasants in that part of the world must manage in every growing season what midwestern U.S. farmers would recognize as excessive rains, drought, and swollen streams.

Neither the evenly spaced rains of the eastern United States corn belt nor the peculiar monsoonal weather system of north China is typical. Each agricultural region has its own unique environment. However, some pattern of drought, heavy rainfall, and high water is more common than not to most of the food producing areas of the world.

This reality means that much of the world agriculture is dependent on supplemental water, artificial drainage, and flood control.

Extra water comes from streams and surface and subsurface reservoirs. Surface reservoirs, luckily, are not dependent on annual precipitation. Major water sheds like those feeding the Yangtze and Mississippi Rivers drain enormous areas and receive water from sources other than seasonal run-off. Most manmade reservoirs are designed to hold enough water for more than one year. My own estimation is that eastern Chinese surface-water sources, with the help of irrigation wells, are presently capable of preventing widespread famine through a three year drought. This is a great achievement. Unfortunately, the probability of a four year drought in any fifty or one hundred year period may be quite high.

Some underground reservoirs or aquifers accumulate water over a long time, and can yield water for extended periods without replenishment. Others such as the Ganges Plain aquifers are regularly filled by river water. These aquifers like surface reservoirs can be restored in a single wet year. Many of the subsurface reservoirs that have accumulated water over long periods of time, or in a different geologic era, cannot be replenished at all. Such water is accurately termed fossil water. Like coal or oil, once it's gone, it's gone forever. This depletion may cause more human sorrow, in time, than the end of recoverable oil and gas. Supplies of fossil water underlie parts of our Great Plains and other arid and semi-arid places on earth.

It is important to note that aquifers capable of yielding sufficient water for large scale agriculture are sparsely scattered over the world. Large areas of the earth, including the humid areas, have little or no extractable ground water.

Temperature refers to the energy or heat units that go into

the food-plant environment. Frost-free days, growing days, temperature lows, highs, averages, maximums, and minimums are all factors affecting crop production. In the temperate zones, the number of heat units, which go into the environment, is a critical factor. For grain crops, this can be more important than the number of frost-free days. However, too much heat imposes another set of limitations.

Not only in the tropics and subtropics, but even in the temperate zone, high temperature and lack of moisture can induce plant dormancy, or death. Few if any of the major food crops do well when the soil and ambient temperatures exceed ninety degrees. Contrary to popular myth, it can become too warm for corn. Of course, many crops are well adapted to tropical and subtropical conditions, but excessive heat and/or lack of moisture limits all plant growth just as effectively as low temperatures.

Ordinarily, sunshine is not directly limiting, but is related to all climatic factors.

In some areas, wind restricts crop adaptation. Excessive wind conditions cause erosion and "lodging," where crops are blown down. But wind's greatest effect is on the transpiration and evaporation rate, evapotranspiration.

Evapotranspiration is the result of temperature, wind, sunshine, and plant cover. Approximately seventy-five percent of total precipitation is transpired and evaporated back into the atmosphere rather quickly. Less than twenty-five percent runs off or penetrates to the ground water reservoir (water table, aquifer, etc.) The evapotranspiration rate vitally affects the amount of water needed for crop growth. In the Dakotas and Minnesota an average precipitation amount of twenty-five inches will yield a good crop most years; on the southern Great Plains the same amount is not enough to sustain intensive cropping without irrigation. Similarly, desert soils are often highly fertile, but huge amounts of water are required for plant growth.

Topography, the features and surface configurations of the earth and the availability of water, generally determines the extent of food production in a nation. Only about fifteen percent of the United States is arable. China has even less arable land, around twelve percent. Arable land is usually restricted to areas of level and gently rolling plains, and also river valleys (flood plains). (However picturesque and admirable mountain terrace agriculture may be, its importance is mostly local and insignificant.) Most of the major food producing areas are characterized by broad plains. Some of these lands have to be both watered and drained, or protected from periodic flooding, but it is only these areas of level to gently rolling lands that are capable of feeding large numbers of people.

The immense area of the earth that is too rocky, too steep, too cold, too dry, or too wet for grain production is still highly important for food production, mainly animal agriculture. It may be even more important in the future. But for now and in the immediate future, its contribution to the task of eliminating world hunger is not great.

An example of how restricted the productive areas are is the fact that four areas in the U.S. produce approximately ninety percent of the total U.S. production of food and fiber. They are the midwest corn belt, the southern Great Plains, the Mississippi River delta, and the California valleys.

The same thing is true in China. The north China plains, the Yangtze River plains, the Sichuan Basin, the northeast (Heilongkiang, etc.), and the Pearl River delta produce the bulk of food and fiber in the "Middle Kingdom." All of this suggests that in evaulating a country's food production capacity, one should look first at places where ample water supply and favorable topography come together.

This chapter has emphasized grain (more exactly, concentrate food) production as affected by climate and geography. I have tried to outline for the reader the most important factors to be noted. However there are a number of misconceptions which should be noted too.

The labels "good" and "bad" soils can be misleading. For example, the deep dark glacial soils of central Indiana are our "best," and the light-colored sandstone soils with a limiting "fragi-pan" in southern Indiana are the "worst." But a good farmer can get consistent high yields from the southern Indiana land, and poor management results in disappointing returns from the "best" soil. Studies done by Purdue University over a long period of time have shown that the person farming the soil is more important in determining production than the soil type.

Much of the popular literature on agricultural production would lead to the belief that if we could only come up with or use a magic seed (or cow!), our food production problems would be solved. Far be it from me to denigrate the efforts of the plant breeders, but an improved seed is of little value unless it is planted in fertile soil, receives ample water, and is protected from pests (weeds, disease, and insects). The Green Revolution is not a multi-national plot; it is simply a term to describe the four factors necessary for successful food production. Improved seed is probably the least important.

We are all fascinated with apocalyptic events, and this includes potential climatic catastrophes. Drastic warming and chilling of the world environment are frequent subjects of conjecture and intellectual diversion. So far as food production is concerned, it is futile to try to ascertain whether any substantial weather changes are going to occur more than a few days ahead. Sunspots, weather cycles, and carbon dioxide in the atmosphere are currently as useless as woolly worms, wasps' nests, and the *Farmer's Almanac* in predicting the weather for agricultural purposes. All we have is probability based on recent reliable weather records. All the wondrous technological advances have not substantially changed this assessment of long range predictions.

Weather forecasts for the next few days are a different story. They are an accurate and valuable agricultural tool.

Another subject of speculation (and dire prediction) relates to the use of tropical soils. In the late 1960's an article in the *Scientific American* speculated that if enough of the Amazon basin were plowed, the oxidizing laterite soils could absorb all the earth's available oxygen! Charles Kellogg, for many years head of the United States Soil Survey and authority on world agriculture, writes that the hazards of laterite soil have been enormously exaggerated. It is of importance in some localities, but the areas of true laterites are relatively small. The tropical areas, as a whole, have many other kinds of soils, many of which are highly responsive to agricultural management.

Artificial fertilizers are often seen as precursors of doom. The limitations, or dangers, lie in what they are not rather than in what they are. All are manufactured, processed, or refined from natural deposits, except nitrogen, which is synthesized from the air by various processes. They are increasingly "pure" so that they consist only of the limiting element. The major elements are ususlly nitrogen, phosphorous, and potash. The secondary nutrients are calcium, magnesium, and sulfur. Only a few contain the micronutrients which under some conditions—particularly in the tropics and subtropics—can be severely restrictive to food plant growth and detrimental to animal health.

Organic fertilizer adds organic matter and some micronutrients. Its chief limitation is that it can be expensive, measured in terms of money or human effort. Moreover, there is simply not enough of it.

Phosphorous fertilizer is especially critical, although nitrogen might be the present most limiting nutrient in agricultural production. But there are many ways including leguminous plants to obtain that element.

Potash and the secondary elements are fairly widely dispersed and available. Significant deposits of phosphorous are much rarer. Agriculture in the humid areas could not long yield adequate food without addition of non-organic phosphorous. The geographic distribution and extent of phosphate deposits may, in the long run, be more important to humankind than the amount and location of fossil fuels.

Self-reliance is a concept to which we are all attracted. Nevertheless, it has severe limitations in our present densely populated world. Self-reliance may have been possible when the emperor of China told the king of England, almost two hundred years ago, "I set no value on things strange and have no use for your manufactures." But that is no longer the case. The driving force behind China's four modernizations was not a desire for Coca-Cola or other "strange manufactures." The realization that China's arable lands may not be able to feed their one billion plus people put an end to dreams of self-reliance.

Population is not the only pressure that modifies self-reliance. Most countries lack one or more critical elements for a self-sufficient agriculture. Phosphate may be the most notable, but there are numerous others.

To be self-reliant, most countries are going to have to have something of value to trade for certain essentials. They must also have the ability to get what is traded from there to here and vice versa. Geographical barriers can be a severely limiting factor in the transportation infrastructure serving a country's agriculture.

Another interesting limitation to self-reliance is the hazard of strictly local diet tied to local production. A lack of iodine in the soil produced bulging goiterous necks throughout the American midwest, just a half-century ago. Today in parts of central China one out of four persons dies from esophageal cancer precipitated by a deficiency of molybdenum in the soil.

The better we understand climate, the more we will come to appreciate the importance of technology in agriculture. But even technology is unable to provide self-reliance. The more we know about the deficits of a given soil, the greater will be our respect for trade and transportation in sustaining life and health.

A self-contained life somewhere on a small neat farm in a green valley may be possible for some, but it is not for most of God's children, particularly the hungry. Hence, the climate and geography of the whole world are our concern. The more we learn about both, the closer we come to a solution to the problem of hunger.

8
Resource Abuse:
"The Land Does Not Lie"

C. Dean Freudenberger

Resource abuse is one of the causes of hunger. Globally, as well as domestically, the magnitude and causality of this abuse is now almost beyond comprehension. Behind us is a long history of resource destruction, climaxing during the closing decades of this century. One merely needs to consider the soil and vegetative losses in the midwestern United States from the early 1930's to understand the effects of destruction in wide areas of Africa, central India, Latin America, and across the major archipelagoes of the Pacific. In part, land, forest, water and soil resource loss is related to ignorance and social neglect. Also, it is due to the impact of modern society's ruthless profit motives which have driven us to irresponsible agricultural resource destruction from the burning of range lands in central Africa to the extraction of timber in equatorial nations. Internationally, there are few environmental controls in operation. Many governments and industrial firms take advantage of this situation beyond their own national borders. As consumption patterns rapidly grow in the wealthy nations, many far-flung industrial giants exert damaging impact upon soil, forest, and grassland resources around the world (not to mention human resources), and thus diminish the earth's capacity for food production.

Global Dimensions of Abuse. Our concern is for food in a hungry world. The soil (like water) is the most basic resource

90

upon which we depend for the growing of food. Yet it is one of our most fragile and scarce resources. There are no practical substitutes if it is lost. This is obvious. But the problem is that we act and react as if it were not so. The worldwide loss of cropland most effectively illustrates the magnitude of the reality of basic resource abuse. We need to be aware of this reality, globally as well as nationally, if we are to hope for change in a dismal historical trend, and for a future without hunger.[1]

Soil is the living, dynamic bridge where crops convert solar energy to human food energy. Soil spans the gap between death and life, between what was and what is.[2] If it is abused, it dies and so die the civilizations!

W.C. Lowdermilk, one of America's great leaders in the soil conservation movement, said many years ago upon his return from a two year study of the history of the abuse of land in Mesopotamia, north Africa, the Jordan Valley, Syria, Cyprus, the Italian and French Alps, and China:

> The land does not lie; it bears a record of what we write on it. In a larger sense a nation writes its record on the land, and a civilization writes its record on the land. . . a record that is easy to read by those who understand the simple language of the land.[3]

There is very little soil upon the dry land of planet earth. The continents themselves represent only four-tenths of one percent of the earth's mass.[4] Of the entire earth's surface, seventy-five percent is covered with water (196.8 million square miles). The remaining twenty-five percent is dry land (fifty-five million square miles). Of this twenty-five percent, one-fifth is too cold to produce food and fiber, one-fifth is too high and rugged to be inhabited, and one-fifth is too dry, leaving only two-fifths useful for human life. But of this two-fifths, there are many areas of poor soil quality, excessive rainfall and marginal grazing resources.[5] It is absolutely wrong to think that soil is in abundance. To the contrary, it is very scarce, and very fragile.

During historic times (the past eight thousand years) one-half of this original soil and vegetative resource was destroyed.[6] We see a fascinating early observation of this process in Plato's *Critias:*

The soil which kept breaking away from the highlands
. . . keeps continually sliding away and disappearing into
the sea. . . . What now remains, compared with what ex-
isted, is like the skeleton of a sick man, all the fat and
soft earth having now wasted away and only the bare
framework of the land being left . . . which now supports
nothing but bees.

Because of humanity's ever increasing demands for food and
fiber, the United Nations Conference on Desertification declared
in 1976:

Estimates of present (soil) losses give rise to a pessimis-
tic outlook, suggesting that the world will lose close to
one-third of its (remaining) arable land by the end of
this century.[7]

This will happen during the next twenty years when our human species will increase in number by one-third while the remaining soil resources, as noted above, will be diminished by
one-third.[8]

The present rates of soil loss through erosion . . . are
over a half a ton of topsoil for every man, woman and
child on the planet.[9]

Of the world's remaining soil resources, the potential for future expansion of cultivatable land remains, as it has for decades, a subject of much controversy. The figures run from eight
to eleven percent of the world's land areas, depending upon
which sets of studies one consults. What is certain, however, is
that what is presently under cultivation is severely stressed, and
what remains in potential can be developed only at great cost
and environmental risk.[10] We must proceed with our agriculture
and other land use plans with extreme caution, always mindful
of humanity's poor historical record and limited future resources. At the moment, "soil fertility on presently used soil resources is declining on an estimated one-fifth of the world's
present croplands."[11] This is a sobering reality.

The pressure for survival increases relentlessly, causing humanity to expand on to more fragile land which in turn causes further deforestation, irrigation with waterlogging and salinization, thinning of soils from oxidization, wind and water erosion and the loss of existing croplands from oil shale and coal extraction and the spread of human settlements (urbanization) onto farmland. Every year we are losing some six million hectares of arable land through the process of desertification. Approximately twenty-nine million acres of agricultural lands were converted to non-agricultural uses in the United States in the past ten years. Between 1960 and 1970 Japan lost more than seven percent of its agricultural land to buildings and roads. In India, six thousand million tons of soil are lost every year from an area less than a quarter the size of that country. We can realize the magnitude of such a loss if we know that nature takes from one hundred to four hundred years or more to generate only one centimeter of topsoil.[12] This means that from three thousand to twelve thousand years would be required to generate soil to a depth of the length of a student's exercise book.

The magnitude of worldwide soil degradation and loss has parallels in descriptions of abuse of forests, semi-arid rangelands, mineral exhaustion, water and air pollution, climatic stress and an impoverished humanity. Four billion people now depend heavily on the earth's forests for firewood, lumber, newsprint and a host of less essential products.[13] Up until now, nearly half of the world's rain forests have been destroyed. At the current rate, between five and ten million hectares are lost every year.[14] Hundreds of species of plants, birds, mammals and insects have disappeared.[15] Normal patterns of rainfall and water retention are broken down, with consequent loss of soil, uncontrollable flooding, and much more. As previously stated, deserts are expanding on every continent as a consequence of abusive agriculture and growing pressures of neglected and exploited human populations. About sixty million people live in these regions. Today, desert encroachment is at the rate of fifty thousand square kilometers a year.[16] We are mining our minerals to exhaustion. For example, in attaining our high level of living in the U.S.A., it is estimated that we have used more minerals and mineral fuel during the last thirty years than all the people of the world used previously.[17] From this kind of consumption, we dump our wastes recklessly. The Love Canal is but one instance of the thirty-two thousand to fifty thousand sites in the U.S. containing hazardous wastes. Of these, anywhere from twelve hundred to two thousand may pose significant risks to human health or to the environment. Fifty-one million tons of hazardous industrial waste alone are produced annually, with 18,500 municipal dumping sites occupying 500,000 acres of land.[18] In addition, generations yet unborn will have to struggle with the unending difficulty of guarding hundreds of tons of radioactive waste that will accumulate, waste that no one yet knows how to store "safely" and will remain dangerous for 250,000 years.[19] We poison our water and air. Wastes introduced into lakes and streams remain for years, if not centuries. As many as two-thirds of the nation's lakes have serious pollution problems.[20] This pollution belies our belief that we are consumers of water. We are not; we are only temporary users of it. We share it with everyone, everywhere, into the indefinite future. The same is true with the air we breathe, for it is in constant motion. For example, the radioactive dust (or sahelian dust) stirred by a nuclear explosion flows great distances. It is in this kind of a continuous flow that all communities are linked together, no matter how remote. "Through the air, the business of each person and each nation has truly become everybody's business."[21] Our climates are threatened in many ways. The delicate balances of the chemical composition of the air and the upper atmosphere itself (the ozone shield) are being shaken. If, as a consequence of chemical changes, atmospheric dust accumulation, or the changes in normal balances of heat and light radiation and reflection increase, the likelihood of significant climatic change increases. An average of only one degree centigrade of temperature change can have major consequences upon our patterns of agricultural production and the prospects of survival of hundreds of millions of people.[22] In terms of human resource abuse and impoverishment, one must look only as far as *The Global 2000 Report to the President,* the eight hundred page study issued in mid-1980 (produced by officials of the U.S. Department of State and the President's Council on Environmental Quality) to appreciate the enormous impact of the continual abuse of the world's resources upon the lives of everyone, everywhere. By the turn of the century, if we do not change our ways, of the estimated 6.35 billion people, 1.3 billion will be suffering from malnourishment and starvation. Five hundred thousand to two million species of plants and animals may die off during the next two decades.[23]

This then, by way of examples, suggests the magnitude of global resource abuse. We are facing immediate problems which, until a few years ago, never entered our imagination. All of our social and technological assumptions are challenged by the reality of global resource abuse.

National Dimensions of Soil Abuse. Lest we conclude that the problem of resource abuse is felt beyond our immediate doorstep, it is useful to look at the national dimensions of the problem. Soil resource loss best illustrates the seriousness of the problem of general resource abuse here in the United States. At the present time, several agencies of the United States government are making what is called "The National Agricultural Lands Study."[24] The problem statement, forming the basis of the three year study, is that ten years from now America could be as concerned over the loss of the nation's prime and important farmlands as it is now over shortages of oil and gasoline. Today, one million acres of prime farmland are lost annually due to urbanization. This is an equivalent to a strip of land one-half mile wide stretching from San Francisco to New York City. In addition, two million acres of less than prime land go into non-agricultural uses for such purposes as roadways and industrial parks. In total, three million acres are lost every year in the U.S., which is an equivalent to three hundred and twenty acres (a half section of land) per hour. If one multiplies this figure by twenty-four hours, the result is a shocking reality that every day twelve square miles of U.S. farmland vanish forever. In the last decade, we lost an equivalent to Vermont, New Hampshire, Massachusetts, Rhode Island, Connecticut, New Jersey and Delaware.[25] Today only one hundred and thirty-five million acres of potential farmland are left in the U.S., of which a mere twenty-two million are considered prime.[26] *It is likely that by the year 2000 all food grown in the U.S. will be consumed in the U.S. and there will be no exports for maintaining a "balance of payments" or for relief in a hungry world.*[27] No wonder the United Nations agencies concerned with the world food problem are alarmed by what is happening in the U.S.A., the world's greatest granary.

Reflections on the Trends. "Since 1935, one hundred million acres have been degraded to the point where they cannot be cultivated, and another one hundred million acres, more than fifty percent of the topsoil, has been lost."[28] Niel Sampson, executive Vice President of the National Association conservation districts says:

> Soil depletion is not just a steady loss . . . it accelerates with each increment of topsoil that is washed away, resulting in less absorptive capacity, organic matter, and plant growth to protect the soil when the rain strikes again.[29]

In 1971, it was estimated that in the north central United States sixty-seven percent of all cropland needed conservation treatment. Since then, highly erosive soils have been placed into export production (grains and soybeans), involving one hundred million tons and twenty-three billion dollars of balance of payment earnings—mostly for oil. Unrestricted land use will give as much as twenty metric tons per hectare of soil loss per year which is twice the "tolerable" level.[30] Therefore, for each ton of grain exported, several tons of topsoil is exported to the Gulf of Mexico.[31] Dudley Stamp, in his classic *Land for Tomorrow,* written nearly thirty years ago, said:

> The watcher of the Mississippi in flood recognized the mud as the once fertile farmlands, the excess of water due to the destruction of forest and prairie, and the swift current as taking the solid burden far out to sea where it can have no value to man.[32]

In January and February of 1979, the U.S. Soil Conservation Service reported that 517 countries reported 3.1 million acres damaged by wind erosion. Ninety-six percent was upon cropland, three percent upon rangeland and one percent at other places. The total land damage in that year was two and a half times greater than wind erosion damage of the previous year. Land reported in 1979 in a condition to blow was 13.5 million acres—forty-five percent on the northern great plains and fifty-five percent on the southern plains.

All this happens repeatedly in our national history when there is low precipitation on semi-arid lands, plowing and land leveling left unplanted, lack of sufficient crop residues, stubble burning, block farming and conversion of marginal land from grasses to crop production and late fall planting due to weather. In addition to soil loss is the impact on fences covered with drifting soil, hazardous driving and auto damage, accumulation of dust in homes, increase in respiratory ailments, loss of farm incomes, soil fertility, damage to wildlife habitat and increased fuel costs for emergency tillage.

When asked about these threatening problems during his tenure as Secretary of Agriculture, Bob Bergland said:

> We're on a collision course with disaster. Our water supplies are being reduced, we have whole watersheds where the ground water reserves are being depleted, and we have mined our soil. In fact, the erosion of America's farmland today is probably at a record, and this simply cannot go on.

Not much later, while addressing the U.S. Congress on the subject of "Environmental Priorities and Programs" in August 1979, President Jimmy Carter said:

> But in emphasizing ever-increasing production we have sometimes neglected to maintain the soil, water, and biological resources upon which the long-term stability and productivity of our agriculture depends. These resources are being degraded in many parts of the country. Our farm and land management practices have led to excessive soil erosion, we have overused chemical fertilizers and pesticides, and some of our most productive farmlands are being converted to non-agricultural uses.[34]

Since the "land does not lie," the loss of soil is the price we ultimately pay for our abusive ways. We shall be like ostriches if we do not change. At no moment in history has the long and oppressive story of soil loss been so threatening. W. C. Lowdermilk raised the following question upon his return from observing the ancient history of human abuse of the land. "If Moses had foreseen what suicidal agriculture would do to the land of planet earth, might he have been inspired to deliver another command-

C. DEAN FREUDENBERGER

ment to establish humanity's relation to the land?"[35] Lowdermilk made this illustration in the form of an "eleventh commandment":

> Thou shalt inherit the holy earth as a faithful steward, conserving its resources and productivity from generation to generation. Thou shalt safeguard thy fields from soil erosion, thy living waters from overgrazing by thy herds, that thy descendants may have abundance forever. If any shall fail in this stewardship of the land thy fruitful fields shall become sterile stony ground and wasting gullies, and thy descendants shall decrease and live in poverty or perish from the face of the earth.[36]

How Resource Abuse Happens. If indeed we are trustees of the resources of the earth, then our purpose and deepest value is to participate in the ongoing process of creation. Our task is that of being compassionately sensitive and to keep alive the moving edges of evolution. We realize that this requires, among many things, the maintenance of the fragile balance of interdependencies of the land—its soil, water and sunlight, vegetation and animal life. But, for one reason or another, we as a whole human species throughout the entire "civilized" history have not related to the resources of the land as trustees: replenishing and improving. Consequently, vital resources are not only abused, but many have been *irrevocably lost.* People are broken, physically and spiritually. Much of humanity is impoverished. We observe that "the technosphere of our creation is out of balance with the biosphere of our inheritance.[37] We cheerfully consume resources, the earth's capital, and call it income.[38]

How great is the danger of resource abuse? Will even a total reversal of the way we relate to each other and to our resources save our world from the destructive processes already in motion? Can we comprehend the human reasoning which might reverse these historic trends, now climaxing in a massive world crisis, of which hunger and poverty are the most obvious signs? Perhaps, if we understand some of the *fundamental causes* of our exploitive attitudes and technologies, we can begin to see the possibility of creative change.

Narrow Anthropocentrism. Our contemporary and prevailing Western religious interpretation of human life has placed nature and its resources in a position of lesser value. Nature exists to be exploited, since human life is interpreted to be central and of highest importance. The folk tales of the conquests of heroes like Paul Bunyan illustrate the point. Humanity conquers nature. We have not slowed down to recognize the vital and fragile interdependencies of the whole of life. Nature and humanity are not seen as a part of one system that needs to be harmoniously maintained. Our ecological innocence, technological assumptions, and indifference are appalling. In a technically oriented world, we grow up with the illusion that somehow, against all laws of nature, infinite growth in a finite environment is possible. The idol of external material growth has been substituted for the concept of trusteeship. Humanity, in its thus far fleeting moment of existence in the history of planet earth, has placed itself at the top of the tree of creation. We perpetuate our propensity to abuse. A narrowly anthropocentric view places human life as that which transcends nature, and that nature (resources) is to be exploited for the pursuits of the human species. Instinctive human inhibitions to exploitation and abuse crumble. We have placed ourselves arbitrarily at the top of an artificial value hierarchy. The value of the stability of the whole creative process, its equilibria and parameters, has been ignored greatly. If we live with the narrow anthropocentric view of evolution, living as though the glorification of humanity is the ultimate purpose of creation, and playing out the transcendent role where all living and non-living things of nature are placed in a lesser hierarchy with the human species above it all, there are few limits to the idea of human regulation and freedom when it comes to the issue of our use of the resources of planet earth.

Sovereignty. Much can be said about our understanding of sovereignty, be it with regard to humanity's relation to natural resources, one another, or the sovereignty of the nation state (nationalism).

> What people do about their ecology depends upon what they think about themselves in relation to things around them.[39]

We often say: "This is my property, my land. I can do with it as I please." King Solomon said this when he took down the cedars on the mountains to make palaces and temples. So say we today when it comes to deforestation, strip-mining, and pumping limited water supplies from ancient aquifers which now, on the U.S. national average, exceed recharge by thirty-three percent.[40] Who has the "full and permanent sovereignty" over the resources? The nation-state does, as affirmed by the New International Economic Order! Is this really a correct assumption?

Security. We drive ourselves to exhaustion to satisfy our need and sense of security. Do we find it in our accumulation of material things, stockpiles of "vital resources," military strength and nuclear arsenals? Or does our security lie in the enduring quality of our relationships to each other and to the resources of the earth? It is obvious in today's world that our security is in keeping alive the evolving frontiers of creation—the intricate regulatory mechanisms of nature involving among hundreds of major phenomena, normal radiation patterns of incoming light through the ozone shield and atmosphere, normal cycles of oxygen, carbon dioxide and nitrogen generation and absorption, a healthy soil microbiology and diversified grasslands and forest complexes, with purity of air, sea and fresh water supplies of the planet.[41] Our security rests, ultimately, in the renewability of our resources use, in living within the sustainable carrying capacity of plânet (spaceship) earth. This security issue touches all people, everywhere, into the foreseeable future. In a word, the issue is sustainability.

New Attitudes, New Ethics, and New Strategies. Where do we go from here? Lester Brown said it best in his *Worldwatch Paper #24:*

The issue is not whether the equilibrium between people and the land ultimately will be re-established. It will be. If the deterioration is not arrested by man, then nature will ultimately intervene with its own checks. *The times call for a new land ethic, a new reverence for the land, and for a better understanding of our dependence on a resource that is too often taken for granted.*[42]

Donald Worster, in *Dust Bowl: The Southern Plains in the 1930's,* put it this way:

> As the world's population moves increasingly onto marginal land ... and already more than half a billion people live in deserts or semi-arid places ... and as unfavorable shifts in climate appear likely, even in temperate zones, *the need for ecologically adaptive cultures becomes all the more crucial.*[43]

Can we develop new attitudes and value systems which will enable us to overcome our narrow anthropocentrism and help us to participate in the enterprise called creation? Can we develop a more inclusive ethic which takes into account justice into the foreseeable future for all life? Are there some guidelines for personal value and social strategy-building that can give us a chance to change abuse to nurture?

Reverence and Responsibility. In the context of our reality of resource abuse and its consequence of hunger, we are reminded once again about the intrinsic value of reverence and responsibility as trustees of the earth's resources. This is the case, be it in the mystical life of a person like Albert Schweitzer,[44] a pragmatic interpretation of responsible anthropocentrism in a W.H. Murdy,[45] or a sense of challenge for the maintenance of the quality of our relationships with the whole environment as reflected in Rene Dubos:[46]

> We must base our actions upon value judgments on the quality of the relationships between humankind and the earth, in the future as well as in the present. This is our noblesse oblige....

Dubos continues:

> The basic need of our time is to develop qualitative relationships and qualitative change. This provides us with a whole new frontier and redirection of science and technology to the goals of quality which are so absolutely essential for survival.[47]

Our task is to participate in the ongoing process of creation itself. We are "late-comers" in the process, but we have a unique contribution to make to it.

Justice and Sustainability. Combining the insights of Aldo Leopold with the new thrusts in ecumenical thought about the "Just, Participatory and Sustainable Society," one can suggest that new ethics address our relationships not only with each other but with the resources of the earth.[48] Perhaps we can say: "Good is that which contributes to justice, participation in the ongoing process of creation, and global sustainability both now and into the distant future. Evil is that which diminishes justice, the right to participate in the ongoing process of our social life and creation itself, and is unsustainable, both now and into the distant future." Aldo Leopold said simply: "A thing is right when it tends to preserve the integrity, stability and beauty of the biotic community. It is wrong when it tends the other way."[49]

With these norms, we can evaluate and reformulate our social, economic and technological policies, our programs and personal involvements in prevailing values and lifestyles with reference to resource use and abuse. Anything less than this kind of basic orientation and change will be band-aid operations, keeping healthy systems of abuse and exploitation so obviously clear in our history.

The needed change from resource abuse to justice and sustainability constitutes an enormous task. The magnitude of resource abuse, a clear cause of hunger, requires us to think and plan in large and new ways. We must:[50]

1. Expand the theory of value far beyond, but including, human centeredness.

2. Expand the concept of value of all life in creation.

3. Expand prevailing theories and practices of justice to include the whole citizenship of the biosphere.

4. Provide explicit rights and guarantees for future generations.

5. Expand human knowledge about the survival of our whole eco-system.

6. Provide clear guidelines for assuring equality of considerations for the use of all life forms (all resources). This means:

a. Identifying the broad, evolutionary limitations, parameters, and goals to which we must be sensitive if we are to survive as a species.

b. Examining the resource limitations and parameters facing us in the next century.

c. Establishing goals for this long-run period, keeping in mind that these goals must be consistent with evolutionary goals and limits.

7. Develop new laws and regulations for the purpose of maintaining the integrity of the eco-systems of planet earth . . . the resources of the land.

Ultimately, doing these things requires a metaphysical and theological understanding of the human role and purpose (our role and purpose) in the whole scheme of things. The challenge of new attitudes, ethics, and strategy is awesome. Can we afford to ignore it? The historical record of resource abuse says no.

NOTES

1. See Lester Brown, "The Worldwide Loss of Cropland," *Worldwatch Paper, #24,* October 1978.

2. Niel Sampson, Executive Vice-President, National Association of Conservation Districts, quoted in *Farming the Lord's Land,* Charles Lutz, editor, p. 123.

3. W.C. Lowdermilk, "The Conquest of the Land Through 7000 Years," U.S. Government Printing Office, 1953.

4. *Scientific American,* March 1977, "The Oldest Rocks and the Growth of the Continents," p. 92.

5. Dudley Stamp, *Land for Tomorrow,* pp. 48–52.

104   C. DEAN FREUDENBERGER

6. M. K. Tolba, "The State of the Environment Report," paragraph 54.
7. United Nations, *Desertification: Its Causes and Consequences*, p. 9.
8. *Ibid.*
9. Tolba, *ibid.*, paragraph 55.
10. W.H. Pawley, "Possibilities for Increasing World Food Production," *Ceres*, November/December 1974, p. 22.
11. Lester Brown, *Worldwatch Paper #24*, "The Worldwide Loss of Cropland," p. 5.
12. United Nations, M.K. Tolba, "Kenya: A Commitment to Conservation," p. 6.
13. Eric Eckholm, *Losing Ground*, p. 25.
14. Tolba, "Kenya: A Commitment to Conservation," p. 6.
15. Rene Dubos, *The Wooing of the Earth*, p. 27.
16. United Nations, "Overview," United Nations Conference on Desertification, p. 3.
17. Utgard and McKenzie, *Man's Finite Earth*, p. 250.
18. U.S. Council on Environmental Quality, *Environmental Quality Report: The Tenth Annual Report of the Council on Environmental Quality*, 1980, pp. 174, 181, and 261.
19. Margaret Mead, *Aspects of the Future*, p. 257.
20. *Environmental Quality Report, op. cit.*, p. 89.
21. Mead, *op. cit.*, p. 253.
22. Lester Brown, *The Twenty-Ninth Day*, pp. 61–65.
23. Presidential Commission, *The Global 2000 Report to the President*, Vol. I.
24. National Lands Study, "Where Have the Farmlands Gone?" Shirley Foster Field, p. 1.
25. Peter J. Ognibene, "Vanishing Farmlands: Selling Out the Soil," in *Saturday Review*, May 1980, p. 29.
26. National Lands Study, *op cit.*, p. 1.
27. *Ibid.*, p. 6.
28. Ognibene, *op. cit.*, p. 29.
29. Niel Sampson, Executive Vice-President of the National Conservation District, quoted in Ognibene, *op. cit.*, p. 31.
30. Cornelius Van Bavel, "Soil and Oil," *Science*, July 15, 1977, p. 12.
31. *Ibid.*
32. Dudley Stamp, *Land for Tomorrow*, p. 19.
33. Interview on "Face the Nation," November 26, 1978 (CBS Television and Radio Network).

34. President Jimmy Carter, Environmental Quality Report, *ibid.,* p. 743.

35. Lowdermilk, *op.cit.,* p.30.

36. *Ibid.*

37. Barbara Ward and Rene Dubos, *Only One Earth,* p. 12.

38. E.F. Schumacher, *Small Is Beautiful,* p. 20.

39. Lyn White, "The Historical Roots of Our Ecological Crisis," *Science,* March 10, 1967, p. 1205.

40. Charles Lutz (ed.), *Farming the Lord's Land,* pp. 132–33.

41. See Lester Brown, *Worldwatch Paper #14,* "Redefining National Security." Also see *The Twenty-Ninth Day* by the same author.

42. "The Worldwide Loss of Cropland," *op.cit.,* p. 42.

43. *Dustbowl: The Southern Plains in the 1930's,* p. 243.

44. See Albert Schweitzer, *The Teaching of the Reverence for Life.*

45. See W.H. Murdy, "Anthropocentrism: A Modern Version," *Science,* March 1975.

46. See Rene Dubos, *The Wooing of the Earth.*

47. *Op. cit.,* pp. 157 and 244.

48. See Aldo Leopold, *The Sand County Almanac;* see also the World Council of Churches reports in Volumes I and II, *Faith and Science in an Unjust World.*

49. *The Sand County Almanac,* p. 217.

50. The outline was taken from William T. Blackstone, Chapter 9, "The Search for an Environmental Ethic," in Tom Regan (ed.), *Matters of Life and Death,* pp. 331–32; the three sub-parts (a, b, and c) in #6 are from Kenneth Dahlberg, *Beyond the Green Revolution,* p. 139.

9
Trade Barriers to Development in Poor Nations

Norman Faramelli

What has trade to do with feeding hungry people? At first glance, the relationship between trade and solutions to hunger seems remote. In fact, the links are often indirect and complicated. Nevertheless, it is essential that we understand the role of trade in solving the problems of hunger, especially as trade is related to agricultural and industrial development in the poorer nations.[1]

This essay first highlights the general connections between trade and solving world hunger problems, and then explores trade barriers and their removal.

I. TRADE AND HUNGER

Trade should be understood as a two-way flow: exports from the developing nations to the industrialized nations, and imports from the industrialized nations to the developing nations. Both flows affect the patterns of economic growth, particularly in the poorer nations.

A. Two Mistakes in Development

To provide some background for the discussion, we should explore two common mistakes in development theory and practice. Ironically, in both of these, the poorer nations usually place *too much* emphasis upon trade.

1. *Ignoring Agricultural Development.* In many of the poorer nations, the Western style of development has been emulated with some disastrous results. In an effort to industrialize rapidly, some nations have placed their primary emphasis upon industrial development and have virtually ignored agricultural development. To get necessary foreign exchange for industrial expansion, the exports of raw materials and, in some cases, of manufactured products have increased. At the same time, food imports to the poorer nations have increased dramatically. Moreover, the high price of imported food makes it difficult for the poorest half of the population to buy it. This type of development could be seen in some Latin American nations. It also occurred in the Commonwealth of Puerto Rico (via its Operation Bootstrap program).

Unfortunately, the advocates of this model of development in the U.S. completely failed to realize that the U.S. became an industrial power only after it developed massive agricultural capabilities. For many years, University of Chicago economist Theodore Schultz has warned against the type of development that ignores the agricultural sector and human resources. His receipt of a Nobel Prize in 1979 indicates that economists and development planners are now beginning to listen.

2. *The Wrong Kind of Agricultural Development.* The second mistake is a variation of the first. In this model, agriculture is heavily mechanized and food production proceeds in a manner that does not utilize the available human resources. In order to get foreign exchange for industrial development and to pay for the expensive farm machinery, crops are grown for export. Crop exporters are capitalizing on what economists term "natural" or "comparative advantage."[2] The crops are exported largely to the richer nations, a practice which has been referred to as "export cropping" or "cash cropping."

This pattern of development results in massive social dislocations in rural areas. It encourages large migration to urban areas. In addition, the emphasis on food exports means that agricultural development is largely devoted to increasing foreign exchange (via cash crops). Meeting the nutritional needs of all (especially the poor) in the producing country is given low priority. High-priced imported food enters the cash-cropping countries, but, like the profit their cash crops produce, the imported food does not reach the poor.

Both types of development are based on the desire for foreign exchange, generated by trade, to stimulate agricultural and primarily industrial development. But in both cases, the increase of exports from the poorer to the richer nations results in unbalanced development. Hence, a myth needs to be investigated, namely, that increased trade between the rich and the poor nations will always enhance the poor nation's ability to deal with its hunger problems. Sometimes the opposite is true. As we shall see, the important question is *what kind* of agricultural and industrial development. Only certain types will result in the feeding of hungry people. Those that keep the nutritional needs of all people in mind when the development program is designed are the ones most likely to help the poor.

Export cropping often sounds like a good idea but usually works to keep poor people hungry. When a relatively poor country devotes disproportionate amounts of land, capital and agricultural labor to the production of food crops (so-called "cash crops") for export (e.g., coffee, sugar, fruit and vegetables), this is done at the expense of production for domestic consumption. This often misapplies available resources to the production of items desired for the tables of the affluent importing nation and forecloses on their application to the production of basic foods needed to satisfy the hungers at home. Moreover, export-cropping typically enriches the owners of the land without returning anything above poverty income to the landless laborers who produce those crops.

B. *The Industrial-Agricultural Balance*

A sound economy needs a combination of agricultural and industrial development. The balance between the two, of course, depends upon human and financial resources, climate, arable land, natural resources, access to capital, and other factors.

Sound or balanced development means productivity (greater output per hour of work) increases in both agriculture and industry. There is no merit in massive subsistence farming as a goal. Such a practice will consign millions to endless poverty. But the development of mechanized farming has to be in balance with the available human and financial resources. That is, there is little value in highly mechanized farming that drains scarce capital resources and proceeds in a manner that is out of balance with human resources. Too much emphasis on mechanized farming usually leads to massive rural displacement and the rapid migration to urban areas (usually to rings around cities). Thus, there is a need to increase productivity (via technology) without resulting in the massive dislocation of people. In order to accomplish that, *both* agricultural and industrial development are needed. But neither has to occur on a large scale in order to be productive.

It is important that the bulk of agricultural development be devoted to meeting the nutritional needs of the wider population, especially the poorest forty percent who do not have the purchasing power to buy imported food. In a balanced economy, the agricultural sector will supply most of the food consumed in the nation, but the use of technology in agriculture will make it possible for an increasing percentage of the population to be employed in the business, industrial, or public sectors of the economy. These jobs will provide people with the money to purchase farm products and the goods they manufacture.

Export cropping should not be categorically dismissed, however, because in some instances it makes sense. But export cropping should not be allowed to dominate agricultural production. When it does dominate, the nation becomes more reliant upon food imports, with the most devastating effects being upon the poorest people.

C. Trade, Capital Formation and Development

As noted, trade can play an important role in providing the foreign exchange needed for the capital outlays in both the agricultural and the industrial sectors. But trade is only one way to get capital. Other sources include foreign investors and aid or loans from the industrialized nations. There are also international sources like the World Bank and the International Monetary

Fund. The problem of loans, of course, is that borrowing increases debt which is already a serious problem to many of the less industrialized nations. Hence, trade is deemed important.

It is important that capital outlays be proportionate to the task at hand and do not unnecessarily drain a limited capital pool. For example, foreign exchange obtained from the export of food, raw materials or manufactured goods can be used to increase agricultural productivity. One way to do that is to accept the Green Revolution lock, stock and barrel. This means mechanized farming (large tractors, harvesters, drying equipment), irrigation systems, hybrid seeds, and chemical fertilizers, plus herbicides and pesticides. The cost of such a package requires large amounts of capital. But does it make sense to desire foreign exchange to perpetuate a style of development that will drain capital, cause social dislocations, and fail to use available human resources?

In many poor nations, appropriate or medium-sized technology is needed. In Bangladesh, for instance, the use of a gasoline pump to irrigate land is needed far more than large tractors. In some countries, the soil has been so depleted of nutrients that organic fertilizers will not work effectively, and the nutrients from chemical fertilizers can play a useful role in increasing agricultural yields. Many times small scale mechanization will be effective and make the giant-size tractor unnecessary.

In the industrial sector, capital is needed to increase the productivity of workers. But if a vast labor pool is available, it makes little sense to mechanize production extensively while many workers are unemployed. As industrial development occurs, productivity increases in the industrial sector *are* essential if the workers' wages are to increase. But balance is needed.

Since the debt is already a pervasive problem in developing nations, and since these nations are attempting to break the dependency patterns associated with development aid, increases in trade are seen as key ways to deal with capital formation.

D. *"Free Trade" Versus "Fair Trade"*

If trade is to be an effective instrument for dealing with world hunger, we should question the notion that "free trade" always works for the benefit of everyone. That is, free trade does not always result in fair trade. Some specific questions to be raised are: What kind of trade? At what level? On what terms? For whose benefit?

Are the needs of the entire society addressed with the foreign exchange received from the expansion of trade? In March 1980, the final report of the Presidential Commission on World Hunger was released. It is interesting to note that four of the twenty commissioners challenged the Commission's assumptions about free trade. The four commissioners noted that the section on trade "assumes a fundamentally free trade approach which by definition camouflages the more appropriate fair trade issues."[3]

The four commissioners also noted that the section on trade in the report:

> . . . largely ignores the need for less developed countries' self-reliant development based upon production for local consumption whether in commodities or manufactured goods. Less developed countries need to develop their own domestic markets by generating indigenous "effective demand" through more jobs and better incomes. On the national level, less developed countries cannot expect to increase individual purchasing power by relying on foreign exchange receipts which seldom "trickle down" to the poor and hungry.[4]

Only when that occurs can *free* trade become *fair* trade.

Another aspect considered by the four commissioners was that higher prices of commodities and even the stabilization of commodity prices, despite their inherent desirability, could lead to more land being devoted to cash cropping while the needs of the people are ignored. Thus, we cannot assume that increased foreign exchange, via increased trade, will always foster social and economic equity either between nations or within a nation.

One still hears the mistaken notion that free trade benefits everyone equally. Inequality between nations has been perpetuated by the price of imports to the poorer nations rising faster than the price of its exports. For example, in 1960 three tons of bananas could buy a tractor, but in 1970, the same tractor cost an equivalent of eleven tons of bananas.[5]

The noted social scientist Gunnar Myrdal has remarked that international development theory has often provided a "smoke-screen" for global inequities. According to Myrdal, the theory of international trade has not offered a satisfactory explanation for the reality of underdevelopment. On the contrary, its effect has been to explain away the problem of international equality and to justify the current inequities.[6]

Although the reduction of trade barriers to agricultural and industrial development will enhance free trade, it is not axiomatic that trade will promote greater equality. Questions on the kind and level of development are needed. Will trade and development create dependency? For whose benefit are they working?

There are often large differences in the benefits to the rich and the poor nations as a result of increased trade. There are also vast differences in income and wealth within a developing nation. Whether foreign exchange is used to meet nutritional needs depends upon national policies. But that issue is beyond the scope of this essay and will not be explored here.

Several years ago, Bread for the World conducted a campaign called "Aid for Self-Reliance." The question was how could U.S. development assistance be provided in a manner that promoted self-reliance. Although the terms "aid" and "self-reliance" seem to be contradictory, assistance is needed before self-reliance can occur.

We now need a similar campaign to highlight "Trade for Self-Reliance," as contradictory as the terms might sound. Self-reliance does not mean autonomy. It simply means less dependency or less reliance upon food imports and imported products and more reliance upon food producing capability within nations. It also means more emphasis on manufacturing of products for local consumption. This, of course, means that trade must be selective. Can the U.S. trade with the developing nations in a manner that promotes self-reliance? The real answer, of course, depends upon what is happening in the developing nations. What kinds of policies are being implemented there? Trade for Self-Reliance assumes that most of the nutritional needs of the people in the developing nation are being addressed by local food production.

II. TRADE BARRIERS AND THEIR REMOVAL

Having set the context for understanding the complex role of trade in promoting agricultural and industrial development, we can now identify barriers to the type of development that might enhance social and economic justice in the developing nations. Then we can address the removal of those barriers.

A. *Trade: The Two Way Street*

We have looked at trade from the standpoint of the less industrialized nations, but we should also recognize the importance of trade to the rich nations.

In 1965, the imports from the third world accounted for thirty-six percent of total U.S. imports. By 1977, the amount had risen to over forty-seven percent, due primarily to higher-priced oil from OPEC.

The U.S. imports from the non-OPEC developing nations, however, had also risen. Between 1970 and 1977, these imports grew at an average annual rate of twenty-one percent, compared to a fifteen percent growth rate of U.S. imports from industrialized nations. The most important fact, however, is that the growth of manufactured goods from non-OPEC developing nations grew twenty-five percent annually between 1970 and 1977. The share of manufactured products in the total U.S. imports from developing non-OPEC nations increased from twenty-nine percent (1965) to fifty percent (1977). Textiles, clothing, footwear, and consumer electronics make up the bulk of the U.S. imports of manufactured goods.

Despite its large balance-of-trade deficit, the U.S. still continues a trade surplus in manufactured goods with developing nations ($14 billion in 1977). In addition, U.S. income from service exports (investment income, fees and royalties, shipping and insurance, interest income, etc.) has a positive effect on the U.S. current account balance.

Even though the capital account of the U.S. payments balance shows new outflows to the developing nations, these outflows are the basis for current and future inflows of income on investment and loans. In 1970, for example, forty-seven percent of the total U.S. direct investment income originated in developing nations. This shows a major U.S. involvement in the development of these nations. In other words, it has been profitable for U.S. based transnational corporations to invest in developing nations.[7]

The U.S., therefore, has a major stake in trade with the less industrialized nations, in terms of both our exports and their imports. For example, imports from the less industrialized nations to the U.S. allow us access to the raw materials we need, and provide consumer benefits through lower product prices. For instance, a recent study found that imported products from all areas are 10.8 percent less expensive than comparable domestic goods.[8] In addition, development of the less industrialized nations provides the U.S. with a market for our exports. Exports account for roughly one in eight jobs in the U.S. manufacturing sector. These exports provide jobs for many Americans. As we shall see below, many labor union leaders and workers do not share this perspective.

B. *Trade Barriers and Some Efforts To Remove Them*

The barriers that are imposed to restrict or regulate the flow of imports can be listed under two categories: "tariff" and "nontariff." In recent years, the U.S. and other industrialized nations have developed an ambivalent attitude toward trade with the less industrialized nations. On the one hand, the concept of "non-reciprocity" has been applied to North-South trade, by which the poorer nations receive the advantage of tariff and non-tariff liberalizations by the industrialized nations *without* being expected to offer similar reductions in their own trade barriers. In addition, the industrialized nations have established a General Systems of Preference (GSP) under which certain developing nations are able to enter the markets of the industrialized nations duty free or with reduced tariffs. But under the U.S. system, some labor intensive manufactured goods, such as shoes and textiles, are not covered, since preferential treatment is deemed to be harmful to domestic manufacturers in those areas.

The benefits of the GSP have been highly concentrated. Among the top beneficiaries of the GSP are Taiwan, South Korea, Hong Kong, and Mexico. In 1978, they accounted for sixty-eight percent of the value of duty free GSP imports. Other beneficiaries were Singapore, Yugoslavia, Argentina, India, and Israel.[9]

The Hunger and Global Security Bill, designed and promoted by Bread for the World for consideration by the U.S. Congress, contains a section on trade. In that section, BFW calls for a wider distribution of the benefits of the GSP. Hence, tariff concessions should be extended to some of the goods, like textiles, produced in the less industrialized nations.[10]

Expanding trade with many of the poorer, less industrialized nations raises a host of domestic issues. For example, there has been a resurgence of protectionism in many of the industrialized nations (including the U.S.) due to their slow growing economies and high unemployment rates. Thus, these nations have erected trade barriers such as quantitative ceilings on imports. The U.S. and other industrialized nations, for instance, have put quotas on imports of footwear and color televisions. In recognition of this protectionist stance, Bread for the World has called for an equivalent reduction in the imports of these goods from other more industrially developed nations so that there will be no net increase in imports.

The ambivalence of the current trade policies is well illustrated by the results of the recent Tokyo Round of Multilateral Trade Negotiations (MTN).[11] A key goal of all the industrialized nations was to allow the developing nations to participate fully in the trading system organized under the General Agreement of Tariffs and Trade (GATT) in order to change GATT's image of favoring only the rich. But the results of MTN were mixed.

As a result of MTN, the tariffs on raw materials were reduced by sixty percent, but the tariffs on semi- and finished-manufactured products were reduced by only twenty-seven percent and twenty-four percent, respectively. In addition, some products are subject to restricted trade through non-tariff barriers. Nevertheless, there were some improvements for the less industrialized nations in the terms of trade set by the MTN.

As part of the MTN, there were significant changes in the GATT framework and agreements on several codes of conduct on specific non-tariff barriers. For the developing nations, there were: (a) inclusion of an "enabling" clause that provides a stronger legal basis for non-reciprocity (i.e., allowing the richer nations to extend selectively differential and more favorable treatment to poorer nations on a non-most favored nation status, and (b) a commitment from the developing nations to assume fuller GATT obligations as their economies expand.

C. U.S. Obstacles to Liberalized Trade

Faced with slow economic growth, high inflation and unemployment rates, labor unions and workers in the U.S. and other industrialized nations are leery of more liberalized trade with anyone, including the developing nations. Hence, "protectionism" or the "buy American" attitude is fast growing. As one bumper sticker put it: "If you are out of a job, eat your Toyota." Labor unions and workers do not want to be sacrificed on the altar of free trade.

The argument that free trade is good for the U.S. since it ultimately provides more outlets for U.S. exports is not convincing to labor leaders and workers. The workers have experienced first hand the flow of U.S. capital out of the U.S. to other countries, by way of transnational corporations, with the corresponding job reductions at home. Hence, they do not believe the argument that everyone benefits from free trade.

In response to the needs of the U.S. based transnational corporations, U.S. trade policy helped to promote the expansion of offshore assembly operations. In 1966, provisions for special offshore assembly were introduced in the U.S. Tariff Schedules, exempting from duty U.S. components used in manufactured goods assembled in another country. The tariffs are imposed on foreign value-added only. Mexico was the largest single beneficiary of these provisions and linked its border development programs to them.[12]

What we are experiencing is the traditional case of foreign imports providing increased efficiency for the U.S. economy at large, *plus* lower product prices to consumers, *versus* the losses of employment opportunities in declining industries. The benefits, which are substantial, are dispersed throughout the economy, while the cost of dislocations of jobs is concentrated in relatively few industries with disproportionate impacts in certain areas of the country.

Economic development in the U.S. and other industrialized

nations has entailed major changes in the economic structure, including a shift in jobs away from labor-intensive industries toward services and more technology-intensive industries. The growth of imports from the poorer nations is not the major factor, to be sure, but it does accelerate the shift.

D. *Steps That Need To Be Taken*

The export of manufactured goods from the developing nations to the U.S. and other industrialized nations might provide the type of development needed for a sound economic base that will allow each nation to meet its nutritional goals. Despite the desirability of providing the developing nations with more outlets for their goods, it is ludicrous to think of increasing foreign imports to the U.S. without addressing the issues of domestic unemployment. Many workers and labor unions are skeptical of the "trade adjustment assistance" that has been provided in the past. As a labor leader once told me, "Liberals talk trade adjustment, but my people face only unemployment."

Hence, the first priority is to get adequate assistance to those who are dislocated. This assistance will involve job training and the creation of new jobs. Retraining for non-existent jobs is a farce. Thus, it is folly to speak of increasing foreign imports as long as eight percent of the U.S. work force is unemployed. We should not forget that the workers most likely to be displaced by imports from the less industrialized nations are likely to be female members of minority groups, the elderly, poorly educated, and low skilled. Thus, slogans about "trade adjustment assistance" make no sense unless they are accompanied by support during transition, job retraining and new job opportunities. Ironically, a *full employment program* at home might very well be the most effective remedy for liberalizing trade with the less industrialized nations so that they can export more manufactured products to us.

There are other issues that need to be considered: Trade agreements need to be integrated with the plans of the developing nation to develop its agricultural and industrial sectors. Similarly, it is essential that the U.S. development assistance program be closely coordinated with trade agreements so that both will foster balanced economic development. Increased trade alone is no guarantee that balanced development will occur and serve the needs of the entire society.

The General System of Preference should be redesigned to favor more than the current beneficiaries. Those countries on the UN list of the "most seriously affected" (MSA) nations—with regard to widespread poverty and hunger—should receive special consideration.

SUMMARY

Trade can play a valuable role in the economic development of the less industrialized nations. But trade has to be selective. It is only one instrument in the overall development program. Rapidly expanding trade of raw materials and cash crops can be counterproductive to a developing nation's ability to meet its own nutritional goals and objectives.

Free trade alone will not lead toward more equity either between nations or within nations. Fair trade that will enhance self-reliance is needed. Furthermore, trade liberalization is particularly needed in the manufacture sector, especially for poor nations not favored by the U.S. General System of Preference. Trade provides a means for a less industrialized nation to acquire foreign exchange without going into debt or without fostering dependency relationships. But trade is a limited instrument of development for the less industrialized nations, especially at a time when overall world trade is not expanding.[13]

At home, the pursuit of full employment objectives is one of the most effective ways to facilitate the liberalization of trade. In the process of achieving full employment it is absolutely essential that adequate transitional assistance, job training, and new job opportunities be provided to those who are dislocated due to the increased imports from the developing nations. Under no circumstances should the poorer workers in this country be asked to bear the full burden of assisting the poorer nations of the world.

NOTES

1. Throughout this discussion a variety of terms will be used to describe the "developing" and the "more developed" nations. For example: poor = poorer = developing = less industrialized = third world; rich = richer = developed = more industrialized. The terms *on each line* are used interchangeably.

2. Discussions of "comparative advantage" could be found in any textbook on international economics. For a critique of this concept, see Frances Moore Lappe and Joseph Collins, *Food First* (Boston: Houghton Mifflin Co., 1977), pp. 181–209.

3. *Overcoming World Hunger—The Challenge Ahead,* Report of the Presidential Commission on World Hunger (Washington, D.C.: Government Printing Office, March 1980). The section on trade is on pp. 55–68. The dissenting commissioners were Harry Chapin, Sen. Patrick Leahy, Congressman Richard Nolan (pp. 215–17) and Congressman Benjamin Gilman (pp. 236–37).

4. *Ibid.,* p. 215.

5. United Nations Development Program, "Changing Factors in World Development," prepared by Don Casey (Development Issue Paper 5, Global I), UNDP, August 1975, p. 2, cited in *Food First, op. cit.,* p. 183.

6. G. Myrdal, *The Challenge of World Poverty* (New York: Vintage Books, 1971), p. 277.

7. This section is based primarily on (a) John Sewell, "Can the North Prosper Without Growth and Progress in the South?" in *The United States and World Development—Agenda 1979,* ed. M. McLaughlin and staff of the Overseas Development Council (New York: Praeger Publishers, 1979) and (b) a paper by John Sewell and John Mathieson (Overseas Development Council) on "The U.S. Stake in Trade with the Third World," presented at a conference sponsored by the Bread for the World Educational Fund, "In Our Interest: The U.S. Stake in a Just Economic Order" (Washington, D.C.: Wesley Theological Seminary, October 12–14, 1979).

8. William Cline, *Imports and Consumers: A Survey Analysis* (New York: The American Retail Federation and the National Retail Merchants Association, 1979).

9. From paper by Helen Kramer, "The Role of International Trade," at the Conference cited in note 7, pp. 11–12. These nations account for fifteen percent of the GSP duty-free imports.

10. See Bread for the World Background Paper #48: "Hunger and Global Security—A Description of The Hunger and Global Security Bill."

11. The Tokyo Round of Multilateral Trade Negotiations, GATT, Geneva, April 1979.

12. Kramer, *op. cit.,* pp. 10–11.

13. See A. L. Malabre, Jr., "Expansion of World Trade Slows Nearly to Halt, Reflecting Slump Overseas, New Restrictions," *Wall Street Journal,* May 28, 1981, for a picture that is not optimistic.

10
Food Insecurity: The Inadequacy and Unreliability of Reserves

Jayne Millar-Wood

During the seven years of plenty the land produced abundant crops, all of which Joseph collected and stored in the cities. In each city he stored the food from the fields around it. There was so much grain that Joseph stopped measuring it—it was like the sand of the sea.

The seven years of plenty that the land of Egypt had enjoyed came to an end, and the seven years of famine began, just as Joseph had said. There was famine in every other country, but there was food throughout Egypt. . . . The famine grew worse and spread over the whole country, so Joseph opened all the storehouses and sold grain to the Egyptians. People came to Egypt from all over the world to buy grain from Joseph, because the famine was severe everywhere.

Genesis 41:47–49, 53–54, 56–57

This chapter[1] is about world food security—and insecurity. Specifically, it is about the importance of establishing a world food reserve system that can, in the twentieth century and beyond, provide the same kind of security for today's poor and hungry people in developing countries as Joseph's storehouse provided centuries ago for the people of Egypt. The following pages briefly describe what a food reserve is and how it works. They also discuss why such a reserve is needed and what efforts have been made to date to establish it, what issues remain to be resolved and what needs to be done, especially by the U.S. and its citizens to assure that an adequate and reliable world food reserve system exists in a hungry world.

Whatever the prognosis for long-term world food production, the inescapable fact is that during the past decade world food consumption has come dangerously close to exceeding total food supplies. For example, during the world crisis of 1974, available year-end world reserves were down to 179 million metric tons (MMT), the equivalent of little more than seven weeks of world consumption. The projected grain reserves for 1981/82 are approximately 272 MMT or 18% of world consumption. (This is the minimum safe level for world security, as stated by the U.N.) Between 1974 and 1980, harvests did produce some surpluses, but prices fluctuated violently during this time due to the rise and fall of production, as well as to the sporadic buying of grain by Russia and The People's Republic of China. The latter is rapidly becoming the major importer of U.S. grain.

Living precariously on this production tightrope are more than 460 million malnourished people, mostly in the developing countries. Many of these countries rely on imports of food grain (primarily from the U.S., Canada, Australia and Argentina) to meet the most basic and minimal needs of their people. For these people, a significant loss or gain in world grain production in a year means the loss or gain each day of precious life-giving calories, since depending on the region of the world grains make up anywhere between 20% and 70% of a person's diet. In some instances, hunger and malnutrition result from the inadequacy and unreliability of food grain reserves. Though grain reserves in themselves do not ensure anyone food, especially the poor, unless food policies within nations are geared to distribute food resources equitably, the establishment of a viable world food reserve system would provide a measure of security heretofore not available. This security, in the form of food available to consumers at stable prices or through short-term emergency food aid, could contribute to an improvement in the nutritional status of poor people. The absence of such a security system, in turn, is a contributing cause of hunger.

What is a food reserve system and how does it work to promote world food security? Simply put, a food reserve is a stock of one or more grains (e.g., wheat, corn) consciously designated as a "reserve" for one or more specific purposes. A world food reserve is not a single stockpile of grain stored up in one place, cared for and controlled by one nation. Rather such a reserve would be a *system* of reserves supported and maintained by producing and consuming countries and operated by the same set of rules. Such a reserve system would require commitments by producing and consuming countries alike to store grain in times of surplus so there will be sufficient supplies in times of scarcity.

The establishment of a world food reserve system is dependent on the amount and availability of surplus food stocks. The existence of a surplus however, does not, by definition, constitute a reserve. Rather, to design and implement an effective global food security system requires a *conscious* effort to acquire and store food for the achievement of specific objectives that would benefit not only the hungry, but the producers and other consumers as well. These objectives include:

1. Provisions of sufficient supplies of food to avert famines in times of scarcity.

2. Provision of a stable supply of U.S. or other donor government food aid, where and when it is really needed.

3. Stabilization of food prices, leveling the steep price rises occurring in times of scarcity that have prevented poor nations from making food purchases on the international market when they need them most.

4. Prevention of an equally steep decline in the price of grain during a glut which prevents the farmer from receiving a fair return on his production.

5. Elimination of one source of inflation which has disrupted development planning.

Two different types of reserve are really required to fulfill these five objectives. First, *an emergency food reserve,* encompassing the first two objectives, is necessary to alleviate specific crisis situations such as those in West Africa and Cambodia. Such reserves could be purchased and held by food donor countries until an emergency situation develops, but might also be held in lesser quantities by developing countries in anticipation of difficult times. Second, a *market stabilization reserve* is also needed to respond to the latter three objectives and to minimize extreme shifts in world market prices resulting from fluctuations in world production. This reserve would also have to be large enough so that when prices go upward, its release onto the market would satisfy demand sufficiently to depress prices. Its beneficiaries would not be exclusively victims of drought or flood, but *all* consumers of grain products, including ourselves. Such a two-tier system of food reserves would contribute substantially to bolstering world food security in both the short and long term.

Why is a world food reserve needed? It is one thing to acknowledge the existence of a world food crisis and quite another to propose and implement programs adequate to resolve this immense problem. Making the developing world's lands more productive is the most promising solution to world hunger. It is a long-term solution, as irrigation schemes are implemented, as governments become committed, and as fertilizer, hybrid seed, and other technological advances penetrate the rural world. For many poor people, however, increasing productivity is very difficult as they lack access to the land, water, capital and agricultural imputs that could make the land more productive. Even with all these goals achieved, sufficient food supplies are by no means guaranteed. The vagaries of climate that have produced famine in Africa also cause a rise and fall in grain production in the United States. The natural, yet unpredictable, cycle of scarcity and plenty, sufficiency and insufficiency, of course, affects more keenly those countries just barely able to feed themselves. Already the developing countries, especially in Asia and Africa, import a growing quantity of food to meet the needs of their people. In 1979, they imported 77 MMT or forty-five percent of the grain traded on the world market.[2] In the future, as rapid population growth continues, these developing country imports are projected to be much higher as their production of staple food crops continues to fall short of consumption requirements.

In times of short-supply, the developing countries depend all the more on the world market and on individual government food aid to make up for the short-fall. When there is a world shortage, the price of grain will be prohibitively high, and as a result the U.S. government aid dollar can purchase only limited quantities of food for distribution abroad. The developing country which requires this food will similarly be less able to buy grain at inflated world market prices that result from the shortfall. Furthermore, the goal of self-sufficiency, where it can be achieved, is also subject to the vagaries of the world market price of grain. This is because in times of surplus many developing country farmers find themselves competing with a deflated world market price for their produce, and thus the incentive for them to increase their production and grow a surplus for their own use is reduced.

Recent history demonstrates the critical need for a world food reserve system. In 1974, world grain production fell as bad weather in southern Asia and Sahelian West Africa brought severe famine. By this time, the large grain reserves of the 1960's had been drawn down as a result of decisions by the wheat-producing nations to reduce production in order to raise prices. Significant grain purchases by the Soviet Union in 1972 and 1973 further contributed to the rapid drain in stocks. Where carryover stocks in 1970 had been sufficient to provide world grain consumption requirements for roughly seventy-four days, by 1974 there remained carryover stocks for only forty-four days.

Grain prices shot skyward, largely due to the low reserve levels. One report has noted that in 1970, at a time when the total stockpile was large, blight reduced corn stocks by seventeen million tons but the price went up only twenty cents a bushel. Three years later, with a relatively smaller stockpile from which to draw, an equal fall in corn stocks pushed the price up to eighty-four cents a bushel, four times as much.[3] All grains were affected. Between 1972 and 1974, the price of wheat tripled and did not return to previous levels until 1976. It is said that price stability has never returned.

Although the entire world suffered the higher cost for foodstuffs, in the end the chief victims, as always, were the poor in developing countries. Industrial country efforts to supply stopgap food aid to famine areas were greatly hindered because aid allocations brought half or less the amount of food than they would under more stable price conditions. U.S. PL 480 food aid, for instance, dropped from 9.9 MMT in 1972 to 3.3 MMT in 1974. What is more, developing countries, untouched by the famine yet dependent on grain imports, lost precious foreign exchange in satisfying their own basic needs. In 1974, developing countries imported as much grain as the previous year, but paid five billion dollars more.

The 1973–74 world food crisis was only the most recent of a series of major fluctuations in grain prices occurring over the years. This time, however, the world's nations were so close to running out of sufficient market and basic food aid supplies that they were provoked into trying to find a solution. As Joseph recommended reserves to the Pharaoh centuries ago when he was faced with seven years of famine, the nations gathered at the U.N. World Food Conference in 1974 urged the establishment of an international food reserve program as essential to world food security. Unfortunately, such a system has still not been wholeheartedly adopted.

If a world food reserve system is so necessary, why hasn't it been established? Despite rhetorical agreement, activity to bring about food security through the establishment of an adequate and reliable worldwide system was slow to occur and greatly limited in scale throughout the 1970's. This is the result of a number of factors that have hindered and continue to thwart the establishment of an international reserve system. These include:

• *Lack of political will in producing countries:* The major grain producing countries must tackle a number of complex domestic economic and political issues if they are going to commit resources to establishing a global reserve. Competing interests within these countries make it difficult to resolve many of these issues. In the U.S., for example, despite the tremendous impression on public opinion made by photos of starving Sahelian and Cambodian children, support for foreign aid continues to diminish. Furthermore, the powerful U.S. farm lobby is concerned that price stabilization will mean loss of profits during years of scarcity and they are not convinced that reserve purchases will lift depressed prices equally in times of glut.

• *Lack of political will in consuming countries:* Many of the consuming countries are also developing countries and they have their hands full just trying to grow enough food to satisfy their immediate needs, let alone plan for fallow years hence. They cannot afford to create an effective reserve of their own, and must rely on the producing nations to act. Also, some developing nations find it difficult to admit that they cannot feed themselves. In two extreme cases, Ethiopia and Cambodia, fear of political embarrassment in the former and international interference in the latter kept political leaders from publicizing their country's dilemmas and permitting international aid.

• *Lack of production to commit to reserves:* The U.N. Food and Agriculture Organization (FAO) has set seventeen to eighteen percent of annual world consumption (i.e., sufficient stocks for sixty-two to sixty-six days) as the "minimum safe level for world food security." During the 1970's this minimum level ranged from roughly 175 to more than 200 MMT. Although an international grain reserve meant to supplement existing carryover stocks for emergency requirements need only be a small proportion to provide a sufficient degree of security, the figure of ten million tons recommended by the USDA and FAO is still too large for accumulation in a short time without having a severe upward impact on the world market price. Acquisition of the reserve would be subject to the availability of surplus on the world market, and following the 1974 crisis adequate reserves did not exist for several years. This argument applies to an even greater degree to the market stabilization reserve which some believe would have to comprise about 60–75 MMT of grain in order to meet its objectives.

• *Lack of storage capacity in many developing countries:* At the present time, most developing countries do not possess adequate storage facilities; in fact, most have insufficient facilities for their own pipeline production. Furthermore, their location in tropical and semi-tropical climates with high spoilage rates makes storage difficult and wasteful.

• *Unpredictable purchases of surplus stocks:* Industrialized countries such as Russia that can pay for food imports in times of scarcity in their own country enter the world market from time to time and make large purchases of what would otherwise be surplus food stocks available for a reason. These unpredictable purchases from major producing countries such as the U.S. are often allowed more for domestic political or foreign policy objectives than to satisfy the food needs of the purchasing country. In any event, these sales have the impact of not only raising the world market price of grain but also of decreasing any potential surpluses that might have been used to stock a reserve. Such purchases also breed mistrust by developing countries and others of large suppliers, like the U.S., when such actions continually occur unexpectedly.

• *Unresolved economic, technical and political issues:* There are a number of issues—economic, technical and political—that must be resolved within and among all countries participating in a reserve before it can be implemented. These include size, location, cost-sharing, acquisition and release mechanisms among others. More discussion of these can be found later in the chapter.

What efforts have been undertaken to date to establish a world food security system? In spite of the difficulties noted above, some movement has occurred in the direction of establishing an international grain reserve system. Efforts have been made primarily on two fronts: (1) to establish an emergency grain reserve, and (2) to establish a market stabilization reserve. To date, the former has met with more success than the latter.

1. *Emergency Reserves.* In 1975, the United Nations Seventh Special Session of the General Assembly set up a small, 500,000 ton, International Emergency Food Reserve (IEFR) as an interim measure pending establishment of a more significant and widespread reserve. Ten nations contributed to this first reserve, including Australia, Canada, West Germany, Sweden, the United Kingdom, and India (the only developing country to do so). The United States contributed twenty-five percent of the original stock and has since continued to assist in its replenishment.

This reserve is, however, inadequate to the task. In the single crop year of 1977–78, the Sahelian nations alone had emergency needs equivalent to the entire U.N. reserve. The FAO estimates the worldwide emergency needs due solely to crop failure amount to 2–3 MMT a year. Already experts are suggesting that the emergency reserve be increased to 750,000 tons, but no automatic replenishment mechanism was instituted with the emergency reserve. In 1981 total reserves in the IEFR were 540,000 tons of grain, thus exceeding the original request for 500,000 MT. New contributors to the reserve include Austria, Italy, the OPEC and Spain.

The United States also independently undertook an effort to establish an Emergency Grain Reserve located in and controlled by the United States to act as a symbolic first step and catalyst for eventual adoption of an emergency grain reserves system on an international basis. Congress established an emergency grain reserve consisting of 4 MMT of wheat. The legislation faced considerable opposition from commodity interests, but after three years of consideration its way was paved by the exigencies of the Soviet grain embargo which had threatened a domestic glut. The replenishable reserve allows a small portion of the reserve (300,000 tons) to be used each year, regardless of the overall supply situation, to meet the urgent unanticipated needs of the developing countries. Required to be used only for the most extreme relief requirements and not for standard foreign economic assistance, this reserve provides for a backstop for additional U.S. food aid commitments in a crisis year, though the legislative provisions do not ensure that it be used in this way. Moreover, if the reserve is unused by a certain time, the Secretary of Agriculture can sell it off in any manner. As of mid-1982, this legislation had not been used, and could expire with no food security benefits.

The record that will eventually be established by these two emergency grain reserve efforts—by the UN and by the U.S.—will no doubt determine whether each should be expanded on a global scale. An emergency reserve should, like the U.S. effort, be released only in times of severe supply short-falls in the developing world and should be of sufficient size to deal with most emergencies. Of course no one can predict on what scale the next drought or flood will be, but both the USDA and the FAO have recommended a 10 MMT reserve as likely to ameliorate developing world demands. In the Food Security Act, the U.S. has essentially taken responsibility for forty percent of an eventual 10 MMT global reserve. But a truly effective reserve should have the participation of the entire international community, particularly all those producing nations which possess the resources for purchase and storage.

2. *Market Stabilization Reserve.* The establishment of market stabilization reserves has been more difficult to achieve than an emergency reserve despite discussions in several forums over a number of years. Clearly there is a critical need in the long run for the stabilization of prices so that develor·nent can take place without the economic disruption and political instability caused by inflationary spirals, diversion of precious foreign exchange to

grain purchases, and widespread hunger and malnutrition, all of which are the result of unpredictable grain price increases. Despite unanimous agreement reached by the World Food Conference in 1974 (and represented often since) that an international food reserve system is essential, no such system has yet been achieved in even a limited form because of the difficulty of resolving the fundamental political and economic issues that its establishment poses. Moreover, even if all parties to the system (i.e., producers and consumers from both industrialized and developing countries) were to agree to the ground rules for storing and releasing the grain, there are still many administrative difficulties in operating the reserve on a day-to-day basis which would make it difficult to achieve all the desired objectives of a market stabilization reserve. It is a very complex undertaking and impinges on the interests of many different groups.

The United States and several other countries moved to establish farmer-owned domestic price stabilization reserves (FOR). The U.S. FOR is administered by the Department of Agriculture. Under the Food and Agriculture Act of 1977, farmers receive loans to hold their produce in reserve during times of surplus until grain prices rise substantially. At that time the farmers are required to pay back loans and the grain is sold, causing supplies to expand and the prices to decline.

The Farm Bill of 1981 established a discretionary cap on the FOR, meaning that a maximum of 700 million bushels of wheat (approximately 25.6 MMT) and 1 billion bushels of feed grains (approximately 19 MMT) may be placed in the reserve. As of May 1982, 557.1 million bushels of wheat (15.1 MMT) and 1461.6 million bushels of feed grains (37 MMT) are in the U.S. FOR.

The FOR has been particularly appealing to U.S. farmers because it offers a price stablization mechanism which might not otherwise be available. For example, in 1982 farm prices were depressed, causing large financial losses for some farmers and bankruptcy for others. If the FOR had not been available farmers would have been in an even more desperate situation. Holding this grain in reserve therefore served as a price stabilizing mechanism because if the grain had been released during a time of depressed prices the effects would be devastating for U.S. farmers and for the U.S. government due to farm payments. However, because the size and function of the reserve is dependent on (1) the discretion of the Secretary of Agriculture, (2) the attractiveness of the loan price to farmer participation, and (3) farmer, not government, response to market fluctuations, the reserve's ability always to provide price stability for the U.S., let alone the international grain market, is questionable.

What issues remain to be resolved if an adequate and reliable reserve system is to be established? The establishment of a large-scale institutional food reserve system poses a number of politically and economically challenging issues for producing and consuming, developing and industrialized countries alike. Before such a system can be established, the following issues must be resolved:

1. *Acquisition prices.* It has been suggested that stocks intended for the reserve be purchased when the market is glutted and prices are at their lowest. This would encourage the industrialized, producing countries to participate because such purchases would help to raise deflated farm prices and would cost them less. Such a policy might also, however, justify the fears of farmers that they stand only to lose by a reserve system—not getting their fair market value during the surplus years and losing the benefit of a price swing to higher levels during a time of scarcity.

To encourage the support of producing nations and to provide an incentive to farmers in the developing world to grow as much as they can, it has been suggested that the acquisition price of grain should be commonly agreed on at a fixed rate yielding producers a reasonable return on their investment. This would also assure producers that when grain reserves are released in the market their price will never be less than the cost of production. The desired result, it is said, would be to encourage high levels of production in both the LDC's and the developed world.

2. *Trigger mechanism for release of grain.* The point at which stocks are released onto the world market must be determined. Most economists agree that the mechanism determining release of stored grain should be based on a trigger price rather than determined by quantity, the former usually being a more accurate and timely reflection of the market situation.

For example, the already existing U.S. farmer-held reserve might serve as a model. In 1980, the trigger price for wheat was roughly 150 percent higher than the purchase price of

$2.50/bushel originally paid (as a loan to be returned when the wheat was released onto the market) by the government. Under the trigger price system the wheat price had to rise to $3.75/bushel before a farmer might begin to sell it. Sale, however, was required when the price reached 185 percent of the original price or $4.63/bushel. The first release price allows the farmer to make a reasonable profit; the second mandatory price is intended to keep the domestic price from escalating. The large amounts of grain entering the market would deflate prices.

In a market stabilization reserve, the trigger price should be set at a level that would assure producers that, while benefiting from price stability, they are not threatened by a premature loss of reasonable profits. Such a high trigger price would also allow supply and demand to work within the bounds of the reserve's stabilizing influence.

Unfortunately, no agreement has been achieved on either acquisition or release figures. When the UNCTAD Wheat Trade Convention negotiations disbanded in early 1979, an impasse persisted. The developing countries favored acquisition and release prices of $130 and $160 per metric ton respectively, and the major exporters supported higher, more profitable acquisition and release trigger prices of $140 and $210 respectively.

3. *The size of the reserve.* Suggestions vary widely, ranging between 15 and 80 MMT. The U.N. Food and Agriculture Organization (FAO) has estimated a stock which adequately protects single-year shortfalls at seventeen to eighteen percent of annual world consumption or, in 1977, 61-73 MMT. The United States and the developing countries have generally favored a reserve of 25–30 MMT at minimum, while the European Economic Community prefers a smaller reserve. Whatever the reasoning, some economists argue that the cost for maintaining such large stocks would outweigh potential benefits. It is perhaps because the benefits of providing secure food supplies are so difficult to quantify that there exists so much disagreement on this subject.

4. *Cost sharing for acquisition and maintenance of reserves.* Constructing storage facilities and maintaining grain reserves is expensive. Were the developing countries to hold only a five to seven million ton reserve, the acquisition and storage construction costs are estimated to be roughly $1.75 billion. It is not surprising that they feel this money could be better spent on

immediate food needs or agricultural development. Most reserve plans would appear to call for acquisition and storage by the developed nations, while the developing countries supposedly reap the benefits. This raises many political as well as economic concerns in these countries. It should be noted, however, that until the emergency or price-rise crisis comes that releases the grain stocks onto the world market, the U.S. and other producing countries have benefited by the purchase of their grain and the higher profit this brings their own farmers. Nevertheless, grain reserve costs are viewed by many as a form of foreign aid and too high a price to pay for some other country's food security.

This is an especially important issue for the U.S. as it is most likely to bear the brunt of the expenses, mostly because it is the world's largest producer and possesses the best storage facilities. An emergency reserve fits within the scope of present U.S. foreign aid commitments. It is the larger stabilization reserve which would possibly be a prohibitively expensive undertaking. Some economists say that when the U.S. government maintained comparable stocks during the 1960's, storage and related costs reached three million dollars per day. No real agreement has been reached on the principles determining how costs could be shared.[4]

5. *International participation.* In earlier negotiations on the reserve issue, the developing and industrialized countries could not agree on the level of developing country participation that should be achieved. However, international cooperation is essential to success of the reserve system. There is concern that a loosely coordinated system of national reserves scattered around the globe would be likely to break down when a food crisis threatens. Furthermore, the developing countries cannot themselves afford the cost of storage facilities and maintenance. It has been suggested that one way to encourage international participation and contributions from LDC's and developed countries alike is to make such participation a requirement for eligibility to purchase from the reserve in times of high prices.[5]

More developing countries must be encouraged to implement national grain reserve policies. Under normal conditions, lack of proper storage facilities deters farmers from producing to their full capacity, preventing self-sufficiency and increasing the need for foreign aid. Furthermore, when a food crisis occurs, the lack of holding facilities has led to enormous waste before food could be properly distributed to the areas where it is scarce. Foreign aid funds from the developed nations and multilateral organizations such as the International Fund for Agricultural Development should be utilized to support developing country reserve projects.

The USSR must also be encouraged to participate responsibly in the international grain market and reserve system. It was the surprise entry of the Soviets into Western grain markets in 1972 that contributed to the sudden draw-down in reserve stocks and escalating prices. In that year, the Soviets became a net importer of grain to the tune of some 19 MMT. Advance information regarding crop production is a vital part of maintaining reliable supply and stable prices. Following the World Food Conference in 1972, a Global Information and Early Warning System on Food and Agriculture was established with eighty-seven member countries. The Soviet Union is not a member, creating a major information gap.

One analyst has suggested that stabilization reserve requirements could be held at significantly smaller levels than anticipated were the Soviet Union excluded from the world grain market or were it to operate its own reserve program. In lieu of these options, the Soviets may perhaps be encouraged to cooperate and contribute to world grain reserves if world opinion places increased responsibility for destabilized prices on Soviet shoulders.[6]

If an effective world security system is to be implemented in the future, the support of all sectors of the international community must be achieved, including the producing and consuming nations in both the developing and industrialized world. All have an important role to play in establishing a food security system.

Because the developing countries cannot themselves afford the cost of storage facilities and maintenance, the Food Security Assistance Scheme (FSAS) was developed to help these countries improve their food security. The FSAS, sponsored by the U.N. Food and Agriculture Organization, works within specific countries helping a country to find funds and provides the technical assistance to implement its own national reserve policy. However, while sixty developing countries have adopted explicit food reserve *policies,* only eight of the sixty—China, Chile, Egypt, India, Indonesia, Kenya, Pakistan, and the Philippines—have actually succeeded in implementing policies and establishing reserves.

6. *Location of Reserves.* Where the reserves will be located is another issue. Current grain storage facilities are found in the industrialized producer countries whereas the need for reserves is most often in poor developing countries. To move the reserves closer to the point of greatest need requires substantial investment in grain storage and distribution systems in developing countries. The only expeditious way to do this is through foreign assistance to these countries to build reserve storage capacity, but this necessary contribution has been a sticking point in negotiations.

7. *Management conditions.* How a reserve should be managed and by whom is extremely important to producing and consuming countries, many of which have opposing political philosophies with respect to the issue. The U.S., for example, has argued that reserves held individually by farmers are adequate to meet the U.S. obligation to "hold an international reserve." Others argue that it would be very difficult for the U.S. to meet its international obligations via such a reserve because farmers will not acquire or release reserves according to specific trigger mechanisms or other international guidelines, unless such actions are in their self-interest. These voices would advocate that a government, not individual farmers, should control stockpiled grain. On the other hand, government control of grain reserves in some countries may lead to its use for domestic political purposes rather than to achieve internationally agreed economic or humanitarian goals.

What needs to be done to establish a reserve? Any serious effort to establish an international system of food reserves is going to involve deeply the United States as the world's largest producer and dominant participant in international grain trade. Moreover, the U.S. acted for years as a *de facto* grain reserve for the world. This was not by conscious design, but rather as a result of U.S. domestic agricultural price support policies that encouraged the expansion of production which, in turn, led the U.S. to hold a large proportion of the world's food stocks.

In the establishment of emergency and farmer-held reserves, the U.S. has, thus far, done more than other producing countries to work for world food security. Although it is the leading producer and exporter of food grains, the U.S. needs the other major producers and consumers to make price stabilization possible by the achievement of a wheat convention and other reserve agreements. Such agreements have not been forthcoming. Also, the U.S. should be more direct in participating in an international grain reserve system. Our nation should use its influence (1) to obtain greater participation in an emergency reserve by its fellow producers, and (2) to achieve a rational world grain stabilization policy through a market stabilization reserve that will benefit not only the hungry in developing countries but inflation-plagued consumers in the U.S. as well.

Final attainment of a stabilization reserve, like the emergency reserve, will probably come to depend on U.S. leadership. Active support for world food reserve must be sought not only from the world community of nations but also from U.S. citizens as well. For example, Bread for the World played a key role in the establishment of both the emergency and the farmer-owned reserves. It is important that more people come to realize that existing opposition interests are outweighed by the benefits that a food security policy will bring to large numbers of people within the U.S. as well as in the developing world.

The American consumer should have a particularly strong interest. The U.S. is the only major producer with a completely open market policy. The highs and lows of grain prices on the world market are therefore directly reflected in grain price levels in the U.S. In this inflationary age, U.S. consumers would benefit by the stabilizing effect that a reserve would have on retail prices. Because reliability of the U.S. as exporter has come into question by the embargo on grain sales to the Soviet Union, and earlier by embargoes on grain sales generally, a grain reserve would restore world faith in the U.S. export market. As a result, our balance of payments situation and the strength of the U.S. dollar, both of which depend heavily on agricultural exports, would be bolstered. Finally, U.S. leadership on the grain issue would benefit our national security by strengthening the U.S. overall relations with the developing world. Few issues could more demonstrably indicate our interest in resolving the basic problem of hunger and malnutrition that beset the developing countries. Grain reserves are more than simply an expression of interest; they are a practical step toward world food security.

The establishment of an adequate global food security system requires major support from the U.S., in terms of surplus grain contributed and of financing the effort in one or more ways. While the issues are complex and confusing, it is important that Christians in the U.S. act to support the establishment of a world food reserve system. Such actions can take many forms including political lobbying and educational programs. The important thing is to speak to the issue of world food security and help others to understand the linkage between the establishment of a food reserve system and the gradual elimination of hunger and malnutrition.

NOTES

1. The author expresses deep appreciation to Curtis Tarnoff, an associate of Development Resources, for his invaluable assistance in gathering data and preparing this chapter.

2. Overseas Development Council, *The United States and World Development Agenda 1980* (New York: Praeger, 1980), p. 59.

3. Interreligious Task Force on U.S. Food Policy, "Grain Reserves," *Hunger-Impact,* March 1977, No. 8, p. 3.

4. Commission on International Development Issues, Willy Brandt, Chairman, *North-South: A Program for Survival* (Cambridge: MIT Press, 1980).

5. Alexander H. Sarris, Phillip C. Abbott, and Lance Taylor, "Grain Reserves, Emergency Relief and Food Aid," p. 208 in William R. Cline (ed.), *Policy Alternatives for a New International Economic Order: An Economic Analysis* (New York: Praeger, 1979).

6. D. Gale Johnson, *World Food Problems and Prospect* (Washington, D.C.: American Enterprise Institute, 1975), p. 58.

11
Crisis of Confidence in U.S. Aid to Poor Nations

James A. Cogswell

Development aid is in deep trouble. Economic concerns at home and U.S. setbacks abroad, along with growing public pessimism about "foreign aid," have resulted in fewer and fewer members of Congress being willing to defend aid programs or resist a growing effort to slash them as a step toward balancing the federal budget.

What is happening in the United States is not unique. As a percentage of Gross National Product, aid from Western governments to developing countries has fallen markedly over the past decade. Faced with unprecedented rates of inflation, rising energy prices, staggering budget deficits, and worrisome unemployment, most Western governments know their electorates well enough to realize that hard times at home take precedence over hard times abroad.

This crisis of confidence in aid to poor nations is growing at a time when the "rich" nations are being urged as never before to increase their help to countries facing unprecedented hunger and poverty. An international commission headed by former West German Chancellor Willy Brandt declares that the present state of relations between the rich nations of the North and the poor nations of the South poses such a threat to global survival that reshaping those relations is the greatest challenge to humankind for the remainder of the century, and that a part of the

response must be at least a doubling of development assistance
by 1985.[1]

The Presidential Commission on World Hunger, in its report
to the President in April 1980, recommends that the U.S. move
as rapidly as possible toward the United Nations' goal of 0.7 percent of Gross National Product for development assistance—a
move which would mean at least a tripling of the present level of
aid.[2] Such goals seem highly unrealistic in the face of present political realities.

Many Americans have concluded that "foreign aid" simply
does not work, whatever the reasons may be. A December 1979
study, related to the work of the Presidential Commission on
World Hunger, sought out the views of the American public on
the problem of world hunger. The findings are surprising. While
the issue of world hunger is not uppermost in the minds of Americans, a substantial minority (39%) sees it as a top world issue
which deserves increased government spending. Yet "foreign
aid" (grossly misunderstood by the majority questioned) ranks
last in the list of programs deserving increased spending. One
out of every six respondents was negative on aid. Obviously, the
American public does not see aid as a major means of solving
world hunger.[3]

Is the problem simply one of misunderstanding? Possibly.
The Presidential Commission Report states, "Few government
programs are as frequently criticized—and as poorly understood—as 'foreign aid.' "[4] Certainly there is need for a much better public interpretation of what "foreign aid" and "development
assistance" are all about.[5] Yet, as Presidential Commission member Eugene Stockwell commented, "While the foreign aid program is indeed frequently criticized because it is *poorly*
understood, it is also often criticized because it is *well* understood."[6] Well-grounded criticism of "foreign aid" and "development assistance" comes from the "right," from the "left," and
even from those who are strong advocates of aid to poor nations.

I. WHY THIS CRISIS OF CONFIDENCE?

First, a brief word about the history of "foreign aid." The
present pattern of aid emerged shortly after the Second World
War. The grand model was the Marshall Plan, a massive and

dramatic effort for the reconstruction of post-war Western Europe. At its height, the United States directed almost three percent of its Gross National Product (GNP) to meet human need and to rebuild the badly damaged European industrial machine. The plan was highly successful in rebuilding war-torn economies, opening the way for U.S. investments and checking the advance of communism.

With the recovery of Europe, the focus of U.S. aid began to shift. Beginning with President Truman's Point IV program introduced in 1949, the emphasis was increasingly placed on technical and capital assistance designed to strengthen the economies of newly independent nations. Later, in the cold war era, the emphasis turned to mutual security. More and more aid was earmarked for military purposes, especially for nations that were considered to be on the cold war frontier.

With the coming of the 1960's, the vision expanded. The United Nations called the 1960's the "development decade." The logic of the Marshall Plan appeared impregnable: If Europe, then why not the newly-emerging poor nations of the third world? This time around, not only the United States but all Western nations could pitch in. The goals set were much the same: (1) move economically weak countries toward development, (2) open new sales and investment markets for Western industry, (3) secure access to strategic raw materials, and (4) bring greater well-being for the poor. Western leaders were also keen to carve out areas of influence in the poor world to undercut any drift in political sympathies to the left.

What has gone wrong? Why is it that, after thirty years and billions of dollars of aid, the third world is still in the cauldron of poverty and hunger? What has brought about this crisis of confidence in foreign aid among the donor nations? Is there any possibility that it can be turned around in order to meet the critical challenge that confronts the world in the 1980's? We need to hear the criticism from all quarters if viable answers are to be found.

A. *Criticism from the "Right"*

From the viewpoint of those viewed to be on "the right," the storm gathering over U.S. foreign aid is attributed to the following reasons:[7]

1. *Anti-American hostility continues to flourish around the globe.* Despite U.S. foreign aid expenditures of billions of dollars (which critics usually expand to include not only bilateral and multilateral development assistance, but military aid, security support, contributions to the Export-Import Bank and aid to U.S. business for expansion in the third world), the United States finds itself facing a rising tide of criticism and opposition within the third world and within the councils of nations. Says Representative C. W. Bill Young (R-Florida): "There is a general feeling the world is ripping us off."

2. *Too often America's generosity has been wasted on unstable governments.* In some cases, billions of dollars have gone to countries without producing any noticeable improvement in their internal stability. Many are still angry over the explosion of anti-American violence in Iran, culminating in the taking of fifty-two American embassy staff persons as hostages. Speaking of the 1.3 billion dollars in aid given to Iran during the Shah's regime, former Representative Robert Bowman (R-Maryland) said, "Iran was a classic example of our foreign aid being made as an investment. Then a new government overthrew the old, and we wasted all that money."

3. *Many aid programs are not advancing U.S. foreign policy.* Some Americans think the receiving nations' support of U.S. policy should take precedence over other considerations: "We should continue to aid our friends; but should we go on aiding our adversaries? We believe that the . . . policy of helping those who hurt us repeatedly is an obvious failure."[8] This position has led to a growing insistence on greater congressional control over the distribution of aid. Each year, restrictions barring aid to a growing list of countries have been tacked-on to aid legislation, and the debate over "country-specific restrictive amendments" has become the focal point of long and acrid debate.

4. *Too often multinational lending banks funnel money to governments that are opposed to U.S. interests.* International lending institutions like the World Bank are financed largely by

industrial nations, with the U.S. contributing about one-fourth. They make low-interest loans to developing nations for major development projects. However, critics contend that these multinational lending groups are making loans to countries deemed hostile to U.S. interests. For this reason, they argue, American participation in such financing should be reduced, if not eliminated.

5. *Domestic needs and other budget constraints require a shift of funds away from foreign aid.* No matter how effective a foreign aid program might be, where would the additional money to finance it come from? Members of Congress feel pressure from their constituents to take care of needs close to home. They are pressured to deal with inflation, to solve the energy problem, to beef up military defense, and to cut back on all government spending for "welfare" whether at home or abroad. Many conservatives take this as "a mandate" to reduce spending wherever possible on foreign aid.

This mood is summarized in a statement issued in December 1974 (immediately following the World Food Conference) by the United States Industrial Council, a nationwide association of conservative business people:

> ... the American people are very tired of all types of foreign aid. Today, the United States faces severe economic difficulty at home. The nation can't afford to be as generous as it was in the past.... To be sure, the problems facing some countries are horrendous. But in many cases, the suffering nations have brought on their troubles.... They lack the leadership, resources, educational elites and the capitalist economic structures necessary for effective production of food and long-term national existence. The United States cannot save all the inadequate nations of the world from their inadequacies or follies.[9]

B. *Criticism from the "Left"*

While the criticism from those on "the right" focuses on the lack of results obtained for our own nation's interests, criticism from "the left" generally is more fundamental and devastating.

1. *The primary purpose of aid has never been to help the poor and hungry, but rather to advance policies for the welfare of rich nations.* This fact is well stated in a 1957 report of the Senate Committee on Foreign Relations on the concept, purpose, and evaluation of American technical assistance:

> The subcommittee has conducted its study on the premise that the sole test of technical assistance is the national interest of the United States. Technical assistance is not something to be done, as a government enterprise, for its own sake or for the sake of others. The United States is not a charitable institution, nor is it an appropriate outlet for the charitable spirit of the American people.[10]

The validity of this criticism can be supported by some sobering statistics:[11]

(a) About two-thirds of official aid is bilateral (arranged on a country-to-country basis). Fifty-three percent of bilateral aid from all aid-giving nations is "tied" to purchase of goods and service from the donor country. In the case of the United States, seventy-five percent is "tied" aid.

(b) According to the General Accounting Office in Washington, for every aid dollar that leaves the U.S., two to three dollars flow back.

(c) Approximately one-third of all aid now is in the form of loans which have to be repaid with interest. Loans by Western governments to developing countries generally are for the purpose of buying rich world manufactures.

Debt repayment on these "export credits" accounts for the single largest outflow of capital from the third world back to the first world—more than $16.2 billion in 1977.

The "Food for Peace" Program (Public Law 480) is cited as a clear case in point. Written into its statement of purpose in 1954 were two principal goals: to dispose of agricultural surpluses and to develop future markets for American agricultural products. As the food crisis intensified in the early 1970's, food aid all but disappeared while food sales skyrocketed. In 1969, revenues from U.S. agricultural exports were $5.9 billion, of which seventeen percent was related to concessional sales under PL 480; in 1974, sales were $21.9 billion, of which only three percent was concessional.[12]

2. *Aid, while spread thinly across a large number of countries, is highly concentrated on a small number of countries where donor nations have high political interest.* "If aid is designed to benefit the poor," asks a critic, "why is it that there are such startling discrepancies in per capita aid figures?" In 1977, India (undoubtedly one of the poorest countries in the world) received $1.60 per person. Meanwhile, Israel received $226, Jordan $134, Egypt $72—and the postage-stamp French colony of Reunion, $661 per person.[13]

The U.S. offers the clearest example of aid as "power politics." Half of U.S. aid goes to ten countries where the U.S. has strong political interests. Israel and Egypt receive approximately one-third of the total. Of the total 7.1 billion foreign aid appropriation bill for FY 81, approximately $1 billion is for military assistance and another $2 billion for the Economic Support Fund to "provide assistance to regions of the world in which the United States has special foreign policy and security interests." Only twenty-one percent of total U.S. aid proposed for FY 1981 went to low-income countries (i.e., those with an average per capita income of less than $300, and comprising one-third of the world's people).[14]

3. *Fundamentally, foreign aid reinforces power relationships.* It fails to help the poor because it is based on the fallacy that aid can reach the powerless even though channeled through the powerful. This is the thesis of the recent book by Frances Lappé and colleagues, *Aid as Obstacle:*

> Official foreign assistance necessarily flows through the recipient governments, and too often (particularly in those countries to which the United States confines most of its aid) these governments represent narrow, elite economic interests. . . . The influx of such outside resources into those countries where economic control is concentrated in the hands of a few bolsters the local, national and international elites whose stranglehold over land and other productive resources generates poverty and hunger in the first place. Instead of helping, we *hurt* the dispossessed majority.[15]

4. *While that part of foreign aid known as "development assistance" focuses on lack of resources, what the poor really lack is power.*

U.S. government aid and agencies such as the World Bank cannot ally themselves with the poor, in part because the definition of the problem of poverty reflected in their projects is wrong. The prevailing diagnosis of why people are poor and hungry is that they have been "left out" of the development process. From this diagnosis flows one solution—bring the poor *into* development. . . . (But) the poor have been an integral part of the process—both as resource and as victim. The poor have provided their labor, their products and often their land. The issue, then, is not to bring the poor into the development process, but for the poor to achieve the power they need to direct a development process in their interests. . . . It becomes clear that what the poor really lack is *power,* to secure what they need. The aid agencies focus on the lack of materials; we focus on the lack of power.[16]

5. *The task of concerned citizens of rich nations, then, should be not to provide more aid, but to remove the obstacles that prevent poor nations from becoming self-reliant.*

We are calling for a halt to all economic and military support for governments controlled by narrowly based elites which use repression to protect their interests and to block the demands of their own people for redistribution of control over productive assets. Such a move would mean cutting off those governments now most favored by U.S. economic assistance and military aid. . . . These economic and military supports actually block efforts by those who are working for a more just sharing of control over resources. As Americans, our responsibility is to remove such obstacles.[17]

C. Criticism from Aid Advocates

Hemmed in by such devastating criticisms from both right and left, those who are advocates for aid to poor nations are strongly tempted to take a purely defensive stance in an attempt to refute the critics. Yet there is growing recognition that this may indeed be the worst approach. Far better to acknowledge the fact that present development aid policies do have some serious problems and shortcomings.[18]

1. *U.S. development assistance continues to be shaped by a narrow concept of national security that frequently conflicts with long-range development goals.* As a result, the development assistance agency (U.S. Agency for International Development) has never been permitted to focus single-mindedly on raising living standards in third world societies which seldom pose direct military threats to U.S. national security. Hence, some of the neediest countries receive last claim on America's political attention and economic resources.

2. *Shamefully low appropriations prevent development assistance from attaining its stated objectives.* During the thirty-year period from the initiation of the Marshall Plan until the present, the percentage of U.S. development assistance in relation to Gross National Product has shrunk from 2.7 percent to 0.27 percent, less than one-tenth of the earlier proportion. During the same period, the annual income of the average American (adjusting for inflation) has more than doubled and the U.S. defense budget has fluctuated between five and ten percent of GNP, or roughly twenty times the level of development assistance. Although the United States is still the world's largest aid donor in absolute terms, it now ranks thirteenth among the seventeen countries of the Development Assistance Committee in development assistance as a percentage of GNP.[19]

3. *Domestic political considerations and economic interests dilute the impact of development assistance.* Too frequently aid programs have been designed with potential benefits to the U.S. economy in mind at least as much as benefits to the recipient nations. To insist that seventy-five percent of aid appropriations be spent on more expensive U.S. goods and services, rather than those from local firms or other developing nations, is to dilute seriously the net impact that each aid dollar can have.

4. *Short-term authorization and appropriation processes impede rational planning and consistent implementation.* The annual Congressional wrangle, first over authorization of the aid program and then over appropriation of the necessary funding, results in the U.S. development assistance program being erratic from year to year. This prevents the kind of long-range planning that is so desperately needed in poor nations if they are to undertake the task of overcoming hunger and poverty.

5. *Adequate priority has not been given to the deeper underlying causes of poverty.* Land reform, which could enable impoverished farmers to own their own land and become more productive, has not been pushed in U.S. development assistance programs. The pressing need to expand employment opportunities has not been given adequate priority, nor has there been any overall strategy to move poor nations from capital-intensive to labor-intensive development activities.

The Presidential Commission on World Hunger, after presenting these and other criticisms of the U.S. development assistance program as it now is, draws this conclusion:

> The Commission is convinced that the developing countries cannot achieve significant self-reliant growth without increased development assistance from the richer nations of the world. For the United States, this means an immediate commitment to doubled resources and a considerably strengthened administrative approach to development assistance activities. Achieving these objectives would provide ample evidence of the U.S. commitment to overcome hunger and poverty and provide the basis for calling upon others to do the same.[20]

II. A REALISTIC VIEW OF DEVELOPMENT ASSISTANCE

What then can be said in the face of this avalanche of criticism? Is there any hope for overcoming the crisis of confidence? Should the effort to provide aid to poor nations be abandoned? If not, in what direction should it go?

Before attempting to suggest future directions, let us first sort through the criticisms and offer several comments toward a realistic view of development assistance.

A. Development assistance by itself should never be expected to
solve the total problems of hunger, poverty and injustice which
oppress the world's poor nations.

Many Americans have expected development aid to poor nations to do the impossible. In the halcyon days following World
War II, it seemed that what worked in Europe would work everywhere in the world, and at a fraction of the cost. Little consideration was given to the basic differences between post-war Europe
and what has become known as the third world:

• Our common cultural heritage with the nations of Europe,
and the totally different heritage of most of the nations of the
third world.

• Our common economic interest with the nations of Europe
in rebuilding the world's free enterprise power bases, compared
to our interest in the third world primarily as a source of raw
materials and an outlet for our products.

• The quick results attainable through massive injections of
aid to countries which already had advanced technology, education, skills and facilities, compared to the extreme difficulty in
poor countries of starting from "below zero" where basic changes
needed to be made in political, economic and social patterns inherited from the colonial era.

Development assistance in and of itself never could and never will be able to do the whole job of curing the ills of the poor
nations of the world. Like putting a bandage on a cancer, it can
cover the wound without healing it, and thus only allow the disease to progress toward a stage beyond healing. "There are no
short-cuts to eliminating hunger," says the Brandt Report. Unless and until the world's developed nations, especially the United States, come to grips with the underlying roots out of which
hunger comes, there will be no solution and development assistance has the potential of being demonic rather than redemptive.

This is why the very placement of this chapter within this
book on "causes of world hunger" is important. Development assistance must be viewed in the larger context of the colonial legacy, the gross maldistribution of wealth and income in the world,
the trade barriers confronting developing nations, the patterns
of overconsumption in the West which rely upon the exploitation
of the third world's raw materials and natural resources, and the

senseless spiraling cost of the arms race. Without a prior consideration of these root causes of world hunger and poverty, development assistance becomes charity without justice and makes a mockery of all our good intentions.

B. Development assistance is inevitably a tool of our nation's political and economic policy.

To argue for aid to poor nations which is purely idealistic and totally devoid of national self-interest is whistling in the wind. Foreign aid, including development assistance, inevitably will be an instrument of foreign policy. The goal then must be not simply to transform or improve development assistance, but to affect the foreign policy of our nation.

When the U.S. Congress debates foreign aid, it often argues the wrong issues. Generally, Congress talks of the world in terms of East-West rather than North-South, interpreting all that happens in the third world in terms of the capitalism/communism contest. Congressional committee reports dealing with foreign aid are dull, dreary and distressingly defensive—"frozen in an essentially defensive posture," as one third world critic comments.[21] Somehow our representatives must be called to a more realistic assessment of the world in which we live and into which we are moving, recognizing that the relationship of the rich North and the poor South is "the greatest challenge to humankind for the remainder of the century."

> The challenge before the international community is to prepare a coherent international development strategy for the next few decades—a strategy that ensures accelerated growth in the developing countries, meeting of basic human needs as a priority item, elimination of the worst forms of absolute poverty before the end of the century, and orderly growth—uninterrupted by excessive inflation or unemployment—in the industrialized countries.... The international community (must be made) conscious that it is possible to combine the legitimate aspirations of the developing countries with the enlightened self-interests of the developed countries and

150   JAMES A. COGSWELL

that a new international economic order can work to the
long-term benefit of all nations.[22]

C. *Development assistance is not only a tool but also a gauge as
to how serious our nation is about the struggle to end world
hunger, poverty and injustice.*

Imagine for a moment the implications of our nation's termi-
nating altogether its program of aid to poor nations. By the developing nations themselves, it would be seen as a breach of
trust, an abandonment of involvement in the United Nations
and other international agencies where aid agreements and commitments are made, a slamming of the door in the faces of the
world's billion hungry people. By citizens of our own nation, it
would be seen as evidence of a new isolationism, based on disillusionment rather than lack of concern, but bringing about the
same result. The prospect of bringing about fundamental reforms for greater international economic justice would be nil if
we were to shut off concern for those now desperately hungry
and development assistance to poor nations.

While development assistance represents only a portion of
"foreign aid" and only a fraction of capital flows into all developing countries, it does represent a very large proportion for the
world's poorest countries.

The rate of economic growth in the poorer developing
countries in the period immediately ahead is likely to be
painfully slow. Reductions in economic aid almost certainly would exacerbate the already serious economic
problems of those countries and impose additional hard-
ships on their people. . . . Development assistance is extremely important to the thirty-nine poor developing
countries (with gross domestic product of $300 per capi-
ta or less . . .). Approximately two-thirds of the cumulative net inflow of capital to these countries from all
sources for the period 1973–78 took the form of concessional loans and official transfers. . . . The economies of
the poor developing countries, which have only very limited access to private capital markets, are thus highly
vulnerable to development aid cutbacks.[23]

It is all too easy to throw the acid of cynicism on development assistance programs in the name of critical analyses which call for radical change, particularly when no one realistically expects radical change to happen outside of revolutionary (and possibly catastrophic) upheaval. With all its failures and shortcomings, development assistance remains one of the positive bridges between the first and third worlds. The collapse of that bridge would mean that the world would enter a stage of stark confrontation between North and South that could be the prelude to chaos.

D. There is a distinctive role for both government and non-government participation in the task of development assistance.

One of the findings of the public opinion study commissioned by the Presidential Commission on World Hunger was that Americans trust volunteer organizations more than either the U.S. government or international organizations to administer assistance funds. This reflects "lack of confidence in the federal government's ability to handle funds effectively."[24]

Undoubtedly there is a distinctive role for private voluntary organizations in this overwhelming task. They are playing it comparatively well. Private voluntary assistance for development from U.S. non-government organizations (NGOs) came to $840 million in 1977, an average per capita contribution of $3.87, placing us fifth among the developed countries.

However, the dimensions of the North/South crisis are so great that voluntary agencies cannot begin to meet the total need. Governments and international institutions must play the major role in providing development assistance at the macrolevel of nations and regions. It is helpful to recall that one legislative amendment reducing a Congressional appropriation for development assistance can deprive poor countries of an amount equal to the total contributions of all non-government organizations for one year.

Governments, of course, cannot do everything. Non-government organizations (and especially the churches through their worldwide programs) can undertake "basic human needs" development programs at the grass-roots level as no government can.

Out of their vision of a better world, they can experiment to build models of people participating in their own development.

> Because they are smaller, they can be more imaginative, more innovative, and above all more radical.... NGO projects can also provide an embarrassing yardstick against which official development efforts may be measured.[25]

It is tempting to think of government development assistance resources being used increasingly through private and voluntary organizations (PVOs). The Presidential Commission estimates, "by 1985, PVOs could probably double the amount of AID funds that they can administer effectively, with little strain or fear of exceeding their absorptive capacity."[26] Yet voluntary organizations must see their role as more than a channel through which governments carry out development assistance. There must be sufficient distance so that PVOs can maintain their freedom to criticize or, if need be, condemn government policies both in general and in their relation to particular developing nations.

E. The critical task is to refine the goals of development assistance (within the context of larger initiatives) with the aim of achieving justice and improving the quality of life for the world's poor.

Year after year, the "hunger lobby" (as it has become known in Washington circles) tries to help citizens understand the complicated process through which aid legislation goes. It also attempts to identify the various programs included in "foreign aid" bills. In addition to development assistance, there is military assistance and security support assistance. The average concerned citizen can easily become confused, not knowing exactly what to be for or against in relation to aid to poor nations. At the beginning of the "third development decade," there is no more urgent task than that of refining the goals of development assistance in the context of larger initiatives.[27]

There is a restlessness among Americans about our present role in the world. A willingness to make a fresh start is emerging. That mood must be nurtured and given articulate leadership. Our people must be helped to move beyond the assumptions of the post-World War II reconstruction period, beyond the mind-set that measured development almost exclusively in terms of GNP and per capita average income increases—beyond that to a new sensitivity that measures aid in terms of achieving justice and increasing life quality for the poorest of the poor.[28]

III. SOME DEVELOPMENT ASSISTANCE GOALS FOR THE 1980's

What then should be the goals toward which development assistance should move in the 1980's if it is to regain the confidence and support of those deeply concerned about the world's hungry? I think the following considerations are most important.

A. Development assistance must place much greater emphasis on empowering the powerless.

Critics on "the left" are correct in saying that what the world's poor lack is not simply resources, but power to determine their own destinies, "to make effective demands on the social systems within which they live."[29] The Brandt Commission Report takes much more seriously than does the Presidential Commission Report both the need for and the resistance to power-sharing.

U.S. development assistance made a small step toward this goal in the "New Directions" legislation adopted in 1973 and revised in 1975 and 1977. Recognizing the shortcomings of the "trickle-down" approach which emphasized large-scale projects aimed simply at increasing the GNP of developing countries, Congress approved a new philosophy for U.S. development assistance which placed primary emphasis on direct help for the predominantly rural "poor majority" in developing countries. Basic needs of the poor were to be met by focusing on food production, nutrition, population planning, health, education and human resources. Somewhere within the legislation, there was mention of increased participation of recipients in the choice of programs and in their administration. Yet implementation of the "New Directions" mandate has been slow and uneven, and the call for the poor to be involved in their own development has gone largely unheeded.

If development assistance in the 1980's is to have integrity, one of its keystones must be empowering the powerless for participation in their own development.

> The poor must obtain new resources in ways which transform them into creators, and not mere consumers, of civilization. Thus any imagery which portrays the poorest billion or the bottom forty percent as welfare recipients is unsatisfactory.[30]

There is no question that such aid will be controversial; it will challenge and in some cases threaten power relationships at the village, state, national and international level. Yet such change is indispensable if the poor are to be the subjects and not merely the objects of their own development, and if development assistance is to drive toward justice.

B. Development assistance should target aid selectively to those poor nations strongly committed to meeting basic human needs and rights.

This "country-specific" emphasis may be one of the major breakthroughs proposed by the Presidential Commission on World Hunger. A minority of that Commission goes a step further and calls for a "Basic Human Needs Agreement," that is, a contract in which aid-receiving nations would agree to pursue development strategies aimed at overcoming poverty and hunger in return for continued assistance from the U.S. The minority commissioners further recommend that countries which sign such an agreement receive special consideration in terms-of-trade preferences and reduced tariffs on their exports. One Commission member proposes that a set of standards for assistance be determined by international agreement among aid-giving and aid-receiving nations, and that the way a country measures up to these standards be determinative of eligibility for assistance.[31]

The need for some such step is evident. Much U.S. aid (accompanied by military and security support assistance) is concentrated on support of some of the world's most repressive regimes. The Interreligious Task Force on U.S. Food Policy undertook an intensive review of eight nations from among the sixty-six countries that received U.S. bilateral assistance in fiscal year 1979, and found that, while all the countries ranked relatively high in terms of need, only two had any standing in terms of government commitment to equitable development, human rights record and agrarian reform efforts. The Task Force suggests that, even if quantity of aid cannot be increased, "now may be a good time to move toward granting aid to *fewer* countries . . . and to direct it primarily to countries whose need, government policies, and performance make such aid more likely to promote equitable, self-reliant development."[32]

It goes without saying that a corollary to such a policy would be the separation of development assistance from military and security support assistance. Neither Congress nor the American public should be misled by a label that lumps these disparate parts together under the ill-defined term "foreign aid." Proper labeling is a first step in focusing development assistance on what Tanzanian president Julius Nyerere has termed "catalyst aid"—development assistance which can be used by poor nations to create more self-reliant societies.[33]

C. Development assistance should emphasize the long-range economic interest of our nation in developing a healthy global economy, and therefore work toward removing short-range economic advantages that hinder this goal.

The Presidential Commission recognizes that national economic interest necessarily plays a part in our relationship to the world's poor nations. Therefore it states, "The United States can maintain its own economic vitality only within a healthy international economy whose overall strength will increase as each of its component parts becomes more productive, more equitable and more internationally competitive. To sustain a healthy global economy, the purchasing power of today's poor people must rise substantially, in order to set in motion that mutually reinforcing exchange of goods, services and commodities which provides the foundation for viable economic partnership and growth."[34]

But such a long-range approach necessitates the sacrifice of some of the short-range advantages which the U.S. has sought through its development assistance program. Our nation is famous for its "tied" aid, that is, aid given on the condition that it must be spent on American goods and services. This tied aid really amounts to subsidizing American corporations. Poor countries dislike it, not only because it means higher prices than on the world market, but also because tied aid encourages greater penetration into developing nations by multinational corporations. Such short-range economic advantage needs to be set aside for the long-range economic interest of a healthier global economy.

A minority of the Presidential Commission offers an excellent additional suggestion: U.S. firms receiving financial assistance for work in developing countries should be required to file a Hunger Impact Statement "to ensure at the very least that private investments in the LDCs do not have an adverse effect on the poor, and, more positively, that the financial aid be channeled toward projects and investments designed to have a beneficial impact on the income and living conditions of the poor."[35]

Undoubtedly, one of the most serious problems facing most developing nations today is their mushrooming debt, much of which is due to past aid received in the form of loans. That total debt has been rising by sixteen percent since 1976 and will approach $300 billion in 1980. Some countries—Canada, Britain, Sweden—have written off past debts owed them by the poorest nations. The United States should seriously consider doing the same, possibly as part of Basic Human Needs Agreements reached with particular nations. Needless to say, major emphasis henceforth should be given to aid in the form of grants instead of loans.

D. Development assistance must take much greater account of ecological sustainability.

Both the Presidential Commission and the Brandt Commission show some sensitivity to the ecological crisis. The Presidential Commission warns, "There can be no lasting solution to the world hunger problem if the world persists in current practices which have already led to increasingly serious degradation of the soils, grasslands, water resources, forests, and fisheries."[36] The Brandt Commission notes, "So far the bulk of the depletion of non-renewable resources and the pressure on the oceans and the atmosphere have been caused by the spectacular industrial growth of the developed countries where only one-fifth of the world's people live. But population growth in some parts of the third world is already a source of alarming ecological changes, and its industrialization is bound to lead to greater pressure on resources and environment."[37]

The realization that we are "approaching the outer limits of the life-sustaining capacity of planet earth" has far wider implications than can be dealt with in the scope of this essay. However, one obvious implication is that it would be sheer folly for the United States and other Western nations to limit development assistance simply to exporting the Western model of development to the third world. In agriculture in particular, the desire to imitate the capital-intensive, highly mechanized approach to farming which has characterized American agriculture has already led many developing countries astray. Edgar Owens of the U.S. Agency for International Development sums up the situation well:

> One of the most fundamental premises of economics is that one should husband the resource which is scarce and use the resource which is plentiful. For developing countries, this means labor intensive, capital saving investment. However self-evident this point may seem, it is unhappily true that most of the low income countries and international assistance agencies have been pursuing the opposite pattern—policies and technologies which are capital intensive and labor saving.[38]

Aid to poor nations in the 1980's will need to seek to share successful models, developed within the poor nations themselves, which maximize use of abundant labor and respect scarce resources and fragile ecological systems. An important corollary is that we be cautious about promoting an export-led development strategy based on increasing consumption of third world materials and products by a consumer-oriented rich world.

E. New avenues must be found for providing the resources desperately needed for development assistance.

Some advocates of aid to poor nations have come to the conclusion that quality of aid is more important than quantity. How much aid is less important than to whom it goes, for what purposes, and with what consequences. The quality questions are right on target. But no one can confront the monumental needs of the third world without recognizing that quantity of aid must be increased at a deliberate pace. Over the past decade, the level of assistance from the United States and other industrialized nations has dropped. The struggle now is simply to keep appropriations from falling to lower levels. Is it time for a completely new approach?

The Brandt Commission Report makes some challenging proposals to establish transfer mechanisms from rich to poor nations, automatic transfers not dependent on acts of periodic and unpredictable generosity. Examples of such transfer mechanisms are:

1. An international system of universal revenue mobilization based on a sliding scale related to national income (i.e., an international income tax).

2. The adoption of timetables to increase Official Development Assistance from industrialized countries to the level of 0.7 percent of GNP by 1985, and to one percent before the end of the century.

3. Introduction of automatic revenue transfers through international levies on international trade, arms production or exports, international travel, and sea-bed minerals.

4. The creation of a new international financial institution—a World Development Fund—with universal membership, in which decision-making is more evenly shared between lenders and borrowers. This would supplement existing institutions and diversify lending policies and practices.[39]

These ideas may seem visionary. But does not the desperate

situation which our world confronts in the 1980's call for some such vision? "The search for solutions is not an act of benevolence but a condition of mutual survival."[40]

Much of the criticism outlined in the early part of this chapter remains unanswered. Suggested goals for development assistance in the 1980s are sketchy and only the beginning of what must be said. Possibly, they can contribute to the lively debate needed among concerned American citizens.

Two concluding remarks. First, aid to poor nations cannot be accomplished without each of us being willing to pay a price personally. Both the Brandt Commission and the Presidential Commission emphasize that the rich and poor nations have mutual economic interests, and this is true. The destiny of all nations and peoples is tied into the struggle for a just, participatory and sustainable world society. Yet we cannot assume that such a society can be built in ways that will benefit everyone and cause loss to none. There must be caution about an easy optimism that says to the citizens of the rich nations, "This really isn't going to hurt." If the basic needs of the vast majority of humankind are to be met and poor nations are to move out of the web of injustice and exploitation toward genuine self-reliance, there will have to be changes in our own lifestyles. There must be an end to consumption patterns that rely so heavily on the victimization of the world's poor. Aid to poor nations begins with the willingness to live more simply so that others may simply live.

Second, and finally, the crisis of confidence in aid to poor nations calls for a new vision of the kind of world we seek. It also calls for commitment to translating that vision into political reality. The appeal to "political realism" in relation to such an issue as aid to poor nations can be stultifying unless it is accompanied by the continual pressure of a higher vision of what the world can be. "High politics," writes William Lee Miller, "is not the art of the possible; it is the art of enlarging what is possible and making what has hereto been impossible come in the range of what can be considered."[41] In times like ours, the U.S. desperately needs citizens with that kind of political realism.

NOTES

1. Independent Commission on International Development Issues, Willy Brandt, Chairman, *North-South: A Program for Survival,* p. 242.

2. Presidential Commission on World Hunger, *Overcoming World Hunger: The Challenge Ahead,* Section IV, "U.S. Efforts to Combat Hunger Through Development Assistance." Also cf. pp. 188f.

3. Market Opinion Research, *Views of the American Public on the Problem of World Hunger and the Role of the United States in the Solution of the Problem,* pp. 1, 5, 16, 20.

4. Presidential Commission Report, *op. cit.,* p. 105.

5. Excellent interpretive materials are available free of charge from the U.S. Agency for International Development: *Agenda,* a monthly magazine on the works of USAID; *World Development Letter,* a biweekly report of facts, trends and opinion in international development. Write U.S. Agency for International Development, Office of Public Affairs, Washington, D.C. 20523.

6. Presidential Commission Report, *op. cit.,* p. 106.

7. See *U.S. News and World Report,* "New Storm Gathering Over U.S. Foreign Aid," March 30, 1980, pp. 59–61.

8. Minority views presented to Committee on Foreign Affairs, of Representatives, re International Security and Development Cooperation Act of 1980, April 16, 1980. Report 96–884, Part I, pp. 100f.

9. *New York Times,* December 2, 1974. Quoted in Jack Nelson, *Hunger for Justice: The Politics of Faith,* pp. 15f.

10. U.S. Senate, *Technical Assistance: Final Report of the Committee on Foreign Relations,* Report No. 139, pp. 18–19. Quoted in Nelson, pp. 16f.

11. From *The New Internationalist.* December 1979 issue, "The Foreign Aid Link: Are We Really Helping the Third World?" pp. 5f.

12. Nelson, *op. cit.,* p. 21.

13. *New Internationalist, op. cit.*

14. Frances Moore Lappé, *et al., Aid as Obstacle: Twenty Questions About Our Foreign Aid and the Hungry,* Chapter 1, pp. 15–18.

15. *Ibid.,* pp. 10f. See also "Aid That Doesn't," in *Christianity and Crisis,* March 31, 1980, and response in issue of May 12, 1980.

16. *Ibid.,* pp. 11–12.

17. *Ibid.,* p. 14.

18. The major points here are drawn from the findings of The Presidential Commission on World Hunger, Section IV, "United States Efforts To Combat Hunger Through Development Assistance."

19. Overseas Development Council, *The United States and World Development,* p. 247. However, Bread for the World, in its September

1980 newsletter, estimates that Italy is the only industrialized country which gives a lower percentage of its GNP for developmental assistance.

20. Presidential Commission Report, *op. cit.,* pp. 148f.

21. Mahbub ul Haq, "A View from the South: The Second Phase of the North-South Dialogue," in Overseas Development Council, *op. cit.,* p. 115.

22. *Ibid.,* pp. 120, 124.

23. Interreligious Task Force on U.S. Food Policy, Statement to Subcommittee on Foreign Operations, Committee on Appropriations, U.S. Senate, April 11, 1980.

24. Market Opinion Research, *op. cit.,* p. 45.

25. Susan George, *Feeding the Few: Corporate Control of Food,* p. 68.

26. Presidential Commission Report, *op. cit.,* p. 123.

27. Several efforts are underway in this regard. The Interreligious Task Force on U.S. Food Policy has prepared a working paper on "Identifying a Food Policy Agenda for the 1980's." Bread for the World prepared a Hunger and Global Security Bill for presentation to Congress in January 1981, seeking to implement key recommendations of the Presidential Commission on World Hunger.

28. C. Dean Freudenberger and Paul M. Minus, Jr., *Christian Responsibility in a Hungry World,* pp. 27f.

29. Denis Goulet, "Strategies for Meeting Human Needs," in Mary Evelyn Jegan and Charles K. Wilber (eds.), *Growth with Equity,* p. 56.

30. Denis Goulet, *op. cit.,* pp. 59f.

31. Presidential Commission Report, *op. cit.,* pp. 115, 188, 227f. See also Arthur Simon, *Bread for the World,* pp. 119f.

32. Interreligious Task Force on U.S. Food Policy, Statement to Committee on Foreign Relations, U.S. Senate, April 23, 1980.

33. *New Internationalist,* December 1979, p. 7.

34. Presidential Commission Report, *op. cit.,* p. 6.

35. *Ibid.,* p. 229.

36. *Ibid.*

37. Brandt Report, p. 113.

38. Edgar Owens, "Development with Social Justice," presented to the International Seminar of Economic Journalists, New Delhi, December 5, 1972. Quoted in Lester R. Brown, *The Twenty-Ninth Day,* p. 225.

39. Brandt Report, p. 255.

40. *Ibid.,* p. 282.

41. William Lee Miller, *Of Thee, Nevertheless, I Sing,* p. 38.

12
The Absence of Political Will in the United States

Mark O. Hatfield

• After a substantial meal, you sit down to watch TV and relax. The show is interrupted for a commercial. An emaciated, hungry child peers forth through hollow eyes. She is surrounded by squalor. The impoverished village in which she lives is as dissimilar from your reality as anything could possibly be. A faceless voice espouses the brutal reality that only your compassion will alleviate her misery, and warns that without it she will die. For a moment, you are captured. Guilt and compassion inspire you to help. But your focus turns to the newspaper and it consumes your attention until the show returns.

• During an election year, a politician attacks U.S. foreign aid as the ultimate "giveaway" program. His televised political advertisement focuses on vandalized and abandoned buildings that were intended to be schools. Next a sheik races by in a car you could never afford. Then an angry mob shouts hostilities at an American television camera. It all takes place in countries which receive millions in U.S. foreign aid.

• A bureaucrat in the federal government comes across a new report on world hunger in his daily shuffling of the mail. The impersonal cover letter warns of a world edging closer to peril and the urgent need to channel more resources toward the hungry poor before instability and the resulting politics of desperation threaten even the rich and powerful nations. The report goes in the trash; there are too many urgent matters to be dealt with.

• A senator goes to the floor of the Senate to vote on a resolution affirming the right of all human beings to a proper diet. The resolution has no cost, nor does it commit the nation to a specific plan of action. Along with the great majority of his colleagues, he votes favorably on the bill. Hours later, another amendment is introduced. It calls for halting development aid to a government which has been leaning too closely to the Soviet Union, even though its people are hungry. The senator votes affirmatively and without hesitation for the amendment.

These examples represent a sampling of the reasons why hunger is on the rise. The failure of will in the face of such massive and unnecessary suffering is not easily understood because it occurs in vastly divergent forms under wide-ranging conditions and circumstances. But one thing is certain: no amount of theorizing over approaches to the problem will yield a solution until the will to tackle hunger emerges on a number of levels where it does not presently exist.

Without will there is nothing. No act or accomplishment has even taken place without it. The most horrendous atrocities and the most glorious achievements claim will as a common denominator. It is born of faith as well as fear. Will is also the most glaring omission in the politics of hunger. One need only note the lack of empathy between various groups in the U.S. in order to understand the inability of affluent Americans to understand hunger. The secure rural inhabitant is unlikely to understand the violence and despair characteristic of urban emptiness and decay. The urban dweller does not comprehend the impact which weather problems that cause crop failure can have on the lives of rural families. So it goes with the average American's sense of connection with the poor of Africa and Asia. His or her existence is simply too far-removed to allow full sympathy. Hunger will never be reduced significantly until developed nations regard the distant poor as part of an indivisible whole.

This detachment of the haves from the have-nots need not be viewed as inevitable or unchangeable simply because of the physical distance between them. But there are factors which act to reinforce the distance; they enable us to rationalize apathy or to close our eyes to the problem altogether. A thorough understanding of these obstacles and diversions can lead to fresh initiatives aimed at a solution.

As a society, we are increasingly living for the moment. At this writing, the nation's political machinery is in the grip of a fierce and all-consuming anti-Sovietism. The country itself, I am convinced, does not as yet fathom the implications of this dangerous ritual. The resounding call to arms originates in the corridors of the Pentagon as well as in the armaments industry and Congress. The call thrives on ignorance and misinformation. It purposefully attempts to divert everyday frustrations regarding family security and economic well-being by focusing on an external threat. This singular focus on the Soviet threat has resulted in massive increases in Pentagon spending. Any overseas revolt against poverty and authoritarianism is seen as invented in Moscow. Moreover, the "Soviet threat" prompts from us a compulsive approach to security agreements with unstable, but anti-Soviet, governments. It goes without saying that if the Soviet Union is the only physical and spiritual threat which our way of life faces, there is little point in marshalling resources toward those who are too weak to stand alone. When a fortress is being built, the gates are not opened to the infirm and the helpless, for they are but an unwanted burden.

Misinformation is a critical barrier to the elimination of hunger. In its evaluation of American public opinion, the Presidential Commission on World Hunger produced two surprising items of information that demonstrate the lack of understanding which most Americans have toward hunger issues. First, "any direct linkage in the public mind of increased foreign aid with social concern is weak." Second, "few Americans are aware how much other nations are doing in development assistance or of the extent to which U.S. aid has declined since Marshall Plan days." Thus, the American public generally believes that the United States is contributing a significant portion of its resources and energy to the eradication of world hunger. In truth, the U.S. ranks twelfth of seventeen developed nations in its development assistance as a percentage of GNP. Less than three percent of total federal expenditures are channeled toward this end. Americans spent less on world hunger last year than they lost at the gambling tables in Las Vegas.

The burgeoning popularity of "underground condos"—the 1980's version of nuclear fallout shelters—illustrates, if in the extreme, the nihilistic thread which runs through modern society. To be sure, purchasing an "underground condo" is not a priority for the average American. But the surprising level of interest in this approach to security is indicative of more profound changes in the national psyche. We are digging in. We are retreating from the threats of nuclear war, economic uncertainty, rapidly changing mores, and violence too close to home. Such an atmosphere of withdrawal is obviously not conducive to the kind of positive reaching out which the world's poor so urgently need.

We live in an age where the "giveaway" is among the most unpopular ideas. Tight pocketbooks and diminished faith in a secure future serve as the underpinning of this development. From food stamps to foreign aid, the public looks with scorn on the doling out of their taxes to presumably ungrateful and unproductive recipients. Many in the middle class who in the past were not particularly concerned over reports of welfare abuse and structural disincentives to working have undergone significant attitudinal changes as inflation and decreasing job security have been introduced into their lives. Foreign aid is perhaps even more suspect than food stamps or federal employment programs; it is regarded by many as little more than useless welfarism.

Another obstacle to developing a national will sufficient to make a significant impact on hunger is the overwhelming nature of the hunger problem itself. Americans tend to focus their energies on "manageable" problems. World hunger is not viewed as a "manageable" problem, but rather as a hopelessly "unmanageable" one. Most prefer to leave grandiose theorizing about magnificent problems to a handful of individuals with a sense of "mission." As for government, few public servants are willing to invest their time and energy in a cause that offers little promise of ultimate realization.

Indeed, the problem is ominous. A number of recent studies, including the *Global 2000* report to the President, the Brandt Commission Report, and the Presidential Commission on World Hunger Report, not only serve to underscore the urgency of tackling the problem, but, in the effort to inform us of its severity, form a picture of almost unfathomable proportions. To quote from the *Global 2000* report:

> The world's population will grow from four billion in 1975 to 6.35 billion in the year 2000, an increase of more than fifty percent. In terms of sheer numbers, the population will be growing faster in the year 2000 than it is today with the 100 million people added each year, compared with 75 million in 1975. Ninety percent of this growth will occur in the poorest countries.

In addition:

> Arable land will increase only four percent by the year 2000 so that most of the increased output of food will have to come from higher yields. Most of the elements that now contribute to high yield—fertilizer, pesticides, power for irrigation and fuel for machinery—depend heavily on oil and gas.

Nowhere is the question of will at the government level more dangerously clear than in our approach to the global resource crunch. One need only look at the thrust of the U.S. response to its dependence on foreign oil and its efforts (or lack of efforts) to curtail consumption. Rather than channeling technology and funding toward conservation and renewable energy resource development at an accelerated pace, we are downplaying such programs and gambling on a military solution instead. The Rapid Development Force (RDF) symbolizes a rejection of the fact that energy is a global problem which mercilessly squeezes the resources of the poor everywhere. While the RDF is designed to meet military contingencies anywhere in the world, vulnerability to foreign oil supply disruptions lies at the heart of the concept. It is a desperate display of will. Not only is it wholly unfeasible to defend and secure six thousand miles of sabotage- and destruction-prone oil pipeline, but the risk of uncontrollable nuclear war, should a U.S.-Soviet conflict occur, is immense. We choose this approach not because it is optimal, but because it is within our grasp. As the late General Omar Bradley put it, "The world has achieved brilliance without wisdom, power without conscience. We know more about war than we know about peace, more about killing than we know about living."

A meaningful discussion of political will must focus on the potential of the anti-hunger community and their advocates in government. It is they who must bear the burden of change. If this chapter has anything to contribute toward a solution, its task must be to influence advocates in ways which might lead to effective policy reform. The anti-hunger community's effectiveness is currently being undermined by a form of psycho-political schizophrenia. It fights for the *concept* of humanitarianism, yet it despises the primary vehicle upon which this concern must be directed: the foreign aid program. It must also deal with a foreign policy apparatus which does not share its goals.

Either the bulk of our foreign aid goes to countries where the need is not particularly great, or, where the need is great, the aid too often does not reach those most in need. Thus, it is neither productive nor accurate to repeat the familiar liberal assertion that cutbacks in foreign aid will affect the hungry. The ten top foreign aid recipients receive roughly half of U.S. foreign aid. The rest is distributed among roughly ninety other countries. With nations like Israel, the Philippines and Pakistan in the top ten, it is clear that strategic concerns rather than development or humanitarian concerns are preeminent. Virtually all of the countries in this category are either notorious for their neglect of the poor and the abuse of human rights, or they are relatively affluent allies undeserving of "development" assistance.

On the one hand, anti-hunger activists are inspired to heed the call of the Presidential Commission on World Hunger or the Brandt Commission to elevate hunger to a high priority status through increases in foreign aid. On the other hand, studies such as Frances Lappé's *Aid as Obstacle* point out in a convincing, almost brutal, fashion that "human rights" and "direct aid to the poor" stipulations in Congressional legislation are usually ignored or distorted in the course of implementing these programs.

But the Lappé prescription fails to provide meaningful guidance for the anti-hunger advocates in an immediate sense. Lappé argues that foreign aid will be useful only if the fundamental orientation of the nation and its foreign policy undergo a revolutionary transformation in which political power is actively sought for the poor. While there is more than a measure of truth in this analysis, it collides headlong with current political reality so far as the activist is concerned. I would not overly criticize this view, however, as it is positive and necessary that a significant portion of the activist community devote its energies exclusively to the long view. The question of whether to devote one's energy to measurable progress in a lifetime, as opposed to sowing the seed for a brighter future, is a difficult one. My personal choice is to do all that one can in a realistic light, but to struggle to maintain a greater vision and keep threatened ideas alive after all immediate avenues have been exhausted.

Lappé's radical view has an "either-or" character about it. Either we abandon the dangerous dance of myopic anti-Sovietism which enables us to rationalize indifference to the poor, or we are spinning our wheels on ice and going nowhere. The question naturally emerges: Is it possible to achieve measurable and significant progress in combating global poverty irrespective of the political climate? The answer is yes. But, more important, this can be accomplished without sacrificing the longer view. In all probability immediate and long-range goals can be promoted simultaneously and independently.

Lappé would urge the anti-hunger activist to opt for more meaningful change-over than that which may be immediately obtainable. But it is necessary to ask what the implementation of such a radical course would actually produce, given certain realities. Lappé ignores the powerful psychological influence which "superpower" status has over national behavior and the pre-eminence of national security considerations in the formulation of every nation's foreign policy, regardless of its rhetoric. Given the current superpower competition and the preeminence of national security considerations, U.S. identification with the forces of revolutionary change in the less developed world could result in destabilizing, selective and manipulative policies similar to the Soviet approach. It may be that the nation-state system itself is a more appropriate reform target for the activist concerned with the long view than the fundamental orientation of U.S. policy.

So the Lappé assessment is very useful and revealing, but it is too far-reaching for immediate application and too unpredictable to be placed in the hands of a nation which is so capable of distorting its itent. Finally, the transfer of power from current elites to those who claim to speak for the poor does not guarantee that conditions will improve or that a more just order will be created.

For their part, liberal-leaning, pro-foreign aid groups usually respond to hunger by intensifying an increasingly blind defense of "foreign aid." According to one such group, "the average real annual growth in the LDC's as a whole has been above three percent. This is greater than the growth rate of the industrialized countries during the same period of their development. Real per capita income has more than doubled in the last twenty-five years." But these figures do not accurately represent the experience of the poorest sector of the populations within these nations. Per-capita income and GNP are virtually meaningless indicators of development because they fail to highlight significant pockets of poverty. Many governments in the less-developed world and their allies in the privileged sector are doing very well, while the people at large, and particularly the poor, face increasingly dire conditions.

It is apparent, then, that the anti-hunger effort is being undermined by (1) a range of psychological impediments, (2) enduring myths concerning the U.S. commitment to the hungry, and (3) two seemingly irreconcilable schools of thought, each clinging to its own illusions. By isolating and understanding these factors, we can begin to chart a path through the obstacle course which has prevented effective reform.

Nothing is more fundamental to tackling hunger effectively than the vision of a just world, free of dire poverty and hopelessness. To some extent, this vision is already an inherent part of the national mandate. Leaders of all political persuasions speak of our commitment to the downtrodden and the oppressed as though it were as much a part of our national character as free speech or freedom of religion. To be sure, there is often more than an ounce of hypocrisy in this rhetoric. But there is cause for hope in the fact that the mandate is firmly implanted in the national psyche. And as the opinion surveys point out, the American people believe that this mandate is being performed in deed as well as in word, however ineptly.

A priority item on the agenda of any hunger education campaign must, therefore, be to dispel the erroneous notion that the U.S. is effectively feeding a starving world. Appealing to guilt ultimately causes more resentment than action, and is, conse-

quently, counter-productive. Exposing how little we actually do
can be effective, but only to the extent that it appeals to the positive vision of justice which already exists. The reservoir of compassion in the nation is capable of absorbing the hunger fight,
but misinformation and the absence of information combine to
prohibit access to the truth. Effective action is impossible without the truth.

Another essential step in the formulation of a strong national political will is to widen the base of individuals who see a commitment to hunger problems as a fundamental tenet of
Judaeo-Christian thought. Those who already serve the Lord in
their immediate surroundings must be reached and shown the
need to expand their conception of the terms "neighbor" and
"community."

We have all been touched from time to time by examples of
"one-to-one" human compassion. I know from experience that individuals who perform these acts of love are often the same individuals who hold the view that we shouldn't spend "another
dime on those ungrateful Africans and Asians." This indifference exists not only because the problem is so far removed as to
be unintelligible, but it is also the result of legitimate cynicism
over the intent and ability of government to do the job. Those of
us who observe government food programs and their effect at
closer range would be dishonest if we didn't admit the partial
truth in this observation. Government does few things well. But
concrete political reforms designed to improve this situation are
possible.

This foreign aid muddle in which good is blurred with the
bad is eroding our effectiveness and our ability to confront the
real issues squarely. Consequently, our will is splintered. This is
why it is so necessary to carve the truly effective hunger programs, such as the Title II food program, the Disaster Relief program and others, away from the foreign aid program as a whole.
We must be able to assert our advocacy with a clear conscience.

Legislation which would accomplish this separation to a significant degree has been introduced and shows promise of being
accepted. The Senate version of Bread for the World's Hunger
Elimination and Global Security Act would direct the President,
in consultation with Congress, to identify those programs which
are exclusively aimed at meeting basic human needs. These pro-

grams would be categorized as "Hunger Prevention and Relief Assistance." Exposing how unconscionably inadequate the purely humanitarian portion of the foreign aid program is would be an important step in the right direction. The Department of State, in concert with the Pentagon, will probably always have so-called "national security" uses for food aid. But let us cease to add insult to injury by allowing it to masquerade as humanitarianism. It is clearly counter-productive for the anti-hunger community to fight the tide against foreign aid, when they could be developing an excellent alternative to sell to the American public. The undesirability or immorality of the current foreign aid program should be challenged, but on a separate battleground. Today we abstain from fighting that battle out of fear that it will cast a dark cloud over foreign aid in general and jeopardize fragile support for the comparatively few worthwhile programs.

The hard-bitten, efficiency-minded sentiment which prevails both in government and in the electorate today offers new opportunities for reducing world hunger. As the defense budget skyrockets and security assistance becomes the linchpin of our foreign policy, the tendency is to recoil in horror. There is need for creative ideas, not the politics of isolation. This challenge first requires the separation of hunger aid from foreign aid. The generation of fresh ideas consistent with an accurate reading of public sentiment must be an integral part of this approach.

Concurrently, the hunger program which emerges should be subject to the most stringent requirements for recipients. Nations which fail to make serious efforts toward food development should be effectively penalized or removed from the program altogether. This is not only a saleable package for those who already support development, it is one which opens the door to individuals not currently disposed to support global humanitarian efforts. Such a hunger program would not include nations like Pakistan, which presently receives its aid for strategic reasons under the guise of humanitarian relief. That aid should be termed strategic aid. The critical difference is that we could tap the reservoir of anti-giveaway sentiment which now burns brightly in the public mind and redirect it toward the counterproductive national security programs without fear.

If we fail to separate hunger relief from foreign aid, we risk drowning our efforts in a sea of anti-government sentiment which is not likely to diminish in the foreseeable future. Surely, if push comes to shove in this age of scarce resources, the high priests of East-West confrontationalism will unhesitatingly sacrifice the meager anti-hunger effort for their strategic designs. Those who grasp the moral and practical dimensions of world hunger and seek to eradicate the problem are not without opportunities in the age of austerity and armament.

Of all the issues pertaining to global survival, the control of nuclear weapons and the elimination of hunger are the most urgent and pivotal. These issues are far from unrelated as the most desperate and hopeless governments feel the most compelling need to acquire an offensive nuclear capability. This desire stems not only from the perceived security value of such weapons but from the recognition that there is no other way to be taken seriously in the global arena, given the impossibility of building a sound economic infrastructure.

The degree to which hunger is reduced in the years ahead will depend on the intellectual cohesion and moral forcefulness which anti-hunger groups display. The degree of success achieved may well determine not only the legitimacy of our historic claim to moral leadership but our very survival. This success will only be possible with an unprecedented display of political innovation and courage. The development of a national will to reduce hunger significantly will not be a question of revolution or budget figures; it will be a question of clarity achieved and opportunity grasped.

13
Refugees: The Uprooting of Peoples as a Cause of Hunger

Eileen Egan

The uprooting of peoples, the man-made disaster of the refugee, has been consistently underestimated, if not ignored, as a causative factor of hunger. Refugees cannot produce food. They can only bring increased need to areas where food is likely to be in short supply. Over ten and a half million refugees, distributed over a vast area of the earth's surface, are part of the world community, and one of its most intractable problems, as it enters the final decades of the twentieth century.[1]

I was in the United Nations Headquarters in September 1980 when Zimbabwe became the one hundred and fifty-third member of the international body. As the flag of the new nation of seven million people was ceremoniously raised at UN headquarters, a startling fact intruded on my consciousness. It was joining the flags of seventy-five UN member nations whose populations were smaller than that of the uprooted, the flagless, the unrepresented. Refugees, comprising at different times segments of the human family, can be seen as a nation of the nationless.

The presentation speech of Zimbabwe's prime minister went to the point. His newly freed country needed immediate and extensive aid to survive. It was estimated that after eight years of war and uprooting, Zimbabwe was three years away from self-sufficiency in food. Contributing to this new nation's problems was the return from exile of thousands of refugees who reached Zimbabwe destitute but with high expectations.

Food shortages and even famine faced seventeen countries of Africa in 1980, from Senegal and Mauritania in West Africa to the Sudan and Uganda in Central Africa to Kenya, Tanzania and Mozambique in East Africa.[2] Contributing to so tragic an outlook were war, drought and a crop of five million refugees whose presence and plight gave high visibility to uprooting as a causative factor in producing hunger. The UN High Commissioner for Refugees, after visiting in the north, south, east and west of Africa in 1980, termed it "the Continent of Refugees."[3]

The African experience highlights the fact that forced movements of people, a continuing phenomenon of the twentieth century, and tragically exacerbated by the Second World War, have been a cause of hunger to many millions and a cause of death to untold millions. For reasons to be discussed, reliable figures of fatalities in the matter of refugees are hard to come by.

There can be no gainsaying the fact that the tearing of people from their home places by mass expulsion, by communal or tribal violence, or by war continues to be a root cause of hunger in many parts of the world. At a time when, for too many, the word "refugee" evokes a tired if not hostile response, it might be useful to underline the causal link between uprooting and hunger.

It is a tragic reality that hunger came to large numbers of former food *producers* who were uprooted and separated from the land they once cultivated. Hunger for longer or shorter periods came not only to the uprooted themselves, but to the denuded areas from which they were driven and to the corners of the world where they brought their need and destitution. Those of us with experience with the world's refugees find the word "uprooting" a valid metaphor in describing their plight. The survival of uprooted people is as threatened as that of uprooted trees. Both are cut off from the sustenance necessary for survival. The word refugee thus becomes synonymous with hunger.

The production of food requires stability, and of this refugees are, by definition, deprived. Again, refugee denotes hunger.

For long periods, refugees, whether from rural or urban settings, face unemployment. Even if there is available food in the areas of asylum, refugees have no income with which to buy it. Once more, the word refugee is paired with the word hunger.

Unless food aid from international, national and people-to-people sources had reached the various groups of refugees, the death toll would have been larger than it was. In addition, the scourges that attack people debilitated by hunger would have spread across frontiers. Even so, the aid was often minimal, giving rise to a saying in the refugee encampments of western Europe after the Second World War, "We are given enough food to keep from starving but not enough to live."

Low Visibility of Uprooting as a Hunger Producer—Europe After World War II. Before returning to the African tragedy, it might be well to examine why uprooting has not been given due emphasis as a cause of hunger, but in fact has too often been de-emphasized. An inescapable reason is that history is written by representatives of nations, and the nationless rarely are given equal voice. Often the ruling groups responsible for uprooting people and forcing them to become refugees are anxious to escape responsibility for the survival of the victims. They would prefer that refugees have a "low profile," or possibly no profile at all, in chronicles of world events.

I was plunged into the dark world of the refugee just before the end of the Second World War when I served in a refugee encampment in northern Mexico. This was the first project of a war-born agency, Catholic Relief Services. Hidden away in an ancient and abandoned hacienda were over fifteen hundred Poles— men, women and children from eastern Poland. They had been snatched from their farms and villages and swept into Siberia after the Soviet armies occupied eastern Poland in 1939 in line with the Hitler-Stalin pact. When Hitler ended the pact by attacking the Soviet Union in 1941, the victimized people were freed from slave labor camps at the insistence of the western Allies. Decimated by hunger and exhaustion, the Poles after a long trek arrived in Iran. The younger men joined the Allied armies and the rest of the deportees were moved to havens across the world. One of the havens was near Guanajuato, Mexico. These simple people came to Mexico by a dizzying route across the surface of the globe. From them I learned first-hand of the horror of a slave labor system that had already held millions of Russians in its net before one and a half to two million Poles were added. I talked with a grandmother who had been deported with eleven other members of her family. She alone survived. These refugee Poles, ready to return to their homes after the Allied victory, found that their home (almost half of Poland) had been ceded by the Allies to the Soviet Union. Here was part of the history of the Second World War that was not publicized.

I came to realize that there are two histories, a history as seen from above and a dark underside of history, part of which was the history of the refugee. Over the years, the hunger caused by uprooting, by the man-made disaster of the refugee, has been consistently underestimated if not ignored.

In the aftermath of the Second World War, the period to which the remainder of this chapter will limit itself, there were an estimated forty million refugees in the world, the most massive presence being on the European continent.

It was hoped that with the cessation of hostilities the dread uprooting of human beings would subside. Germany was pockmarked with refugee camps. Barracks, requisitioned schools, and warehouses were jam-packed with men and women dragooned into forced labor in ammunition factories and farms. They had worn the word "OST," meaning that their origin had been eastern Europe, predominantly Poland. The majority of the "OST" people refused repatriation. Other refugee installations sheltered the remnant of Europe's Jews, saved as "brands from burning" from the unspeakable onslaught of murder known as the final solution. The term "displaced persons" was applied to them and they merited the active compassion of the world.

Mass uprooting, however, was accepted as a policy of the victorious Allies. Its basis, morally unjustifiable, was that of collective guilt.

History books give scant attention to the hunger and death caused by the mass expulsions of Germans and German ethnics from Silesia, East Prussia, the Sudetenland, and Yugoslavia. The expellees, as they were called, left behind their livelihoods, many consisting of farms that had been fruitfully cultivated for countless generations. Certainly, post-war hunger in Europe and the need for long-term and massive relief was caused by the expulsion of over fifteen million expellees, twelve million of whom descended in an avalanche of need in Western Germany. Food needs in the annexed territories of Poland and Czechoslovakia and in such depeopled areas as the Voivodina of Yugoslavia were intensified because farms were no longer working and new settlers needed time to assume control of their new holdings and produce crops. Crop production is not an overnight matter.

Meanwhile, the weakest among the expelled people perished as they clung to the edges of life in destroyed communities of defeated Germany, as well as in neighboring Austria. Here the role of American voluntary agencies, notably Lutheran World Relief, Church World Service and Catholic Relief Services, was absolutely crucial. While the decision on mass expulsions was made by the Allied powers, the responsibility for the care and maintenance of the expelled was placed explicitly and harshly on the German community. If the resuscitated German welfare agencies, in particular Evangelisches Hilfswerk and Caritas, had not been mightily buttressed by voluntary aid shipments from the United States, the chronicles of death would have been more harrowing than they actually were.

This sorry episode of modern history is only cited to indicate how those who cause the uprooting of peoples, including in this case the democracies who acquiesced in the program of mass expulsions at Potsdam, do not accept responsibility for the fate of the uprooted. Very often the uprooting is seen as a repayment, according to the morally questionable concept of mass guilt, for acts committed by the governments of the expelled groups.

It is amazing that even in this age of mass communication the annals of the uprooted are so sadly meager. The nations overlook any uprooting they have caused in the annals they choose to broadcast about themselves. In a life spent experiencing the effects of mass uprooting, I have been shocked at the lack of knowledge, not only of the facts of so massive a scar on the face of the planet, but of its intimate connection with hunger and all the ills, medical, social and even emotional that hunger produces.

Uprooting in Asia: The Indian Sub-Continent. To leap across the world to Calcutta, where all the problems of Asia meet in heart-stopping intensity, it is necessary to remind people that the hunger of its homeless street-dwellers is related to a massive uprooting. A million people, mostly villagers, uprooted from East Bengal at the 1947 partition of India, swamped Calcutta. They were part of the four million uprooted Bengalis who found refuge in West Bengal, and only a small part of the sixteen million people uprooted when the two wings of Pakistan were carved out of the subcontinent of India.

Accompanying Mother Teresa through the Sealdah railway station, in the 1950's, I talked with simple villagers whose home was the station floor. They squatted in family groups in the cavernous waiting hall, the living space often marked out by rows of small stones. The fumes of arriving steam engines, the smoke from countless cooking pots over dung-burning stoves and the stench of diseased and sweating bodies settled like a pall over the scene. As the station was periodically cleared by city authorities, new groups of refugees arrived from across a poorly marked border, bringing their starvation to a city besieged by the hungry and homeless. In successive visits over the years, I saw how Sealdah housed new refugees in the same misery. Across the continent, several millions of the uprooted streamed into newly-formed West Pakistan, inundating the city of Karachi. The newcomers, formerly agricultural people, were no longer producing the food needed by themselves and by society. I visited a Haji camp near Karachi, a camp intended to shelter the pilgrims in transit for Mecca. It was filled with enforced pilgrims barely kept alive with a daily dole of food. These were in better circumstances than those who had commandeered sections of the city sidewalks as their home places. A Karachi murder case concerned a man who had killed a fellow refugee. He explained his crime by asserting that the murdered man had pre-empted the corner of the sidewalk on which he habitually made his home.

Between Europe and Asia, of course, cluster the shelters (which they still consider temporary after over three decades) of the Palestinians dispersed in the upheavals and wars that accompanied the founding of Israel. Here is probably the most intractable concentration of refugees. Their hunger, year after year, must be met by a pipeline from the outside, in particular from the UN Relief and Works Agency. Those of us who have visited the Gaza Strip, where a quarter of a million men, women and children are crowded into a tiny area, fear the sparks that arise from seething hearts. It is these sparks that may imperil world peace.

To return to the partition of India, a partition that many

trace to misguided colonial policies, the uprooting of 1947 was almost equaled by that of 1970, when the east wing of Pakistan was militarily occupied by the west wing. Ten million East Bengalis, chiefly Hindus, streamed into a province that because of the earlier influx had become one of the neediest areas on the face of the globe. They left their rice paddies amid the chaos of what was then East Pakistan—soon to become Bangladesh. The military thrust by India in December 1971 had as one of its main aims the return of the ten million refugees. Their presence had made life insupportable in the Bengali-speaking province. They threatened to sink Calcutta under the weight of their misery. A quarter of a million of them were encamped in swampy Salt Lake at Calcutta's gates, threatening the overburdened metropolis with plague, with infection from lack of hygiene and sewage facilities, and with intensified hunger. Mother Teresa's sisters took care of orphaned and unaccompanied children as well as those who were famished and desperately ill. Almost every day some of the refugees were carried to the hostel for the dying in Calcutta where they could at least die in dignity.

Eventually the Indians saw to it that all were induced to return to their home places, mostly Hindu enclaves in Islamic communities. Some of the returnees found their small holdings already commandeered by their neighbors. On a crowded railroad station, at Bongaon near the Bangladesh border, I interviewed many who had slipped back over the border into India, after their repatriation. They were about to add their hunger to the pervading hunger of Bengal. There were certainly no oases in a crowded province where their village skills of cultivation could be used. They were the victims of the "two-nation" thinking that had originally given rise to partition, namely, that there should be one nation for Muslims and another, India, for Hindus. When the Hindus returned to what became Bangladesh, people in some localities, already entrenched in the temporarily abandoned plots of land, drove them away. "Go back over the border," they were told. *Your* country is over there."[4] The new government of Bangladesh was not able to police such unofficial expropriations. Calcutta was the destination of the returnees, and the street would undoubtedly be their home.

Death, Need, Bread: Vietnam, Europe, Korea, Hong Kong. Is there need to remind anyone of the near-million North Vietnamese who fled south of the 17th parallel when the country was partitioned in 1954, or the four million Koreans who fled south of the 38th parallel during years of upheaval and war? Do people still remember the hunger and plagues that raged through the largest refugee camp in the world, Hong Kong, until help converged from many parts of the developed world? It may be that only those who were involved with the world's refugees remember their plight. Unforgettable sights were the Vietnamese refugees selling small cords of wood on the road outside Saigon and scurrying to throw together schools and homes from bamboo and thatch, or the Korean elders, their families destroyed, wrapped in white mourning garments and waiting like corpses in a freezing open-air market for someone to buy a few beans or a cheap comb, or the sixty thousand Hong Kong refugees made homeless in one night after a fire destroyed a hillside that had sprouted with shacks of wood and cardboard.

Wherever solutions could be found, and where the weight put on the receiving area was not irreversibly tragic, solutions were found. In Europe, the expellees brought to a destroyed land, whose remaining productive capacity was lamed by dismantling for reparations, the energy of those whose very survival lay in work. That energy helped confect what was termed the "wirtschaftswunder," the "economic miracle," of Western Germany. The advice given in earlier generations to the emigrants from Germany who sailed for North and South America was "Todt, Not, Brot," "First Death, Then Need and Finally Bread." This now applied to the Germans and ethnic Germans coming into Germany itself.

In Vietnam, the people displaced from the north, with unparalleled energy, built their villages in spaces hacked out from the jungle and soon made maximum use of fertile soil. Talapia fish were stocked in rice paddies. Fishermen constructed new boats, bending the beams with the old, slow method of applying fire. They were soon faring into the South China Sea, from the southern coastline, as they had done earlier from the northern coastline of Vietnam. The South China Sea is bursting with fish, and many of the displaced northerners became rich.

In Korea, resettlement projects allowed people to survive in a landscape where twelve hundred villages were no more than ashes and fifty-two out of fifty-five cities were mercilessly battered. Some projects brought in pigs for new pig farmers; other projects introduced sheep and eventually a flourishing wool industry. In Hong Kong, incredibly industrious Chinese made the rocky colony a beehive of production for the world at large. Voluntary agency effort was crucial in helping these diverse groups of uprooted people reach self-reliance.

World Refugee Year. Many of the achievements on behalf of refugee groups could be credited to the World Refugee Year. The suggestion for a World Refugee Year was first made by the director of Catholic Relief Services, Bishop Edward E. Swanstrom, in Assisi, Italy, at the 1957 meeting of the International Catholic Migration Commission.[5] Bishop Swanstrom pointed out that the International Geophysical Year declared by the United Nations had served as a unifying force for scientists of diverse political strands so that they could aid the human family in coping with the vagaries, weather and other, of its planetary home. He proposed that an International Year for the Refugees could create a community of compassion on behalf of the refugees of the world.

Various groups took up the idea, and eventually the World Refugee Year was declared by the United Nations. The year was 1960, when the globe-girdling refugee problem had sunk by sixty-five percent from what it had been in the immediate wake of World War II. The refugee presence in Europe had diminished to the "hard core" of the displaced persons, the survivors of the wartime forced labor battalions who were ineligible for migration schemes. Abandoned to cold, trapped existences in sixty camps in Germany and Austria, these "unproductive" men and women, often tubercular, or broken in mind and body, were an unwanted reminder of a past tragedy. The World Refugee Year focused a searchlight on their misery, and they were resettled on a purely humanitarian basis. They were lifted out of damp barracks and placed in protective homes in nearby localities or in such countries as Sweden and Belgium.

The "hard core" of the displaced persons offers an example of how uprooting can cause disability, dependence and consequent hunger on a long term basis. The resilience needed to put down new roots was simply extinguished in people who were humiliated by forced labor and then by rejection in successive migration schemes. The scars inflicted often ended only with death.

Volumes could be written on how the World Refugee Year

generated funds not only from governments and intergovern-
mental agencies but, above all, from voluntary sources to help
lift refugee groups out of enforced dependency. Voluntary fund-
raising initiatives, exhibiting striking creativity and generosity
on behalf of the world's homeless, sprang up in the United
States, Australia, Canada and the countries of Western Europe.
The community of compassion showed its power on behalf of
those who felt themselves sloughed off by the world community.
Enclaves of North Vietnamese in South Vietnam and of North
Koreans in South Korea used the new funds as enabling grants
to become self-reliant.

It was assumed by many that with the enormous outpouring
of aid following the World Refugee Year, the challenge of the refugee would be less daunting. There would still be enclaves of the
uprooted, and there would still be a trickle of refugees here and
there, but these could be taken in hand by the enormously effective Office of the UN High Commissioner for Refugees as well as
by the ever-active voluntary agencies, in particular the church-
related agencies.

This did not happen. The beams of the searchlight, however,
which for a comparatively short period had been focused on the
refugees, were turned off. Uprootings continued and the trage-
dies of helpless people, chiefly agricultural people, went largely
unrecorded, particularly in the continent of Africa where new
borders had been drawn and new nations had come to birth.

A New Surge of Refugees: Vietnam, Cuba. The challenge of
the refugee was highlighted once more for Americans in April
1975 when a new generation of refugees was born in Vietnam
with the fall of Saigon. Many thousands of Vietnamese were heli-
coptered out of Saigon while thousands took to the sea from Vietnam's long coastline. While the 1954 escape by sea had led from
North Vietnam to southern ports, the 1975 exodus led to the
open sea. The earlier escapees were picked up from the waves by
the U.S. Seventh Fleet. The 1975 refugees were saved by ships of
many flags and airlifted to the U.S. In a brief period 140,000
Vietnamese were housed in Army forts throughout the U.S. I
talked with some of the Vietnamese awaiting resettlement in
Pennsylvania. For many, it was the second experience of uprooting within two decades.

A small wiry man, with deeply ridged, walnut brown skin,

told me he was a fisherman. His ancestors had been fishermen in a village not far from Haiphong. His family had fled at the division of Vietnam at the 17th parallel in accordance with the Geneva truce accords. He had then operated a fishing boat out of Phan Thiet about a hundred miles up the coast from Saigon. At the approach of the Northern forces, he had bundled fifteen members of his family into his boat, along with rice and drinking water. At the island of Con Son, an American naval ship picked them up and deposited them in the Philippines. From there the family group had been flown to the United States. He was waiting for a placement with a fishing fleet in Florida. A brother-in-law and his family had found a sponsor there. Through the computer terminal operating at Fort Indiantown Gap, Pennsylvania, relatives all over the United States were being reunited. This was how a rich country utilized computer technology to bring together families whom the application of war technology had scattered.

Eventually, the United States became the country of first asylum for three hundred thousand uprooted people from the area known as Indo-China. It also found itself the country of first asylum for Cubans and Haitians who arrived in Florida in flotillas of every type of craft from tiny fishing boats to small yachts. The problem of the refugee became front page news once more and the United States, a rich country, learned once again the difficulties of assimilating the uprooted who arrive with nothing but their need and their expectations. The Cuban influx had barely begun when Florida was officially declared a "disaster area" and thus was eligible for special federal funds. At the same time, the Cubans were evacuated by plane to the same army forts that had housed the Vietnamese refugees.

The U.S. Senate Committee on the Judiciary called its 1979 report the "World Refugee Crisis." It urged that an International Refugee Year be sponsored by the United Nations. United Nations officials must have been dismayed, to say the least. The history of the massive refugee effort of nineteen years earlier had seemingly been lost to history. A tragic fact had become clear to UN agencies, as it had become clear to voluntary agencies whose overseas programs englobed refugees, namely, that every year, in a world of upheaval, is a refugee year.

Countries of Asylum, Rich and Poor: Thailand. If a country as developed as the United States encounters problems in meeting the needs of refugees, particularly in a time of unemployment and inflation, what of less developed countries whose resources are barely able to meet the needs of its own people? As the mounting tide of "boat people" took off from Vietnam, such receiving areas as Singapore and Malaysia found that they simply could not supply the encampments of refugees that were growing on their shorelines. There were cases of boatloads of famished people being towed out to sea from shore points in Malaysia. In one case, two hundred Vietnamese drowned when their boat, which was not allowed to land, fell apart a few hundred feet from shore. Hong Kong, once called the "largest DP camp in the world" after the 1948–1949 influx, was forced to open refugee camps for close to seventy thousand refugees from Vietnam. These were chiefly Vietnamese of Chinese origin. Agencies which had closed their aid offices in Hong Kong found that they had to reopen them, and the international aid pipeline which had saved the earlier crop of refugees from death by hunger now had to be reinstituted to rescue a later crop.

Thailand was the country of first asylum not only for Vietnamese refugees fleeing from a new regime, but for Kampucheans (formerly Cambodians) escaping from a "murderous Utopia." A few Marxist ideologues, unhindered by humanistic or other values, imposed a new regime "by the forcible overthrow of all existing social conditions."[6] Banks were shut down, currency outlawed, schools closed. The "liberation" of Phnom Penh was the signal for its complete emptying. Even hospitals were emptied of patients and all were deposited on the roads leading to the countryside. There they were ordered to start an immediate cultivation of the soil amid the chaos of mass uprooting. In addition to those who died on the roads and in the unprovisioned countryside, a systematic liquidation of "class enemies" was carried out. Examples occurred of execution of those wearing spectacles, a sign of education and of possible resistance. A doctor who reached Thailand explained that he had not been able to treat the sick and dying around him in Kampuchea lest he betray his class origins. This might mark him as a "class enemy" and therefore as a candidate for execution. The death of between two and three million Kampucheans recalled to many the mass death of Jews in Europe's holocaust.

The massive influx into Thailand spawned a series of camps where Kampucheans, often the remnants of families, could survive. Khao I Dang, the largest Kampuchean camp, was at first a collection of huts thrown together from pieces of corrugated tin and any scraps of bamboo or waste material. Before the heavy rains of the monsoon descended on the area, the UN High Commissioner for Refugees supplied bamboo and thatch so that the huts could be reinforced. The UNHCR also supplied food, chiefly rice and fish and oil, for the one hundred and thirty-three thousand refugees. Catholic Relief Services provided a pediatric ward for the sick among the forty-seven thousand refugee children, as well as a hospital kitchen to supply food for all the hospital wards in the camp. A dozen medical teams flown in by Catholic Relief Services strove to heal the ill and wounded and stem epidemics along the crowded border. The International Rescue Committee was one of the most active voluntary agencies. It would be impossible to detail all its services; one example was the operation of the hospital at Nong Khai camp. This camp, directly across from Laos, sheltered Lao people and such tribal groups as the Hmongs. Schools were opened in the camp for child refugees from school-less Kampuchea. A gift of the Japanese government consisted of food for the mind—one hundred thousand Khmer books so that the children would not lose their cultural heritage.

Thailand, a country meeting problems in bettering the lives of its own citizens, became a country overrun with refugees. The newcomers not only brought their own hunger but caused hunger by displacing about two hundred thousand Thais from their border villages. The map of Thailand came to be marked by refugee camps from its border points adjoining Laos, along the length of its border with Kampuchea down to southern points on the Gulf of Thailand facing Vietnam. The remote northern camps, Chieng Khong and Chieng Khan, were filled with primitive and illiterate hill tribesmen fleeing from the Pathet Lao.

Nearly six hundred miles southward from Chieng Khong is Songkhla, where Vietnamese "boat people" found temporary refuge after fleeing across the Gulf. Songkhla was described by a visitor as "a desperately crowded place—about six thousand people on an acre of land. It is literally on the beach. The people are housed in makeshift shelters. All sorts of materials are used to put these shelters together—corrugated iron, thatch, plastic, tarpaulin, even plain cloth as a curtain or front door. The shacks are placed one right next to the other and the 'streets' or passages between are not more than two feet wide. The camp is alternately baking in the sun or awash with rain."[7]

The Thai authorities did not recognize Songkhla as a refugee camp but as "an encampment on the beach." They allowed it to exist only because various countries were already engaged in arranging for overseas resettlement. Those Vietnamese could not have survived without the regular shipments of fish, rice and oil provided by the United Nations High Commissioner for Refugees. The most helpless of the Songkhla refugees were unaccompanied children, many of whom lost their parents during the escape, first by land and then by sea. A missionary priest of the Redemptorist Society opened a shelter for these children where there was a regular school and where documents could be prepared on the children. Many were placed in foster homes in the United States while efforts were made to locate surviving relatives.

Songkhla was not the poorest of the camps in which "boat people" found refuge. Besides the Hong Kong camps already mentioned, tens of thousands were given refuge in Singapore, Malaysia, and Indonesia. Somehow, over seven thousand managed to come ashore in crowded Macau. As of August 1980, the UN High Commissioner for Refugees reported that five hundred and fifteen thousand Indo-Chinese refugees had been resettled since the first of the "boat people" entrusted themselves to the South China Sea or the Gulf of Thailand or, as border-crossers, fled from Laos or Kampuchea. Over half of these came to the United States, with large numbers going to France, Canada and Australia in that order, and the remainder finding homes in thirty other countries. There were just about as many left in camps and makeshift shelters throughout Southeast Asia—close to three hundred thousand in Thailand, about two hundred thousand in Malaysia, Indonesia, Hong Kong, the Philippines and other areas. For how long would their hunger have to be met by shipments from food surplus nations channeled through UN and voluntary agencies? Would their period of hunger be an interim or long-term experience? How many of them would find it possible to return to their home places? Would any considerable number be allowed to put down roots in the country of first asylum, giving the existing needs of these developing areas? As with the fate of many uprooted groups, only history will provide the final answers. Before the final answers, there is only interrogation.

Before leaving Thailand, it is useful to glance over the border in Kampuchea. After the chaos of mass uprooting, starvation took the lives of an uncounted number of Kampucheans. Though massive food shipments were stationed at the Thai-Kampuchean border, they were not permitted entry to the stricken country. Eventually, when the revolutionary forces of Pol Pot were no longer in complete control, large numbers of Kampucheans (estimated at a near million by Dr. Homer Jack) congregated at border areas.[8] Trucks laden with food supplies, taking advantage of poorly marked borders and the continuing chaos, patrolled the borders. At soft points they pierced the border and, on a compassionate "hit-and-run" basis, distributed life-saving supplies and darted back to Thailand. This bizarre life-saving operation had to be conducted by Catholic Relief Services month after month for people uprooted from their homes but not actually refugees, people squatting in a sort of "no-man's-land" near a permeable border. The agencies were able to use purchased foods as well as stocks donated by the U.S. government. They showed once more the flexibility of voluntary agencies in reaching the needy in delicate and precarious situations.

Pakistan. As noted earlier, Pakistan received an influx of millions of refugees after the 1947 partition of the Indian subcontinent, an influx that beggared the resources of a newly-born nation. In 1979 the inflow of refugees was from Afghanistan. Soviet tanks provoked a tragic exodus from Afghanistan similar to that from Hungary nearly a quarter of a century earlier. By September 1980, Pakistan had provided asylum for more than one million Afghans. The receiving areas were the windswept northwest frontier province and the desert-like areas of Baluchistan province. Working against time, the UN High Commissioner for Refugees was hard put to it to supply thousands of tents and hundreds of thousands of quilts for Afghans arriving at the rate of eighty to one hundred thousand monthly. The most minimal protection against the elements and a basic ration of food presented almost incredible challenges. An Inter-Aid Committee composed of Protestant and Catholic Churches within Pakistan appealed for emergency help from their overseas co-religionists.

American church-related agencies began shipments of tenting and quilts for some thousands of refugees as well as funds for urgently needed medical supplies.

Pakistan itself has not reached self-sufficiency in food. Its richer agricultural areas, watered by the Indus or by irrigation, are far too limited to share with newcomers. There are no plans to resettle the Afghans overseas. Again the world is faced with inescapable interrogations: How long will the hunger of nearly two million people have to be the concern of the world at large? What will be the long-term effect of the Afghan exodus as a producer of hunger across generations?

Somalia. The million and a half persons uprooted in the Ogaden region of Africa were only one reminder that violent overturnings of regimes and civil strife have given Africa a continuing refugee presence. Much of the post-colonial history of the continent could be recorded in the calligraphy of agony traced by refugees as they crossed and recrossed new-made frontiers.

The tragic reality was that the nations which sprang from the colonized areas, with the UN acting as midwife, were heir to colonial errors in drawing borders. The borders carved by the overseers from Europe cut across tribal, religious and linguistic groupings, and also joined groups harboring immemorial enmities. Hostilities erupted between north and south Sudan for such reasons, with the south Sudanese taking refuge in all surrounding countries including the Central African Republic. The racial and religious mix of Africa's most populous nation, Nigeria, contributed to the secession of a province and consequent civil war.

Almost every African nation has accepted its wave of refugees for longer or shorter periods, now in flight from Angola or Mozambique, now from the Sudan or Nigeria, now from Zimbabwe-Rhodesia, Guinea, Zaire, Uganda, Chad or South Africa. The UN High Commissioner for Refugees entered these explosive situations over and over again with healing and help. The agency avoided becoming a political instrument for any side and became recognized as an objective instrument to serve purely humanitarian ends. Its monumental effectiveness was achieved with a limited budget for which it had to struggle annually. Its humanitarian credentials were validated when it was awarded the Nobel Prize for Peace. Its program becomes more necessary each year.

As Zimbabweans were able to return to their home places, a

stream of refugees poured out of Chad, some one hundred thousand to Cameroon and over six thousand to the Central African Republic. It was in the Horn of Africa, in Sudan, Ethiopia, Djibouti and Somalia, however, that famine became a spectral presence.

Sudan, which a decade earlier had seen an outflow of its people, now became burdened with an inflow of an estimated five hundred thousand people from the Eritrean province of Ethiopia. Sudan was already experiencing severe food shortages, and at least fifty percent of its child population suffered from some degree of malnutrition. The tiny nation of Djibouti, situated strategically between warring Ethiopia and Somalia, could not escape an influx of refugees. Already devastated by a severe drought, Djibouti was host to one hundred and fifty thousand refugees. The refugees came to number over ten percent of the population and comprised two groups—the first, primarily refugees from the Ogaden and Eritrea, and the second, nomadic herders. The nomadic group, displaced from their grazing land by hostilities and by the shortage of water, arrived with the sad report that they had lost up to ninety percent of their camels and goat herds.

Part of the emergency aid program for the refugees in Djibouti was the provision of water storage tanks.

Somalia, however, presented to the world a face of agony more intense than anything in recent African history except perhaps that of the emaciated civilians of Biafra, so many of whom perished during the 1960's. That tragic tide of death could not be held back despite the enormous feeding program of Joint Church Aid during the Nigeria-Biafra civil war. Somalia, one of the world's least developed nations, was classified as one of the half dozen poorest countries on the planet in terms of per capita income. Its balance of payments was in deficit. The arrival of the refugees coincided with a drought already causing hunger to the Somali people. The total of refugees in makeshift camps reached one million, with another half million simply attaching themselves to Somali villages. The word "camp" may denote a series of firm buildings, supplied with water, light and sewage disposal. In Somalia, refugee "camps" consisted of no more than flimsy brush huts thatched with grass. The refugees themselves went to work to dig wells. Since sixty percent were children and another thirty percent were women, only the male ten percent, many of them aged, were available for well digging. The remaining males were trying to find work in towns and cities or were encamped with fighting units. The necessary work implements were supplied by the UN High Commissioner for Refugees with the cooperation of UNICEF. In Somalia, as in so many other parts of Africa afflicted by the man-made disaster of homeless refugees, the UN High Commission for Refugees carried on its day-in-day-out task of saving human lives. As always, it did not put the refugees to any exacting test of eligibility before extending aid, but mobilized the help in the shortest possible time.

To the World Food Program of the UN fell the task of operating an enormous supply line of thousands of metric tons of sorghum, maize, wheat flour, rice, oil and powdered milk.

Typically, the voluntary agencies supplied adjunctive services including medical aid. In this case, the almost immeasurable need gave rise to a cooperative group called the Inter-Church Response for the Horn of Africa, comprising Church World Service, Lutheran World Relief and Catholic Relief Services. The very survival of these uprooted people depends on the uninterrupted concern of governments and the UN agencies they support, and on the compassion of the citizenry of such countries as our own. This compassion fuels the American voluntary agencies which have an admirable history of rescue and service on behalf of the uprooted, a history that can be barely hinted at here. Again there are interrogation marks. How long will the uprooted people of Eritrea and the Ogaden bring their own hunger to Somalia and increase the hunger of the Somali people? How long will it be before the considerable number of nomads among the refugees find livelihoods that will involve settling into one place should there be no possibility of a return to the only existence they have ever known?

The Persistence of Hunger as Reality, Not Myth. In surveying the hunger and need of the ten and a half million refugees in the world, the 1979 Report of the U.S. Senate Committee of the Judiciary was correctly entitled "World Refugee Crisis." Despite the proposal that the United Nations declare an International Refugee Year (evidently in ignorance of the WRY), there are no plans for a reprise of a UN year devoted to refugees.

That the refugee crisis may be of long duration is recognized by many. In a searching article on refugee and migration issues in *Foreign Affairs,* Michael S. Teitelbaum stated:

> There is a growing realization that immigration and refugee issues may prove to be among the most important and troubling world problems of the next decade. The recent large flows of refugees or expellees from Indochina, Afghanistan and Cuba, all typically treated as short-term crises, instead may be harbingers of long-term trends of profound proportions. . . . Domestic or international conflicts may produce real or only pyrrhic victories, but they always produce refugees. Increasing strife, coupled with populations that are today more than twice as large as those of 1950, portends burgeoning numbers of refugees seeking asylum in the coming decades.[9]

The burgeoning numbers of refugees, especially as they descend on the poorest and often most afflicted parts of the globe, will not only bring their own hunger, but, as mentioned earlier, will exacerbate food problems in the receiving areas.

There are those who take an optimistic view of hunger in the world, pointing out that "if only" this or that panacea were adopted, the international agencies, or the countries themselves, could not only diminish but actually end hunger. I cannot share this optimism. One of the "if only" books that is quoted as almost the final word is *Food First.*[10] It presents a policy for developing countries recently freed from colonialism. The authors are largely correct in their condemnation of colonial policies of enforcing export cropping on dependent countries. I have no disagreement with the authors that the aim of all aid, including food aid, should be the self-reliance and empowerment of the peoples aided. They see a solution "if only" there is rapid agricultural change-over by mass initiative of liberated peoples to put food first. This involves a dismantling of the profit-first system, a deceptively simple sudden cure-all. The point of adverting to *Food First,* and to the well-publicized work of the Institute for Food and Development Policy (founded by the *Food First* authors), is the fact that the refugee crisis is not mentioned in their analysis. The worldwide refugee tragedy simply does not serve their thesis. The programs of voluntary agencies, especially feeding programs, are poorly understood and are often attacked by them as inimical to development. Also poorly understood and even attacked is the fact that American people-to-people agencies may draw on American agricultural stocks, under Title II of the Food for Peace program, to feed the hungry overseas. These feeding programs, utilizing food acquired by tax monies, deal with people whose very survival is at stake and who have been removed from the production of any crops, whether for self-reliance or export. The "myth of scarcity" propounded in *Food First* is not myth to the uprooted millions of the world.

The emphasis on self-reliance and on empowering the powerless is of basic importance and should undergird every aid effort. It is to be hoped that those who promote the goals of self-reliance will include in their purview those from whom all power has been taken, namely the refugees, to say nothing of the uprooted rural people who form slum communities around the world's cities. Very often the refugees reflect a legacy of colonialism as persistent as the legacy of export agriculture. Feeding programs must continue while refugees need to be kept alive until they can either return to their home places where empowerment is a possibility, or until they benefit from resettlement. It is the private voluntary agencies which have, in resistance to oppressive governmental decrees, preserved for refugees the right of asylum and the freedom of choice as to their future, and have then thrown their resources into programs of empowering the refugees to put down new roots.

Another book decries "mere charity" in the generating and distribution of private voluntary resources and urges the agencies to allow local groups greater autonomy in the use of donated funds.[11] The points taken have merit, and private voluntary agencies have had, perforce, to avoid paternalism since they did not have the resources to send in squads of staff members as overseers. Local initiative and autonomy were the backbones of most voluntary agency programs. The hidden premise seems to be that the days of relief and emergency aid have passed. Neither book confronts the very real possibility, as described by Teitelbaum, of a burgeoning crop of refugees as part of the world's future. Such publications, assumed to be authoritative by many Americans supporting church-related private voluntary agencies, may result in destroying confidence in such agencies. This is a disservice not only to the constituencies of these agencies but to the dispossessed and uprooted who will be hurt by diminished aid.

People concerned with hunger must beware of projects to end hunger which omit a persistent cause of hunger; they must beware of a map of the future which omits a crucial factor of reality.

The plight of refugees owes its origin to the darkest forces in human nature, forces that breed a wrong concept of the human person and wrong relationships among the groups comprising humankind. These include ethnocentrism, a nationalism expressed in hatred for enemies rather than simply in patriotic love of one's own people, the fear of other national or political groups and the desire for conquest and control over them. Such drives, long operative in human history, will hardly disappear in this or future generations. Borders will continue to be considered sacred, while human beings, driven over them to destitution and exile, will not be seen in their inviolable sacred reality.

The acceptance and succor of refugees calls for the highest qualities possible to human nature. These include charity, which is never "mere" in its true sense of loving "the other," particularly the homeless, for the sake of Him "who had not whereon to lay his head."

Charity is one with compassion. It involves a "feeling with" the agony of the other, and this gives rise to the works of mercy. Mercy is love under the aspect of need. It is charity that inspires transcendence in the human heart, the power to transcend the narrow tribal, cultural and national barriers that separate humankind, and from this transcendence arises the feeling of unity with all—especially with those who suffer. It is such transcendence that moves people to sacrifice their goods and time for people they will never see in this life, and to make such sacrifice in addition to the programs financed through their taxes.

In my opinion, there will be more need than ever for mercy and such transcendence in the coming decades, especially on behalf of the uprooted. Such organizations as Bread for the World, while not operating in the sense of relief and rescue, are crucial in their power to speak in moral terms to a government that can decide by its food and aid policies who will live and who will die.

Bread for the World is one of the private agencies that speaks for those who hunger and who are victims of history. Those most threatened by hunger, and who have no voice among the nations of the world, are, and will be, the uprooted.

Thomas Merton placed the plight of the refugee in context for the followers of Jesus:

> Into this demented inn, in which there is absolutely no room for him at all, Christ came uninvited. But because he cannot be at home in it . . . his place is with those who do not belong, who are rejected by power because they are regarded as weak, those who are discredited, who are denied the status of persons, tortured, exterminated. With those for whom there is no room, Christ is present in this world. He is mysteriously present in those for whom there seems to be nothing but the world at its worst.[12]

Bread for the World and other private agencies act out of awareness of the presence of the divine in the person of the refugees. Though I do not see the end of hunger in the world as a realistic hope, there are other reasons for hope. I have in mind the strength and vigor of private voluntary agencies who every day of every year work to lessen hunger. They not only show those who see only "the world at its worst" another world, a world of compassion, but they work to have the larger community reflect this other world. The world of compassion is concerned not only with assuaging the hunger of the uprooted but with building a more just world. We have to work for a world where wrong concepts of the human person will not prevail, where further uprootings will be discouraged, and where the already uprooted will receive the help they need to put down new roots. The uninterrupted programs of compassion for the uninvited and uprooted, sponsored by private voluntary agencies, represent a vision of the world at its best, even a sign of the reign of God.

NOTES

1. *United Nations High Commissioner for Refugees Report,* September 1980.

2. *New York Times,* September 26, 1980.

3. *UN High Commissioner for Refugees,* UN Headquarters Office, October 1980.

4. Interviews by the author in Bongaon, Bengal, and Calcutta, March 1972.

5. *Migration:* Report of the International Catholic Migration Conference, Assisi, Italy, Published by ICMC, Geneva, October 1957.

6. *Communist Manifesto,* Karl Marx & Friedrich Engels, German text by Samuel Moore. Translated from 1948 Pocket Books, Simon & Schuster, Inc., New York 1971.

7. *Report on Visit to Thailand,* Jean Gartlan, Catholic Relief Services, August 1980.

8. *WCRP Report on Kampuchea,* Dr. Homer Jack, World Conference on Religion and Peace, 777 UN Plaza, New York, N.Y. 10017, 1980.

9. *Right Versus Right: Immigration and Refugee Policy in the United States,* by Michael S. Teitelbaum, *Foreign Affairs,* Fall 1980.

10. *Food First: Beyond the Myth of Scarcity,* by Frances Moore Lappé and Joseph Collins (Boston: Houghton Mifflin Co., 1977).

11. John G. Sommer, *Beyond Charity, US Voluntary Aid for a Changing Third World,* Overseas Development Council (Washington, D.C.: ODC, 1977).

12. Thomas P. McDonnell (ed.), *The Time of the End Is the Time of No Room: A Thomas Merton Reader* (New York: Doubleday Image Books, 1974).

14
The Arms Race

Eugene Carson Blake

The fact that in 1980 the nations of the world spent approximately four hundred and fifty billion dollars on arms is one of the most obvious causes of world hunger. The disturbing correlative fact is that an amount equal to less than five percent of that figure goes for development assistance.[1] It is not only wealthy nations which year after year increase their expenditures on what is now usually called "defense." Nations both small and poor also divert their limited resources and labor from producing food for their hungry. Instead they grow and export such things as sugar cane and carnations, bananas and coffee, to pay for the cost of supporting and equipping ever larger and more expensive armies, navies and air forces.

Even in the wealthy countries of Western Europe, even in Canada and the United States, there are people malnourished and hungry because too great a percentage of the Gross National Product is spent each year on defense.

One of the reasons nations so distort their budgets, despite the hunger and poverty they cause, is that generally speaking the ones who will suffer have neither the economic nor the political power significantly to affect their nations' decisions.

But a more important cause for national support of militarism is the widespread fear of what other nations will do to us if we are weak. This is not a groundless fear. Military and economic power has been used historically by the strong to exploit weaker nations. Those peoples which have preserved some measure of independence and freedom have reason to suppose that they may very well lose it if they have insufficient power to resist their neighbors, both near and far.

This is the argument used each year by the generals and admirals in the Pentagon to persuade the Congress of the nation, already the strongest in the world, to spend even more on defense. The requests become so outrageous that even the Congressional military committees begin to ask such questions as why we need bombs to destroy an enemy five times over when we already have enough to do it twice.

When this common sense begins to jeopardize the military budget, the usual military argument consists of an exaggeration of the military strength of our enemies and a belittling of the loyalty and power of our friends and allies.

Let us not, however, be unfair to the admirals and generals. They are required by their civilian bosses to keep the nation safe. This means that they must have enough military strength successfully to combat any possible eventuality of a combination of enemies and even of former friends and allies. With that kind of assignment, what self-respecting general or admiral will ask the Congress for too small a military budget?

The U.S. defense budget for the 1982 fiscal year exceeded the two hundred billion dollar mark. The President has approved defense spending of two hundred and forty-five billion for 1982. Faced with such a federal prospect of an ever increasing military expenditure, what then is the right and intelligent response of the Christian citizens of a nation such as ours?

I

Some Christians take the pacifist position. It is easy to state: War is wrong; therefore we should not prepare for war. Under no circumstances is war ethically justifiable.

Forty years ago when I was a young pastor newly come to California, I found the Christian community there sharply divided between those who thought it was our Christian duty to support in every possible way the war effort which had begun a year before in Europe, against Hitler's Germany, and those who took a pacifist position. It was my second Sunday afternoon in town when I found myself in my own pulpit presiding over a large gathering. The speakers were two of the leading pastors in Pasadena who were debating the issue. Both were eloquent and quite persuasive. It was evident that very soon I would have to take a position on the war issue and make it clear to everyone in the church and community.

Even though I admired the preaching of two New York pastors of that day more than that of any others—Harry Emerson Fosdick and George Arthur Buttrick—I found I could not follow them into the pacifist position. It was not that I became a warmonger; I remembered too well the embarrassment of the Church after the First World War was over. In fact, I found during the years 1941–1945 that I was preaching about the same thing as those pacifists whom I admired. Our task was to minister to all the families in our churches. These included fathers and mothers, wives, brothers and sisters of young men at war, some of whom lost their lives fulfilling their patriotic duty. But there were other families (not so many) in the church I served who had pacifist sons—some in prison for the sake of conscience, others doing dangerous forms of alternative service. I was glad that the Gospel included comfort and hope for all our members.

But there are two kinds of pacifists. One kind is perhaps the most admirable of all Christians. St. Francis of Assisi, Gandhi, and Martin Luther King are names that come immediately to mind, and there are countless others, whose names we do not know. These are those who because of their faith in God find some alternative way of love and service even in the worst of circumstances. Some become martyrs. I have always hoped that I would myself turn out to be that kind of pacifist.

But there is another kind of pacifist, much less attractive. These are pragmatic pacifists who argue that one should be a pacifist because pacifism works. During those war years, I had a neighbor pastor who was always giving pacifist military advice to anyone who would listen. Sometimes even the Society of Friends falls into this trap of arguing that everyone should take their position, at the very moment that they and their interests are being protected by professional or volunteer soldiers. The pacifist of Philadelphia Quakers in the eighteenth century seems hardly a model for us all when, protected by poverty-stricken Scotch Irish immigrants on the Indian frontier, they were accumulating some of the largest fortunes in the new world. Pacifism, especially of the pragmatic variety, is not the Christian citizens' response to larger and larger defense budgets.

II

A much more popular response among American church members is the pharisaic or hypocritical stance. This is also an easy position to state: the United States is the hope of the world; our enemies are the enemies of mankind; therefore vote the military budget no matter what it costs the poor in hunger and malnutrition.

I have dared to call this widespread American opinion hypocritical because our enemies are never as bad as we like to think nor are we as good as we claim to be. The scenario of a cheap western movie does not represent the real world. The cowboys who wear white hats in the real world are not always heroes. Nor are the black hats sub-human along with the Indians.

In the first year of the decade of the 1980's, our most irritating opponents in the world were the Iranians. But it does not require a long memory to recall when the Chinese or the Arabs were enemy number one. And ever since the end of World War II it has been the Russians whom we most fear and hate. Through the cold war, detente, and invasions of Hungary, Czechoslovakia, and now Afghanistan, the Soviet Union has been the powerful enemy. We say: we are Christian, they are godless. We are free, they are totalitarian. We are the friends of small nations all over the world. They have no friends, only satellites who fear them. We stand for freedom. Thus do our corporate and political leaders argue. And so in times of crisis almost all church members are persuaded to support the increase of our defense expenditures at the expense of the hungry poor.

But let us remember that in the eyes of the leaders of the U.S.S.R. and in the eyes of a surprising number of Russians, Asians, Africans and Latin Americans, we and the Western Europeans are the imperialists and they, the Russian socialists, are the friends of the poor. We are the exploiters while they establish justice. We are rich and getting richer, while the poor get poorer; so their argument goes.

I realize as I write this that I open myself to the common charge of being at the least a bleeding heart liberal, or, worse, an unpatriotic pro-Russian communist. I am neither. It should be understood that to be critical of the United States and its policies vis-à-vis the U.S.S.R. does not imply that you approve all that the Russians are and do. But the question which is relevant to the military budget of the U.S.A. is whether the Russians are really more of a threat to us than the U.S.A. is to them. What I am saying is that the two superpowers are more alike than different. We both want to dominate the world. We both claim that it is for their own good that we want the third world friendly to us and dependent on us.

My conclusion is that the most popular so-called Christian response to ever larger defense budgets for our nation is hypocritical and pharisaic. It is also the most dangerous, as we shall see below.

III

The American church member's correct response to the ever-increasing defense budget of our nation rises out of three convictions which are based upon realities of the twentieth century world. These are:

A. We live in a world neighborhood. All nations are so interdependent that the day of competitive nationalism is past. All human beings are our neighbors.
B. Human beings (all of us) are sinners and all of us are redeemable by the grace of God.
C. Peace is much more dependent upon justice than upon military or economic power.

A

Let us begin with the uncontested facts of the interdependent world neighborhood and follow them with the vision of one world community that rises out of faith in God.

Instant communication, jet travel, interdependence of all nations for raw materials and for markets to support a rapidly multiplying population: these are realities in 1980 which are very different from those of 1910.

In 1910, most of my relatives were just beginning to be dependent on distant people. My mother's brothers had left the isolated farms and villages of the middle west and moved to Kansas City which had become an important center of the new modern railroads. Before the railroad most people never traveled any great distances. Although they read books and a few magazines, there was no way for them to respond or react to events on other continents until so much time had passed that what would now be current events was for them already history.

Everyone ten years or more younger than I has taken worldwide radio for granted all his life. I can remember that first crystal set I heard. It was a new wonder that began to make the whole world a neighborhood. And I can remember the first airplane I ever saw in the sky above. There were some few parts of our normal diet in Missouri, such as tea, coffee, spices, bananas and oranges, which came from far away, even from other nations. But my relatives, living on isolated farms, could live pretty well without store-bought exotic items.

Looking at trade from the other direction, American exports had begun. In the early 1890's my father supported himself for a year in London selling American manufactured typewriters. But now all of us are dependent on foreign oil and uranium, aluminum, and many other imports in order to live comfortably as we have become accustomed, and we cannot sell enough computers, cars, or grain to pay for what we want. This is a popular reason for selling guns and planes to nations which can't afford them.

Worldwide communications, travel and trade have made the world a neighborhood. The question is: Can it become a community?

The vision of one worldwide community is not new. That vision rises out of faith in God, our Creator, Redeemer and Judge. It is a faith as old as Abraham and as new and fresh as morning prayer. Prophets in every generation have preached the word of the coming of the day when peace will replace war; the day when God will redeem his people; the day "when no more shall be heard" in God's city "the sound of weeping or the cry of distress" (Is 65:19); tbe day when "the wolf and the lamb shall feed together, the lion shall eat straw like the ox; they shall not hurt or destroy in all my holy mountain" (Is 65:25); the day when "the dwelling of God is with men. He will dwell with them, and they shall be his people, and God himself will be with them; he will wipe away every tear from their eyes and death shall be no more, neither shall there be mourning nor crying, nor pain any more, for the former things have passed away" (Rev 21:3-4).

This is the vision arising from faith in God. It is the vision of a new world.

Can one take such poetry seriously? We are living in a skeptical and realistic time. Much religion fails modern men and women right here. No one should be asked to take the poetry of faith literally. But the tragedy of our days is that too many of our contemporaries no longer take seriously such faith in God or such vision of God's world. Too many have come to the conclusion that there is no God, that human history has no meaning or goal, and that men and women are only higher animals and not very high at that.

But Christian faith takes history seriously and believes that history has both a beginning and an end: an end which is a goal, not merely a finish. Christian faith holds that history finds its meaning in the reality of God and eternity. But eternity does not follow time. Eternity is a present dimension of life. "This is eternal life: that they know thee the only true God, and Jesus Christ whom thou has sent" (Jn 17:3).

An important difference between Christianity and most other forms of religion is this paradoxical conviction that God and eternity are real *and* that human life and history find their full meaning only in God and eternity.

The Greeks believed that history was going nowhere but in circles. Death was not the end of each individual life but rather a path to that oblivion which would let a soul begin again, forgetful of its past, in a reincarnation.

The Indo-European tradition, the Aryan bridge between Europe and Asia, brought this religious view to India where its variety of Hindu faiths have reincarnation as a common conviction. Gautama Buddha was essentially a Hindu. His followers in Ceylon, India, Tibet, China and Japan shared this view which makes history meaningless and directs all human effort toward the end of release from the world into identity with God.

This is why Christianity is a faith which requires both prayer and good works, spiritual witness and human service, bread and cup on the Communion table, and bread, milk, and water for the sustenance of physical life.

This is why Christianity is a faith which calls us to view the whole world as one neighborhood and all men, women and children as our brothers and sisters. Christianity holds that God our Father loves all his children and that all of us, no matter how evil we are or have been, are potentially brothers and sisters, friends and servants of Jesus Christ. This is our hope within history.

B

Does this sound so romantic and unrealistic as to be nonsense to the modern educated mind? If Christianity held that all human beings were naturally good, so that of their virtue they would achieve sufficient perfection to save the world from hatred, fear and war, the facts of life, past and present, would prove to any thoughtful person that Christians were blind to reality.

Our faith holds rather to the potential redemption of all and to the coming of God's kingdom through the goodness, power and grace of God. But equally Christian faith holds to the fact of the sinfulness of all people and peoples, including the better and the best.

I realize that my Calvinistic background is liable to an overemphasis of this aspect of our common Christian faith. Nevertheless, biblical faith, however interpreted, does not hold to a romantic view of human nature. All human beings in the biblical view are sinners and need God's grace and power to enable them to avoid personal and social catastrophe.

This combination of realism and hope is, as I have written, a matter of faith. It cannot be proved. But it can be lived. The skeptical secular mind argues that its view fits better with all of the facts of life than any view which holds that human life has meaning or that there is hope at the end of the story of mankind.

But how does the skeptic mind rest satisfied with its intellectual conclusion that human intellect itself means nothing? As a young man studying philosophy, both metaphysics and logic, over fifty years ago, I came to a conclusion which I hold today: that it is more logical to find meaning in human life than not. And this conclusion does not rest on Christian faith so much as upon logical thought.

Therefore faith in God the Father as revealed by Jesus

Christ gives humanity sufficient hope, both in time and eternity, that a martyr's death has ultimate meaning and dedicated lives have historical value, even ultimate success. But that success does not depend on human strength or value but rather upon the grace of a loving Creator and Redeemer God.

C

Ever since Hiroshima, the mushroom cloud of atomic destruction has threatened human survival, casting its dark shadow over all the future. Peace has become the obvious goal of us all. War, in an atomic age, has become unthinkable.

If that is true, how then can peace best be assured? Complete assurance is of course impossible. What then is the most likely path to peace?

So far the nations of our world have based their hope of peace on military and economic power—a balance of power. The U.S.S.R. and the U.S.A. first tried to keep atomic capability to themselves. But now it is clear that the great powers neither have, nor can have, a monopoly on nuclear bombs or weapons.

So far the balance of nuclear power has been even enough so that, despite mutual provocation, neither the super powers nor the lesser powers have seemed likely to want to run the risk of the nuclear destruction of the world. So long as mutual fear prevents even the limited use of nuclear weapons, two other choices have become attractive. One is the development of more traditional weapons and armies to use them. The other is the use of economic power to force the weaker powers to submit.

The first of these choices is the one more closely related to my subject. The ever increasing expenditure for military purposes all over the world is, as I indicated at the beginning of this chapter, a direct cause of hunger even in the comparatively wealthy nations. Fear and/or greed makes governments spend more than they can afford on arms at the expense of the hungry poor. I suppose most nations would continue to think that such military expenditures were worthwhile if they would guarantee peace and freedom. But in a world dominated by military force, both civilians and weak nations have begun to experiment widely on how to force the powerful to capitulate to the comparatively weak. The taking of hostages is today the most common way to do it. Even though the capture of the United States embassy in Teheran by Iranian "students" is the most recent, embarrassing and longest lasting action of this kind, we should remember that kidnaping for ransom has been with us for a long time. Germany and Italy have had more of this type of "political" hostage-taking than most well-ordered nations. The danger of hostage-taking becomes more and more severe if it is supported by governments against governments as was the case in Iran.

In return, the powerful tend to use economic power against the weak rather than expensive military forces on land, sea, or in the air. Long range economic blockades are very powerful weapons. But such economic pressure was considered relatively ineffective against both Iran and the U.S.S.R. in Afghanistan. Whenever you push an economic blockade effectively, the danger of a change of weapons by your opponent increases. This change is apt to be hostage-taking by the weak, or military action by the strong.

What then is the way to peace in the late twentieth century? It is the Christian faith that justice rather than power is the way to peace. The report of the Presidential Commission on World Hunger contains this statement: "The Commission believes that promoting economic development in general, and overcoming hunger in particular, are tasks far more critical to U.S. national security than most policy makers acknowledge or even believe. Since the advent of nuclear weapons most Americans have been conditioned to equate national security with the strength of strategic military forces. The Commission considers this prevailing belief to be a simplistic illusion."[2]

The often quoted statement of President Dwight D. Eisenhower just after he retired is pertinent here: "If we put one more dollar in a weapons system than we should, we are *weakening* the defense of the United States" (italics added).[3] Even more to the point is Eisenhower's statement made in a speech early in his presidency: "Every gun that is made, every warship launched, every rocket fired signifies, in the final sense, a theft from those who hunger and are not fed, those who are cold and are not clothed."[4]

One could add this: if we sell guns or any military equipment to poor nations which cannot feed their hungry, we are laying the foundation for Iran-type revolutions all over the world. The more arms we make and sell or even give, the surer is coming the long-range hatred of us by their common people, even though their own governments are their worst enemies.

And, worse, if we try to outbuild the greatest powers with sophisticated weapons, the more we succeed, the surer the result will be that the peace is broken and civilization destroyed. There are two reasons for this. The first is that if the Russians or Chinese (or even our European allies) see us spending more and more for arms, the surer they will be that we intend to dominate the world by our military might. The result will be fear of us sufficient to make them try to destroy us before it is too late.

The second reason is closer to the theme of this book and of this chapter. If we, wealthy as we are, continue to spend billions for armaments, billions that could feed the hungry and give justice to the poor, the surer will there come disaster to our nation and to the whole world. Buying and selling more and more arms and armament is suicidal.

My conclusion can be very briefly stated. Despite all our very real and legitimate fears of living as we are in a world of hatred and greed, the peace we long for will not come from success in an arms race. A continuing arms race will be a prime cause of hunger all over the world. And such injustice and suffering will destroy those who depend on military power.

NOTES

1. For estimates and reference points, see the Brandt Commission Report, *North-South: A Program for Survival* (Cambridge: M.I.T. Press, 1980), p. 14. For measures, definitions and international comparisons, see Ruth Leger Sivard, *World Military and Social Expenditures 1980* (Leesburg, Va.: World Priorities, 1980), pp. 20–33; working definitions of national military expenditures are given there on p. 30.

2. Report of the Presidential Commission on World Hunger, *Overcoming World Hunger: The Challenge Ahead* (Washington: Government Printing Office, 1980), p. 4.

3. This excerpt from the former President's 1961 speech at the Naval War College is quoted in Arthur Simon, *Bread for the World* (New York: Paulist Press, 1975), p. 122.

4. Address entitled, "The Chance for Peace," delivered to the American Society of Newspaper Editors, April 16, 1953.

15
Population and Poverty: Exploring the Relationship

J. Bryan Hehir

The fact and the challenge posed by increasing global interdependence has become one of the key characteristics of foreign policy in the 1970's and 1980's. A distinguishing mark of interdependence is the existence of transnational problems. Food and population issues, energy, monetary and trade problems—all classify as transnational. A transnational problem is one which no single nation, no matter how powerful, can resolve; it requires the cooperative planning and action of several nations, indeed of the international system as a whole.

The population problem is one of the politico-moral issues which comprise the fabric of interdependence today. Christians concerned about shaping the moral fabric of interdependence are required to develop a systematic view of the population question as it relates to other issues of interdependence. Few issues are more sensitive for individuals, for governments or for non-governmental organizations than the population question. This chapter will discuss the population debate, relate it to the broad lines of the development debate and, finally, comment on the ecumenical debate about development and population.

I. THE POPULATION DEBATE

In the decade of the 1970's, the population debate moved ahead on several fronts. The U.N. Population Conference at Bucharest in 1974 was a catalytic force which focused worldwide attention on the issue. By the end of the decade a consensus position had appeared on the nature of the population problem.[1] The consensus surely did not mean an identity of views on policy priorities or moral perspectives but it did provide a widely shared definition of the population question.

By the end of the 1970's there was also a generally agreed upon set of statistics to indicate where we had come from in terms of global population growth, where we are now and what may reasonably be expected for the future. The statistical description of the problem needs to be understood in terms of the changing dynamics of the population problem. The *numbers* are quite straightforward: the present population of the globe is about 4.3 billion and is expected to rise to about six billion by the year 2000.

The *dynamics* of the population issue were analyzed in some detail by Robert S. McNamara at M.I.T. in 1979. In his comprehensive address on the population question McNamara sought to depict the way in which that question had assumed new dimensions in the twentieth century.

> It took mankind more than a million years to reach a population of one billion. But the second billion required only 120 years; the third billion 32 years; and the fourth billion 15 years. . . . At the current global growth rate of about 2% the world's population will add a fifth billion in about 11 years.[2]

The striking fact to note about these statistics is that while the predictions McNamara makes about the immediate future are generally accepted, it is equally important to know that by the end of the 1970's a second trend was evident. The report on the "State of World Population" issued by the U.N. Fund for Population Activities in 1979 opened in the following way:

> A decline in world fertility is now confirmed. Both in the developed world and in many areas of the developing world where the largest numbers of the planet's population live, the trend toward smaller families has become evident, and there is no reason to expect a rever-

sal in the foreseeable future, if we were to ignore minor temporary fluctuations.[3]

As we enter the last twenty years of this century, therefore, there has been a fundamental shift in the dynamic of the population question. The shift will not change the projection for the year 2000. The long-run estimates of the level at which global population will stabilize still run between eight and fifteen billion by the year 2090. The determination of the stabilization level will be a product of *personal choices* by millions of individuals and *policy choices* by governments and other social insitutions.

The personal choices on a question like family size are a product of religious conviction, cultural traditions and a sense of what gives meaning and purpose to life. In the debates on population the poor are usually the focus of attention, very often in a simplistic and prejudicial fashion. McNamara spoke to the question of personal choice in a way which highlights some of the complexity of the issue:

Poor people have large families for many reasons. But the point is they do have reasons. Reasons of security for their old age. Reasons about additional help on the land. Reasons concerning the cultural preference for sons. Reasons related to the laws of inheritance. Reasons dictated by traditional religious behavior. And reasons of personal pride.[4]

At the level of policy decisions and policy perspectives the evolution of the policy debate was summarized in the report of the U.N. Fund for Population Activities cited earlier: "The changing population picture over the past three decades may be usefully viewed in three thematic frames: The Fifties was the decade in which the 'population problem' was perceived and studied by demographers primarily as questions of morbidity and mortality. . . . The rapid increase in population growth that became apparent in the decade of the Sixties demanded and brought about a shift of emphasis to the fertility factor population growth. . . . In the Seventies the awareness of the need to regard population as an important and integral factor in the entire process of development increased and was given universal political recognition."[5]

This summary of the history of the policy debate reflects a deeper political-moral argument which has structured the population debate and produced the consensus position on population by the end of the 1970's. While the consensus can be identified today, two other positions continue to influence the population debate. It is useful therefore to provide an exposition of these three positions to illustrate how the policy consensus was generated, and how it relates to the other two perspectives. Each position involves a definition of the population problem, a target group within the problem and a means for resolving the problem.

The first position argues that population is the problem. It treats population as an independent variable, then contends that if only one could deal with the population issue it would be possible to reduce poverty, hunger and perhaps even warfare. With this independent status accorded population, it becomes clear that the people who threaten the world are those having too many children, and in aggregate terms at least, this means people in developing countries where the growth rate is 2.2% as opposed to industrialized countries where it was 0.8% for 1975. Given this definition of the development-population problem, the solution for this perspective lies in a massive and direct attack on the population front, providing multiple methods of control accompanied by information, persuasion incentives, and, in some versions, coercion to induce the target group to alter its procreative habits.[6]

The second position argues that population is no problem. This position is the antithesis of the first since it treats population entirely as a dependent variable. In this view, often depicted as a Marxist or a Roman Catholic position, poverty is the problem. If poverty can be addressed in depth, the population question will be cared for as a by-product. Given this definition of development-population, the target group which is "the problem" includes those who hold economic power in society, either internationally or within developing societies. The solution to the development-population problem involves radical structural change in patterns of political-economic control.[7]

The third position argues that population is part of the de-

velopment problem. It treats the population issue as significant
in itself, but not possible of resolution apart from the fabric of
the broader question of socio-economic development. In this view
there is not a single target group or a single set of measures
which can deal with development and population. What is required is an integrated policy of development, involving multiple
measures treating both poverty and population as interdependent variables.[8]

The third position, dominantly reflected in the U.N. Conference on Population at Bucharest (1974), is commonly referred to
as the consensus position.[9] The supporting arguments for the position draw upon past historical success and failure in the population area. Negatively, it points to cases where a frontal but
unilateral attack has been made on population and failed to produce the desired result of reducing population growth.[10]

Positively, it is argued that both the history of the demographic transition in the West and current cases where population growth has been curtailed have involved instances where
the improvement of the socio-economic condition of the populace
has resulted in a declining rate of population growth.[11] Three
qualifications are needed to understand this argument. First,
such an argument does not presume that the pattern of the demographic transition in the West can be simply replicated in the
developing world.[12] Second, to argue that rising standards of socio-economic welfare contribute to declining population growth
does not mean that it is necessary or possible to find a magic
number of per capita GNP which must be reached before the impact will be felt on population growth. Such a number does not
exist; rather, the more nuanced position holds that if people are
given some sense of control over the rest of their lives (i.e., a minimal level of security regarding food, health care, education, employment) they will exercise control in the area of reproductive
behavior. Third, this means that in assessing the relationship between development policies and population, effective development strategy is not defined in terms of aggregate economic
growth or even per capita GNP, but is to be judged by what Arthur Dyck has called distributive criteria aimed at improving the
distribution of income and social service in a society.[13] McNamara has stated the case in the following way: "While economic

212   J. Bryan Hehir

growth is a necessary condition of development in a modernizing society it is not in itself a sufficient condition. The reason is clear. Economic growth cannot change the lives of the mass of the people unless it reaches the mass of the people."[14]

The third position, therefore, is a consensus position in two ways: first, it locates the population issue squarely within the framework of development but it recognizes population as a distinct element in the development question, one which requires specific attention; second, this developmentalist view of population has taken the commanding role in the population debate. To understand the meaning of the consensus position it is necessary to relate the population debate to the development debate.

II. THE DEVELOPMENT DEBATE

In summarizing the population debate it was possible to distinguish the views of the 1950's, the 1960's and the 1970's. The development debate follows a parallel course. Indeed the consensus position on population is closely related to conceptions of development policy which appeared in the 1970's as a critique of and to some degree in reaction to the development strategies of the 1950's and 1960's.

In the 1950's and 1960's the development debate was carried on in terms of "trickle-down" and "takeoff" theories. Both concentrated on GNP as the measurement and essential component of development policy. Both terms were short-hand devices for communicating complex conceptions of the development policy. Without seeking to delineate the details of these policies it is sufficient to describe their essential thrust. The "trickle-down" model argued that if the aggregate economic growth of a nation proceeded rapidly, the results would be that the benefits of aggregate growth would sooner or later reach the mass of the population. The key to development, therefore, was to use a mix of instruments, national and international, to achieve rapid and sustained economic growth.

The "takeoff" theory was an allied notion which depicted the development process for the less developed countries as a path of copying the historical process through which the developed countries had passed. The essential idea was that the initial stages of development required massive infusions of outside assistance (capital and technical assistance), but in time the developing country would reach "takeoff" or self-sustained growth.

By the 1970's both "trickle-down" and "takeoff" were under fire in the development debate and two quite different themes came to dominate the debate. The first theme began with a critique of the trickle-down approach, contending that it failed to touch the lives of the lower forty percent of the population even when high growth rates had occurred.[15]

This critique of trickle-down in turn produced proposals for a development strategy which would focus a direct attack on mass poverty. The primary objective of the policy was to meet "the basic human needs" of the "lower forty percent" of the population. These needs were generally defined as nutrition, health, education, housing and employment.[16] While the designation of which needs should have priority in policy varied, the basic thrust of this approach was that development policy should be consciously directed to those who found the trickle-down effect least likely to reach them.

The consensus position on population fitted nicely into a basic human needs strategy. Rather than isolating population as an independent issue which posed a threat to economic growth, the new argument was cast in terms of finding the resolution of the population question in terms of a strategy of development. To meet the basic human needs of a population was to give them the capability to deal with choices about family size in a new context.

The second theme in the development debate of the 1970's also linked population and development. It was explicitly argued at the Bucharest Conference and was rooted in the earlier U.N. debate on a "New International Economic Order" which had occurred at the U.N. General Assembly six months before Bucharest. Beginning with the U.N. Sixth Special Session in 1974 the developing countries cast the development debate of the 1970s in terms of a call for a "New International Economic Order" (NIEO).[17]

The NIEO approach framed the development argument as a question of distributive justice *among* nations rather than emphasizing in the first instance distributive justice *within* a nation. The NIEO argument stressed the need for structural, systemic change in the international economy. It focused on questions of trade relations, commodity prices, control over raw materials and foreign investment policies and practices. But the NIEO also had a political dimension, contending that the developing countries were unable to influence the major international institutions of trade and finance which set the terms for the global economy outside the communist world. One of the developing world's most incisive and moderate voices has said: "The poor nations have only a pro forma participation in the economic decision making of the world. Their advice is hardly solicited when the big industrialized nations get together to take key decisions on the future of the world economy; their voting strength in the Bretton Woods institutions (World Bank and International Monetary Fund) is less than one-third of the total."[18]

The NIEO framework was the way the South encountered the North in a whole series of negotiations in the 1970's; population was no exception. At the Bucharest Conference the developing world advanced the consensus position of population and development, and sought to situate the debate within an NIEO perspective of development.

By the end of the 1970's there were efforts in the development debate to establish linkages between the Basic Human Needs concept and the NIEO argument. There are complementary themes between the two views but also much suspicion. For the purposes of this chapter, however, it is sufficient to recognize that the consensus position on population found its place in both conceptions of the development debate.

III. THE ECUMENICAL DEBATE ON POPULATION AND DEVELOPMENT

There is an ecumenical debate about population and development, but it is not about the consensus position. The main voices in the Christian community, Protestant and Catholic alike, support the consensus position in the sense that they recognize two distinct problems, population and development, each of which has to be addressed, but the approach requires that they be addressed in tandem.

Writing as a Catholic, I am sensitive to the question whether the Catholic position can be said to fit within the consensus position. I believe that the Catholic position has its own distinctive characteristics, but in its general outline it can be shown to fit the consensus model.

The analysis is found generally in the social teaching of the Church; the principal documents relating to population policy are *Gaudium et Spes* (1965), *Populorum Progressio* (1967) and the addresses of Pope Paul on the occasion of the World Population Year (1974) and the World Food Conference (1974). These documents manifest a structural analysis of the population issue, seeking to place demographic variables within a broadly defined socio-economic context. The tenor and style of analysis are exemplified in the following passage from Paul VI's message for the U.N. Population Year (1974):

> The true solutions to these problems—we would say the only solutions—will be those which take due account of all concrete factors taken together: the demands of social justice as well as respect for the divine laws governing life, the dignity of the human person as well as the freedom of peoples, the primary role of the family as well as the responsibility proper to married couples.[19]

The perspective dominating all of these statements is that the population problem is one strand of a larger fabric involving questions of political, economic and social structure at the national and international levels. While acknowledging the existence of a population problem, this view asserts that it is morally wrong and practically ineffective to isolate population as a single factor, seeking to reduce population growth without simultaneously making those political and economic changes which will achieve a more equitable distribution of wealth and resources within nations and among nations. To cite Paul VI's message to the World Food Conference:

> It is inadmissible that those who have control of the wealth and resources of mankind should try to resolve the problem of hunger by forbidding the poor to be parents or by leaving to die of hunger children whose parents do not fit into the framework of theoretical plans based on pure hypotheses about the future of mankind.[20]

To cite these papal texts is to find the structure of the consensus position, but it is also to see reflected the substance of the
ecumenical debate about population and development. The debate is about the weight to be given the population issue, the priority it should have in the policy equation and the means used to
address it.

These questions exist *within* the consensus position, but
they do exist. It is easier for the Christian churches to address
the development debate as a united front than it is to address
population and development. While a detailed review of the specific positions the Christian churches take on population and development is not possible here, it is possible to suggest a strategy
for managing the debate.

The strategy involves three steps: that we agree to disagree
on certain aspects of the population side of the population-development equation, that we formulate procedural rules to handle
our differences on population, and that we promote vigorously in
the American political debate the agreement we have about development and the fact that the population issue must be treated
in the context of development.

Disagreement is not inevitable but likely on two questions:
How forcefully should the population dimension of developement
strategy be pushed and what means should be used to promote
the policy? On the first question, it should be possible to maintain the consensus position of population-development while recognizing that the emphasis given the population issue will be
much less in official Catholic positions than in most other Christian churches. The prudent course here is to keep stressing the
overall consensus case but not try to obtain identical advocacy
from all sources in the Christian community.

The means question is the most delicate and volatile issue. It
will be easier in this area to establish a position on what we can
oppose together than it will be to find means we will support together. On procedural grounds, I would advocate the following
principles to govern the ecumenical differences; all the principles are meant to apply to U.S. population-development policy.
First, we should keep the abortion issue out of the population-development debate by continuing to prohibit it as a means in U.S.
foreign policy. The moral differences which are so deep among us

on this question point to the need to maintain present legislation against abortion in U.S. policy. Second, it should be possible to develop a common position against coercion in population policy; a more difficult task but one which should be addressed is the question of incentives. It is quite likely that an incentives policy can easily become coercive when dealing with the poor; I would propose excluding incentives on these grounds. Third—a more difficult objective, to be sure—I would propose that U.S. funding not be used to support *government sponsored* sterilization programs. The basis of this position in an ecumenical context would not be opposition to contraception in principle, but opposition to granting governments the authority to regulate sterilization programs. Fourth, for other aspects of population policy, it would seem that we will again have to agree to disagree.

On the development side of the equation the ecumenical strategy in support of a consensus position should be aggressive advocacy of a just and forthcoming U.S. policy toward the developing world. In this area strong substantive agreement exists on the need for restructuring North-South relations in accord with principles of justice and equity. Equally important is the need which exists in the American political debate for a strong and consistent voice on this question of U.S. relations with the developing world. The extensive work that has gone on in the churches in the 1970's on issues of hunger and human rights questions establishes the basis for extending both of these policy initiatives to a consensus position on U.S. development policy.

The specific policy position which should be espoused is not self-evident. The churches have been and will continue to be participants in the debate about development strategy—Basic Human Needs and NIEO. But these specific, difficult and necessary questions for analysis should be pursued on the presumption that U.S. development policy at present is clearly inadequate in terms of its perspective, direction and funding. Redirecting that policy requires attention to the issues of how the U.S. conceives its basic relationship to the developing world, how it relates this conception to the East-West competition, what kind of development it seeks to support, what degree of international cooperation the U.S. is prepared to share in, and what resources we are willing to commit to the development issues. None of these questions are being well answered in the early 1980's. The churches should use the ecumenical agreement we have on the consensus population-development position to push vigorously for a comprehensive view of development in U.S. policy which can and will implement the consensus position as part of a new U.S. initiative toward the developing world.

NOTES

1. For a description of the several positions in the debate, including the consensus position, cf. M. S. Teitelbaum, "Population and Development: Is a Consensus Possible?" *Foreign Affairs* 52 (1974), pp. 742–60.

2. R. S. McNamara, *Address on the Population Problem to the Massachusetts Institute of Technology* (Washington, 1977), pp. 5–6.

3. State of World Population, 1979, *Development* (1979–3), p. 24.

4. McNamara, p. 40.

5. State of World Population, 1979, p. 32.

6. Teitelbaum describes this position as "The Population Hawk" position; cited, pp. 752–53.

7. Teitelbaum's description of "The Revolutionist Position," "The Overconsumption Position," "The Accommodationist Position," and "The Social Justice Position" shows them to be cognate views of this second position; cited pp. 751–52.

8. Teitelbaum's description of "The Population-Programs-Plus-Development" position or "The Social Justice" position accords most closely with this third position. This is the consensus position. It is also described by Arthur Dyck as the "Developmental Distributivist" position: A. Dyck, *On Human Care* (Nashville, 1977).

9. Cf. P. Henriot, *Population/Development After Bucharest: The Search for Linkage* (Washington, D.C.: The Center of Concern, 1979), pp. 2–3 (mimeo.).

10. Dyck, pp. 41, 43, 44.

11. Dyck cites the examples of South Korea and Taiwan; J. Howe and J. Sewell cite Sri Lanka, Singapore, Egypt and Barbados, "Let's Sink the Lifeboat Ethics," *Worldview* 18 (1975), pp. 13–18.

12. McNamara illustrates the complexity of the factors involved in the demographic transition, cited, pp. 19–21; also Teitelbaum, cited, pp. 744–745.

13. Dyck, pp. 43, 49; cf. also W. Rich, *Population Explosion: The Role of Development* (Washington, D.C.: Overseas Development Council, Communique #16, 1972).

14. McNamara, p. 34.

15. The critique can be found in several places: M. ul Haq, *The Pov-*

erty Curtain (New York, 1976), pp. 27–47; R. S. McNamara, *1973 Address to the Board of Governors,* IBRD (Washington, D.C. 1973.

16. For a discussion of the basic needs strategy cf. J. Mathiesen, *Basic Needs and the New International Economic Order: An Opening for North-South Collaboration in the 1980s* (Washington, D.C.: OverSeas Development Council, 1981), pp. 17–30.

17. Cf. M. ul Haq; cited, pp. 137–220; J. Mathiesen, cited, pp. 7–16.

18. M. ul Haq, A View from the South The Second Phase of the North-South Dialogue, *The U.S. and World Development: Agenda 1979* (Washington, D.C., 1979) p. 117.

19. Paul VI, Message on the Population Year, *ORIGINS,* 3 (1973), p. 671.

20. Paul VI, Address to the World Food Conference, *ORIGINS,* 4 (1974), p. 351.

16
The Unequal Distribution
of Wealth and Income
in the World

John C. Calhoun

Wealth consists in assets that promise a future stream of income.[1] Wealth resides in resources—land, labor, capital. Not all resources, however, are wealth. Fifteenth century Spain was flooded by money in the form of silver from her American colonies. Yet she failed to convert that resource into wealth—the source of future income. Other nations, through industrialization, worked that wonder into wealth, while Spain fell back into poverty.

Oil is discovered on marginal land. Fashion determines *this* style of jeans suddenly to be "in." Greater value comes to be placed on a systems analyst's skills than on those of teachers. New metals threaten steel's hegemony. Resources once not income-producing suddenly become wealth. These new income sources may in turn advance the process of creating new wealth. George Gilder captures this phenomenon in a striking analogy: "Wealth is governed by mind but is caught in matter. The market, as it generates 'news'—its ceaseless play of prices and ideas—passes its wand over the world of human possessions, conferring capital gains as some things become profitable in the new light of time and knowledge, and casting giant shadows of loss over the looming wealth works of the past."[2] Thus English and New England textile mills, inner cities based on steel and automobile economies, and railroad systems—assets once symbols of wealth and its power—now lack much of their former promise.

Wealth and income are both unequally distributed within and among nations and societies. Assets like land, yielding rent, and capital bearing interest tend to become more concentrated in the population than do incomes earned annually through the sale of labor. Whereas the United Kingdom and the United States have similar inequalities of income, the United Kingdom has a much greater inequality of wealth than does the United States. In part, this is due to certain peers and tycoons in Britain owning tremendous concentrations of land and other properties. Yet even in the United States the top ten percent of our wealthy get almost a third of the total American income, and own more than half the total wealth. While the bottom ten percent owe more than they own, the top one percent own twenty-four percent of the U.S. wealth. Further, the lowest twenty percent of U.S. families get only six percent of the total income, while the most affluent twenty percent of the families get forty percent. The second fifth gets only twelve percent of income, and the third gets only eighteen percent, but the fourth gets twenty-four percent. The top five percent—the very rich—get no less than fourteen percent, more than the income received by the entire bottom third of the population.[3]

This distribution of income is highly dependent upon the initial distribution of property ownership. Property ownership, moreover, is dependent on one's ability to acquire or inherit, on educational opportunities, and on the presence or absence of reacial and sex discrimination.

Socialist countries like China and the Soviet Union have much less private concentration of wealth. Yet a very careful study of wage inequalities in Russia's communist economy showed inequalities and dispersions between the best-paid and poorest-paid workers not unlike those of our own society. The inequality of political privilege among Soviet bureaucrats, military officers, party members and the Soviet public at large may not be susceptible to precise numerical measurement but it is nonetheless real.[4]

Distribution, then, may mean either the pattern according to which wealth and income are divided up among the members of society or the process by which the distributive pattern is brought about. *Wealth* is a stock of goods and financial claims (assets) to property. *Income* is the total of net payments a person receives in any given period. There are ambiguities, however, connected with defining wealth and income which ought to be noted.

Taxpayers are familiar with problems affecting the practice of placing a money value on an estate as well as the experience of categorizing income per annum as part of the "April filing ritual." There are inherent difficulties associated with expressing wealth in money terms as the total value of a stock of possessions. Often prices fluctuate, as with land or an art collection, and many possessions are of a type not easily tagged for sale.

Further, certain conventions are involved in defining these terms. Wealth, for example, usually includes physical and financial assets, but excludes "human" wealth of acquired knowledge and skill, though these may be just as productive as other assets. Thus, how does one measure the "brain drain" of professionals from the developing countries? In politically unstable lands it is difficult to bring forth the human qualities—the commitments and loyalties—upon which long-term yields rely. "Qualities of thought and spirit in an economy can overshadow all the qualities of capital and contracts of labor."[5]

Wealth and income, moreover, seem to be mixed at times. Hence, obstacles in evaluating property arise from the fact that wealth may augment income at the same time that income augments wealth. This is true both for an individual and for a whole economy. Thus, on a national scale, many of the real estate assets that constitute the nation's wealth are employed in producing income. Thus, additions to the national wealth often increase the national income. At the same time, part of the national output consists of additions to the national wealth in the form of durable goods. In this sense, part of the national income is used to increase the national wealth. Finally, *costs* of earning income must be exluded from the income measured, yet significant problems arise about determining the depreciation of fixed assets in calculating business profits.

National income accounting furnishes measures of the income and production of a nation.[6] National production, as output, is the total of *end products* produced by a nation during a specified period. The totals are expressed in monetary values, since these provide a common unit for summing the wide variety of goods and services produced. Gross National Product (GNP) is a country's total output of goods and services valued at market prices. It includes also output produced abroad to which residents of a country have a claim. For some purposes it is desirable to count only the output produced within the country; the resulting total is called Gross Domestic Product (GDP).

Both of these measures are referred to as "gross" because they make no allowance for the amount of fixed capital (buildings, equipment, inventories) used up in the process of production. Statisticians try to estimate Net National Product (NNP) by deducting an allowance for capital depreciation.

The foregoing concepts of national output measure it in terms of market prices. Yet the prices at which goods and services are sold include a substantial amount of indirect taxes (sales, turnover, payroll, some property). These may be subtracted from the net national product to arrive at a figure that reflects the actual cost of production at factor prices (or factor costs). This is generally known as National Income, since it is the sum of wages, salaries, profits and other incomes received by the population of a country.

Excluded from the GNP are goods and services not intended for sale in the market, e.g., domestic services by a member of the family. The treatment of non-monetary items raises difficulties in the measurement of the less developed countries (LDCs), where many types of productive activity that are channeled through the market in Western countries are performed within the confines of the individual households.

A word of warning! Because countries differ greatly in their economies and patterns of life, comparisons of their GNP or income are apt to be somewhat misleading. For this reason, one should be wary of quoting *indiscriminately* tables showing national income per capita for a number of different countries expressed in U.S. dollars. There are difficulties here even when there is no doubt about the value of the various currencies and the accuracy of population estimates.

In addition, countries use varied definitions of their national product. The national output statistics of the Soviet Union and other communist countries, for example, cannot be directly compared with those of the United States and other Western industrial countries because of the broad difference in what is included. However, the United Nations and the World Bank are working to stabilize a world statistical system that will be more useful for international comparisons.

The distinctive elements of modern economics make important the distribution of wealth and income within a society. "In a vital sense, the distribution of income has been a key issue that has pervaded Western society since the beginning of capitalism. In fact, the development of the modern welfare state reflects a continuing trend in modifying the distribution of income to achieve more equality."[7]

Paul Samuelson observes that left alone the market puts goods in the hands of those who can pay the most, who have the most money votes. When democratic society does not like the distribution of dollar votes under *laissez faire*, it uses redistributive taxation to rectify the situation.Hence, ours is not a pure price economy but a *mixed economy* in which elements of government control are intermingled with private ownership in organizing production and consumption. "Democracies are not satisfied with the answers to the questions: 'what is to be produced, how and for whom' when given by a completely unrestrained market system. Such a system . . . might dictate that some people starve from lack of income, while others get inadequate or excessive incomes."[8]

Lester Thurow's *The Zero-Sum Society*[9] examines income distribution and possibilities for economic change in a "stagflated" American economy. He contends that none of the problems that bedevil the U.S. economy can be solved without making many Americans worse off, even though society as a whole might gain. "Since government must alter the distribution of income if it is to solve our economic problems, we have to have a government that is capable of making equity decisions. Whose income ought to go up and whose income ought to go down? To do this, however, we need to know what is equitable. What is a fair or just distribution of economic resources? What's a fair or just procedure for distributing income? Unless we specify what is equitable, we cannot say whose income ought to go down. Unless we can say whose income ought to go down, we cannot solve our economic problems."[10] Thurow holds that all solutions thus far advanced to U.S. economic woes have one characteristic in common: a "win-win" for all groups. This, he declares, is impossible. "Win-lose" is the unpleasant remedy. In the U.S. today, everyone wants everyone else to suffer the inevitable economic losses, and as a consequence none of the possible solutions for restoring economic vitality can be adopted.

Whatever might be said for or against Thurow's analysis, quite evident is the importance of income distribution/redistribution in economic decision making. Bothersome to many Americans is the knowledge that when looking at the earnings gap between the top and the bottom ten percent of the population, West Germany works with thirty-six percent less and Japan with fifty percent less inequality than the United States. Only France surpasses us in terms of inequality. Further, there is the view that Marxism's appeal lies in its radical challenge to the alleged failure of capitalism to achieve distributive justice. Vast disparities in the distribution of income and wealth have created environments ripe for social disorder (El Salvador, Iran, Brazil). Indeed, it is part of the socialist claim, and hence its appeal to so many developing nations, to fashion an egalitarian society in which wealth and income distribution are resolved positively.

The marked inequality often existing in the distribution of wealth and income within the economies of the industrial nations is paralleled by the disparity between "North and South"—a shorthand way of referring to the developed and developing nations of the world. Yet, the same holds true for distribution within the last developed countries (LDCs). Some figures may be illustrative here.

In India, the richest five percent of households receive twenty-five percent of national income, while the poorest twenty percent receive five percent of the income. Forty-one percent of the Indian population lives in absolute poverty. In Sierra Leone, the richest five percent of households receives nearly twenty-nine percent of income, with only two percent going to the poorest twenty percent. Thirty-two percent of the population lives in absolute poverty.

More difficult to obtain from many countries are indices reflecting wealth distribution, e.g., land. It is estimated that in Brazil forty-five percent of the land is owned by the wealthiest ten percent of the owners. About one and a half percent is in the hands of the least wealthy ten percent of land-owners. In the Dominican Republic, the top ten percent of the land-owners hold nearly sixty-three percent of the land.[11]

Understandable, therefore, is the admonition of Nevin Scrimshaw and Lance Taylor: "Although technological advances in food production, food conservation, and food processing will be needed to ensure food availability, meeting food needs will depend even more on greater social equity and fairer income distribution within the developing countries themselves. External assistance can be of some help, but the outcome in each country will be determined by the effectiveness of measures undertaken by the country."[12]

It is important for our purposes in this book to make special note of the fact that *income distribution and family diet correlate.* Family consumption studies demonstrate the extent to which food consumed by a household varies with income. The source of supply can be either the market or foodstuffs produced at home, but in either case the consumption of protein and the total calories *increase with family income.* Up to a certain income level, roughly from $250 to $300 per person per year (in 1980 U.S. dollars), the calorie intake from the local staple-food energy source tends to increase. At higher income levels, calories from fats, sugars, fruits, vegetables, and animal products play an increasing role. Careful studies in selected regions, for example Brazil, show that both the amount and the nutritional quality of protein rise directly with income.[13]

I want to comment briefly on the mechanics of income distribution/redistribution in various economic systems and then consider the wealth/income distribution gap between the developed and developing countries.

Under capitalism, the capital equipment of society (wealth) is owned by a minority of individuals (capitalists) who have the right to use this property for private gain. Capitalism relies primarily on the market system, not only to allocate its resources among various uses, but also *to establish the levels of income* (such as wages, profits, rents) of different social classes. In short, the pricing process operating in the market for economic resources—land, labor, and capital—is paramount in determining income distribution. *Redistribution* is effected through taxes and transfer payments.

In a socialist economy distribution is in the hands of the people through its (ideally) representative government. The use of prices to regulate income distribution is considered wasteful and undesirable. Distribution can be effected through regulating wages, social services, and taxes. Then, too, socialism, unlike capitalism, depends primarily on planning, rather than on the market, both for its overall allocation of resources and for its distribution of income. It should be noted, however, that planning is becoming ever more important for advanced economies generally; consider, for example, the Japanese government's private enterprise cooperation in planning.

Capitalist nations are as unlike one another as Sweden and South Africa. Socialist differences are evident to anyone who contrasts Russia with Tanzania or China. Yet taking capitalism and socialism here as "types" of economic systems, certain specific problems do seem to cluster around representative societies of each type. For capitalism, the problems center on (1) inflation or unemployment (now, unhappily, both), (2) the struggle between the private and the public sector and, (3) the highly uneven division of incomes between the property owning and working classes. Socialism's problems highlight the pains of (1) controlling unwieldy state bureaucracies, (2) avoiding inefficient production and distribution directives, and (3) promoting motivation in the absence of a "profit incentive."

Like all human activities, each type has it own oppressive side to it.

In a capitalist market economy, high prices are placed on scarce agents of production while low prices are assigned by the market to plentiful agents. Persons whose skills are scarce, relative to demand, receive a high level of income. Individuals whose skills are readily available receive low levels of income. People are rewarded, then, on the basis of their contribution to marketable *output*. This reflects consumer preferences and incomes. The implication is clear: persons whose productivity is low, in reference to goods or services the market values, will earn little.

Income flows from two sources: wages/salaries and self-employment/property income. Property income is a stock of claims on the value of wealth, whether natural resources or man-made capital and consumer durable goods. Examples of property claims on wealth are stocks (individual claims on wealth owned by corporations), bonds, notes, and mortgages. Labor income, on the other hand, takes the form of wages and salaries from the sale of human effort. Thus, there is a fundamental dichotomy between labor and non-labor income.

The fundamental premise of the welfare state in capitalist countries is that this dichotomy calls for government intervention to achieve economic and social objectives. As Robert Heilbroner remarks, the market is an inefficient instrument for provisioning societies with those goods and services for which no price tag exists.[14] Moreover, the market applies a strictly economic calculus to the satisfaction of human wants and needs. Further, the market does not cope well with certain social costs that the private sector thrusts on the public. Examples of this would be pollution, traffic congestion, and the disposal of chemical wastes. Briefly, the market system, left to itself, fails to formulate effective stimuli or restraints other than those which arise from the market place.

Achieving redistribution of income to those who suffer from capricious economic and social changes takes the form of graduated income tax, inheritance taxes, transfer payments, and a variety of government expenditures. In the opinion of some, these same transfer mechanisms might well be adapted to financing third world development.

The Overseas Development Council's *Agenda 1980*[15] indicates that the gap between the world's poor and its affluent is wide and, as measured by many (though not by all) indicators of well-being, is growing wider. Thus in 1978 some one hundred and forty developing countries in Africa, Asia, Latin America, and part of Europe and Oceania (some seventy-five percent of world population) accounted for only twenty-one percent of the global world product. In contrast, the thirty or so developed countries of North America, Europe, the Soviet Union, Japan, Australia, and New Zealand (with only twenty-five percent of the world population) accounted for seventy-nine percent of the global GNP.

In *North-South: A Program for Survival,*[16] the Brandt Commission advanced recommendations for an increased flow of development finance using mechanisms familiar in redistributing income within countries, now to be employed between countries:

1. an international system of universal revenue mobilization based on a sliding scale related to national income in which

East European and developing countries—except the poorest countries—would participate (world tax);

2. the adoption of timetables to increase Official Development Assistance (ODA) from industrialized countries to the level of 0.7 percent of GNP by 1985, and to one percent by the end of the century;

3. introduction of automatic revenue transfers through international levies on some of the following: international trade, arms production or exports, international travel, and the global commons, especially sea-bed materials.

Resource transfers should be made more predictable. This would involve long-term commitments to provide ODA, increasing use of automatically mobilized revenues, and the lengthening of the International Development Agency (IDA) replenishment period.

Consideration should be given to the creation of a new international financial institution—a World Development Fund—with universal membership and in which decision-making is more evenly shared between lenders and borrowers. This would supplement existing institutions (e.g., World Bank, International Monetary Fund) and diversify lending policies and practices. The World Development Fund would seek to satisfy unmet needs in the financing structure, in particular that of program lending. Ultimately, it could serve as a channel for such resources as may be raised on a universal and automatic basis.

The U.S. government is at one with the British government in opposing the Brandt proposals to shift billions of dollars from rich to poor nations pressing for a New International Economic Order (NIEO). Recently Myer Rashish, U.S. Under-Secretary of State for Economic Affairs, rejected as impractical and inefficient the demands of the developing nations for (1) lower trade barriers and higher prices for their products, (2) a large increase in foreign aid, and (3) rehsaping of the International Monetary Fund—all proposals of the group of seventy-seven. Rather, "the philosophy of this administration from its very beginning is enterprise and the allocation of resources through free markets."[17] Instead of new pacts, raw-materials producers should apply for loans from the International Monetary Fund when their exports drop. Such loans, maintains Rashish, require borrowers to "respond to market signals," cutting output when prices fall and increasing it when they rise. Further, "we are not sympathetic to a proposal from the poor nations that would give them more votes without increasing their contributions to the IMF." Whether this initial attitude against wealth/income redistribution will prevail through the 1980's as America faces the dynamics of the international politics in an ever-hungrier world remains to be seen. At present, however, the government's position is that growth of Asian, African, and Latin American economies depends on creating *more wealth,* not on sharing existing resources.

NOTES

1. George Gilder, *Wealth and Poverty* (New York: Basic Books, 1981), p. 48.
2. *Ibid.,* p. 57.
3. Paul Samuelson, *Economics* (New York: McGraw-Hill, 1973), p. 84.
4. Abram Bergson, *The Structure of Soviet Wages* (Cambridge: Harvard University Press, 1944).
5. Gilder, *op. cit.,* p. 51.
6. For statistical detail, see: *The World Bank* (Baltimore: The Johns Hopkins Press, 1980); *World Statistics in Brief,* 4th ed. (New York: United Nations, 1979); *World Development Report* (Washington, D.C.: The World Bank, 1980); *Encyclopaedia Britannica,* 15th ed., 1974), s.v. "National Income Accounting."
7. Martin Schnitzer, *Income Distribution: A Comparative Study of the U.S., West Germany, East Germany, and Japan* (New York: Praeger, 1974), p. 6.
8. Samuleson, *op. cit.,* pp. 46–47.
9. Lester C. Thurow, *The Zero-Sum Society* (New York: Basic Books, 1980).
10. *Ibid.,* p. 17.
11. *Socio-Economic Indicators of Basic Needs, Progress, and Commitment for 92 Developing Countries* (Washington, D.C.: Department of State—Office of Development Planning, 1979).
12. Nevin S. Scrimshaw and Lance Taylor, "Food," *Scientific American* (September 1980), p. 78.
13. *Ibid.*
14. Robert L. Heilbroner, *The Making of Economic Society,* 4th ed. (Englewood Cliffs, N.J.: Prentice-Hall, 1972), pp. 237ff.

15. John W. Sewell *et al., The United States and World Development: Agenda 1980* (New York: Praeger, 1980).

16. Willy Brandt *et al., North-South: A Program for Survival* (Cambridge: MIT Press, 1980).

17. Bernard D. Nossiter, "Haig Aide Says US Opposes Sharing the Wealth," *New York Times,* August 7, 1981.

17
Overconsumption in the Developed Nations

Myron S. Augsburger

On one of her visits to the United States, Mother Teresa of Calcutta was interviewed on a television talk show. She spoke movingly of world hunger and the particular plight of the poor in India. Along came a commercial interruption. The message promoted a diet formula for overweight Americans. Back on camera, Mother Teresa first paused, then remarked that it would appear that the teachings of Jesus need to be heard in America as well as in India.

Overconsumption in the affluent nations has a causal relationship to the problems of the hungry poor. Various commentators have chosen different emphases in making this point.

• Doris Longacre, a Mennonite writer, had extensive overseas relief experience in Asia. Her *Living More With Less*[1] is a searching call to serious economic discipleship amid affluence. She argues that even the image of Western affluence is a disturbing influence in the global village. It contributes to the struggle between the "haves" and the "have nots" in third world countries. She cites a missionary with years of service in East Africa: "North Americans find it very hard to believe that their wealthy ways of living affect poor people on other continents. But in Africa, people are fully convinced that North Americans and their actions strongly influence their lives."[2] The mechanism is trade. North America imports many of the resources which underpin the African way of life. We get those resources at low prices from economically impoverished countries and export to them higher-priced manufactured goods.

• A Korean writer, Pyong-Choon Hahm, voices a third world complaint about our recent concern for ecology. "It is a supreme irony of world history that the concern for environmental pollution on the part of the industrially advanced portion of the globe is now being thrust into the path of industrial development of the underdeveloped world which has finally succeeded in forging a commitment to ethnological salvation of its own."[3]

• Denis Goulet puts it this way: "Hunger among starving masses can be permanently abolished only if the privileged rich minority gives up its present standards of wasteful abundance and restructures its own economic incentives around priority needs. No amount of 'trickle down' of its surplus can ever suffice to feed the hungry or enable them to reach a decent level of development."[4] On another occasion, Goulet wrote: "Buried deep in the consciousness of the third world masses is the conviction that poverty is the by-product of wealth, the fruit of exploitation and injustice."[5]

• Bruce C. Birch and Larry L. Rasmussen contributed *The Predicament of the Prosperous* to a series of books that provide a biblical perspective on current issues.[6] For them, the "big picture" is simply this: "We, the human family, cannot afford the modern world, and neither can the rest of nature."[7]

• In Kenneth Boulding's view, "The only way to make the poor richer is to make the rich poorer."[8]

• And many others, Charles Birch among them, are credited with the remark, "The rich must live more simply so that the poor might simply live."[9] Why should this be so? What are the mechanisms at work relating their poverty to our prosperity? There is no need to assign blame; there is great need to undertake analysis.

The Presidential Commission on World Hunger, cited elsewhere and often in this book, showed that the United States during the Carter presidency was spending about one and a half billion dollars each year in economic and technical aid to assist less developed nations in feeding their people. Another half billion went directly each year to food assistance. In contrast, the U.S. was at that time spending one hundred and fourteen billion on national defense and more than forty billion a year on medicare and medicaid. There is good reason, of course, for a nation to take care of its own. But excessive spending for defense is bound to shift dollars away from aid. Ironically, more aid for hungry nations may, in the long run, prove to be our best national defense. This is all the more true to the extent that the friendship and respect of less developed nations for us is a response to our love and respect rather than our power and privileged position in the world community. As Eugene Carson Blake reminds us elsewhere in this book, world military spending is now well over one billion dollars a day. This is a sixty percent increase over 1960. Sadly, the U.S. is one of the pace-setters for this increase. Such spending, while millions starve, puts a new dimension on the words of Jesus, "They that take the sword shall perish with the sword" (Mt 26:52). Those who stockpile the swords run a risk to themselves; they also quite literally cause others to perish now in a way not anticipated in an earlier age of less complicated technology and less interdependent economy.

The Hunger Commission report urged greater concern for the development of more self-sufficiency on the part of needy nations. This is easier said than done. It involves much more than military, economic and technical assistance. It is complicated by inflation, population growth and resource depletion. Allan Walker sees the worldwide problem of inflation as "basically caused by the population explosion outstripping available food and energy resources."[10] He deplores the misplaced emphasis of past development efforts which set Western-style affluence as a goal for all while not recognizing that the wastefulness thus generated would fast exhaust the resources of the planet.

By the year 2000, the population of the world will, no doubt, exceed six billion. At Western rates of consumption there are simply insufficient resources to sustain that large a population. Perhaps new technology and undreamed of uses of outer space will relieve the pressure on such a heavily populated globe. Or will a return to the simple, sustainable life mean that four million people will simply have to get off the globe? Isaac Asimov discussed both possibilities in a 1979 lecture. His call for the advancement of technology and the development, for peaceful purposes, of outer space is exciting. His vision of space-station manufacturing with the locational advantage of better access to solar energy has great appeal, but it would be extraordinarily costly. Would not a return to the simple life (with no present occupants invited off the planet) be a practical first step in the face of diminishing resources? The fact that a "giant step" would be required of us and not of others should not be viewed as an unreasonable demand. Literally and figuratively, we have the energy to take that step. The hungry poor do not.

Such a step on our part would be an affirmation of solidarity with our poorer neighbors in the global village. This is the call of Christian concern.

Naturally, the reduction of life-style has little appeal. Conservation of resources never comes easily. Sharing of the wealth is not a natural impulse. But the global village is here to stay. The resource pie is not getting larger. The voice of the poor is bound to be heard. If the necessary response will not come naturally, why can it not emerge supernaturally? To ignore this possibility is to render the Christian message meaningless.

Richard Neuhaus has an essay in this collection on the colonial legacy. I should like to mention that the end of the colonial period shifted responsibility to the local community, ready or not! By collective action on the local level, there can be the discovery of the way to lasting development. This is so because in collective action persons recognize and come to respect each other's contribution. After empire, the imperial powers need to discover a relationship of support to the former colonies while refusing, on the one hand, to exploit and, on the other, to impose a foreign standard. If we, from our present position of power and influence in the world, are to avoid condescension to and manipulation of the weaker nations, we must learn to serve people as *they* want and need to be served. If only the affluent nations would respect the potential of the local communities and offer means of support that have the integrity of searching for the well-being of the dispossessed, it may be that the global village could be on its way to becoming a supporting fraternity. Maybe.

If we want self-sufficiency for others, we should begin by demonstrating this sufficiency ourselves. We over-consume oil and gasoline. Much of this excess is due to our penchant for structuring our way of life around the automobile. Our affluence is characterized by excessive consumption in many other areas. Typically, these excesses involve the use of resources of other nations with no commensurate benefit in return. Some explain all this in terms of good trade. Some rationalize our advantage by pointing to the short-term benefits to the supplying countries. Often overlooked in such analysis is the injustice of a small elite in the exporting country benefiting from the trade while the multitudes in that country remain poor. What I am saying is that the affluence of the "haves," both here and in the exporting nations, makes it more difficult for the "have nots" in those nations to use their own resources for their own well-being. To make matters worse, our disproportionate use of their resources widens the gap between rich and poor in the global village.

Today's problems necessarily focus the mission of the Christian church in a specific way on the physical well-being of people. Food, clothing, shelter and health invite ministries of compassion and concern which, in turn, witness to and participate in the church's mission to needs of the spirit.

We in the West find it difficult to think seriously of sharing the material benefits of creation. Thus we cause a delay and denial of that sharing. We have no sense of stewardship. We think instead of ownership—our ownership. Moreover, our consumer economy, preoccupied with our Gross National Product and with increases in production and profit, fails to concentrate on ways of improving the lot in life for all peoples. We simply produced, consumed and ignored the possibility of exhausting the resources which support our affluence. We are slowly coming to the realization that ecological exploitation is a form of violence. People are getting hurt, some irreparably.

To deprive people of dignity and freedom is violent. To rob people of respect is violent. To use people for our affluence is violent. To pursue high-energy agriculture and thereby limit the distribution of energy resources for the less affluent is to do violence to them.

While the evangelistic priority of Church missions in the third world remains rooted in the love and peace of Christ, services for the physical well-being of third world people must expand far beyond the traditional medical services. Recall St. John: "Who so hath this world's goods, and seeth his brother in need, and shutteth up his bowels of compassion from him, how dwelleth the love of God in him?" (1 Jn 3:17). Many contemporary writers are giving this question the reflection it deserves.

Ronald Sider's *Rich Christians in an Age of Hunger*[11] is encouraging that kind of reflection. Sider sees our causal involvement in the problem of world hunger in the following ways: our consumption of natural resources, our level of food consumption and the extensive food importing that supports our consumption, our excess profits from foreign investments, and our reinforcement of fundamentally unjust international trade arrangements.[12] How does the love of God dwell in us? Sider and others argue that we have the power, by changing our consumption and trade practices, to stop third world power elites from denying the poor of their countries access to the land and their native food resources. Stanley Mooneyham, president of World Vision International, calls this situation the "stranglehold which the developed West has kept on the economic throats of the third world."[13] This is a misuse of power. Instead of using our power to contribute to world hunger, our Christian conscience should impel us to use our power to end hunger.

The creative Mennonite theologian John Howard Yoder presents the Old Testament Year of Jubilee as a relevant guide for an understanding of the messianic answer to the problems of inequity and hunger. This guide invites us to relate our mission today to problems of injustice anywhere in the world. The Jubilee Year included prescriptions to (1) leave the soil fallow, (2) forgive debts, (3) liberate slaves, and (4) return land to the family of historic ownership. More of an ideal, perhaps, than a practical reality, the Jubilee Year was intended to be an instrument employed once every five decades to remedy injustices and remind the people that the land belongs to God.[14]

The Judaeo-Christian tradition has contributed to the development of productivity and the practice of management in the West. Perhaps this influence has also unwittingly fostered the secularization of the West. Rather than simply accepting the current critique of the Judaeo-Christian tradition and its alleged failure, we can rediscover within this tradition the perspective and the principles needed to contain human selfishness and correct the abuses of power which not only hurt the hungry but threaten to destroy the free enterprise system itself. In the Hebraic tradition, the Year of Jubilee was offered as God's design for restoring equity and reinforcing individual freedom. This was intended to be an "intervention" into the very fabric of the economic lifestyle of the people of God. Every half century an end would be put to the accumulation of extensive land holdings. Thus small land-owners would not be systematically and structurally deprived of the opportunity to make a living from the land. It would require a social revolution in our time, but imagine what life would be like today if we had, every five decades, a national reassertion and reaffirmation of the right to land, to freedom and to food.

In Luke 4:16–19 Jesus declared his mission. In that declaration he universalized the principles of social justice contained in the Jubilee motif. In the Sermon on the Mount he taught the active nature of love. In all he said and did, he rejected the secular quest for power and status over others. He called his disciples to a servant role in the social order.

Voices from the third world, especially in liberation theology when it attempts to reinterpret violence as aggressive action for change, constitute a desperate cry of the dispossessed. A Latin American evangelical leader, Samuel Escobar, says: "The new element in the awareness of poverty is that there is after all no desire on the part of the wealthy nations to raise the poor nations because raising the poor would endanger their own wealth and undermine their power. . . . Poverty is no longer a simple datum that you consider neutrally. Mission has to do something about it."[15] It remains for the wealthy nations to discover ways to help the poor.

Another voice from Latin America, this one in the person of Jon Sobrino of El Salvador, calls for a discipleship of praxis that will follow Jesus in real life. This means denouncing injustice and demonstrating the new quality of caring exemplified by Jesus of Nazareth, the one in whom we understand God.[16]

The question before us is whether the words of Jesus in Matthew 25 will be taken seriously by those of us who enjoy the benefits of affluence.

Voices from Asia, Africa, Latin America and, indeed, from the depths of conscience itself are suggesting: "It is necessary that some of us live more simply so that others of us may simply live." If we reflect on that statement and wonder how our consuming less will help others in need, we will have to admit that there is no immediate evidence that our less will make any difference. But acting out of Christian compassion and taking less because others have so little can begin the devlopment of a consciousness that will encourage others to do with less. Thus a cumulative effect will be the availabllity of "more" for the needy and the motivation to work out the problems that must be solved if the needy are ever to receive it. It will begin with individual choice. Such choices will touch upon amount and types of food, size and use of automobiles, the separation of necessity from utility and luxury, and the questions of production, accumulation and distribution. But beyond the question of distribution is the simple fact that God respects those who have compassion for the poor. Countless Scripture passages attest to this; one among the many is the angel's comment about Cornelius: "His prayers and his deeds for the poor had come up as a memorial before God" (Acts 10:4).

One thing, apparently, that is not being overconsumed in the developed world is the word of God. Micah has not yet been heard here, nor fully understood. When he is heard in the affluent West, our causal connection with the problem of hunger in the underdeveloped world will be broken. "He has explained to you, O man, what is good, and what the Lord does require of you: to do justice, and to love mercy, and to walk humbly with your God" (Mi 6:8).

NOTES

1. Scottdale, Pa.: Herald Press, 1980.
2. *Ibid.*, p. 22.
3. John V. Taylor (ed.), *Enough Is Enough* (Minneapolis: Augsburg, 1977), p. 5.
4. "World Hunger: Putting Development Ethics to the Test," *Christianity and Crisis* (May 26, 1975), p. 128.
5. "The World of Underdevelopment: A Crisis in Values," *The Christian Century,* April 24, 1974, p. 452.
6. Philadelphia: The Westminster Press, 1978.
7. *Ibid.*, p. 33.
8. Quoted by Birch and Rasmussen, *ibid.*
9. *Ibid.*
10. *The New Evangelism* (Nashville: Abingdon Press, 1975), p. 28.
11. Downers Grove, Ill.: Inter-Varsity Press, 1977.
12. *Ibid.*, p. 139.

13. Quoted by Elaine Israel in *Hungry World* (New York: Messner, 1977), p. 128.

14. See Leviticus 25:8–17, 29–31. See also John Howard Yoder, *The Politics of Jesus* (Grand Rapids: Eerdmans, 1972), pp. 64–77.

15. *Christian Mission and Social Justice* (Scottdale: Herald Press, 1978), p. 39.

16. *Christology at the Crossroads* (Maryknoll; Orbis Books, 1978), p. xxv.

18
Toward a Solution: Bread for the World

Thomas J. Gumbleton

Malnutrition has been called the hidden holocaust of our day. As much as we might want to avoid this grisly truth, honesty requires us to face up to it. Let me explain.

Today's holocaust from world hunger surpasses, in fact, the horror of the World War II holocaust of Nazi Germany. Right now over four hundred and sixty-two million people are actually starving, and over half of these are children under five years of age. That breaks down to thirty children who die of starvation every minute. And it is getting worse. The World Bank now projects that by the year 2000, seven hundred and fifty million people will live in absolute poverty, "barely surviving on the margin of life, afflicted by disease, illiteracy, malnutrition and squalor—a condition of life so degrading as to insult human dignity."

We don't like to think about it, but in fact how else can we describe, if not as modern death camps, those places where starving people huddle together in such misery? Besides these acutely malnourished people there are also the chronically malnourished—those who survive but suffer the afflictions brought on by daily hunger: blindness, retardation and disease.

There are two other factors that make our present situation like the holocaust. First, it is avoidable. We might like to connect what is happening to some natural catastrophes—disasters that

241

none of us can do anything about. But this is not the case. This holocaust is happening because of *human decisions.* Some of them were made in the past with perhaps no knowledge of their consequences. But some are being made right now, and implemented day after day. We look back in shock at the "bystanders" in Hitler's Germany and throughout the world. Is this generation of bystanders much different?

The second similarity is that those who are well fed seem to need to avert their eyes. Writing about World War II Germany, Albert Speer made it painfully clear: "We *wanted* not to know." Sometimes a picture in the paper, a poster in church or a forty-five-second newsclip on TV forces this holocaust on our attention, but most of the time we casually over-consume as we make sure that the starving are kept out of our sight.

Anyone who has read this far in this book, of course, is determined not to be a "bystander." And the number of people with a highly motivated sense of concern is steadily growing.

But then what can one person *do* about it? It is no help just to feel guilty, or to feel numbed by the enormity of the problem. Bread for the World can help. It is a movement founded on the realization that suffering from chronic hunger and malnutrition can be reduced, even eliminated. It is a Christian citizens' movement that works to reduce hunger by influencing public policy. Bread for the World's strategy is to use the political process to influence thought, change policy, effect legislation, and ultimately attack and obliterate the causes of hunger. The movement enlists individual Christians to contact their elected leaders about issues that vitally affect hungry people. We also help local churches to keep the cause of hunger before their congregations, and to encourage citizen advocacy as a legitimate and effective response to the Gospel.

As you have seen from the preceding chapters of this book, the causes of hunger are complex, interrelated, and, consequently, difficult to overcome. But the conviction of Bread for the World is that these causes are, nevertheless, the results of human choices. Generally, these choices are made in the context of our economic system and developed into public policies. In our society this means that these decisions are made through a political process. And it is primarily through that same process that new decisions can be made and new policies developed which will begin to eliminate the causes of hunger. President Carter's Commission on World Hunger put it this way:

> There are no physical or natural reasons why all the men, women, and children in the world cannot have enough food to eat. . . . The issue of ending world hunger comes down to a question of political choice. . . . The quantities of food and money needed to wipe out hunger are remarkably small in relation to available global resources. . . . The Commission agrees with other studies that if the appropriate political choices are made, the world can overcome the worst aspects of hunger and malnutrition by the year 2000.

There is something special about Bread for the World. It is consciously designed to motivate people to action on the basis of their Christian beliefs. The Gospel foundation for our Christian concern in Bread for the World is summarized in the Beatitudes. It is reinforced by the conviction that the kingdom which Jesus calls us to build will come only in terms of the peace we achieve through the way we treat others, the way we perceive others, the way we are concerned for others. In the dramatic scene of the Last Judgment in Matthew 25, Jesus makes extraordinarily clear what will really count on that momentous occasion. He makes it clear that the hungry person we help is never an anonymous stranger. It is Jesus. As Paul puts it, our love for Jesus more than anything else *drives* us to help.

Bread for the World has recruited tens of thousands of direct members to become concerned and actively involved in the political process. We are currently engaged in the following immediate activities:

- broadening our membership;

- deepening that membership's awareness of the causes of hunger;

- designing more effective courses of action to follow;

- developing more and more "covenant" and similar type relationships with more and larger bodies of Christians for larger scale political and economic efforts;

- developing effective relationships in collaboration with the hundreds of other hunger-centered movements and groups who share our goals.

The number one activity, of course, centers around the political actions we ask our members to carry out. More than anything else we want to help shape public policies that respond to the causes of world hunger. The very first thing we must look at is the distribution and the consumption of the world's resources. If the goods of the world really were put here for the benefit of all, how can a Christian in the United States not be actively working for a better distribution of the world's goods? There are ample resources in the world to support a decent life for many times the present world population, but not when there is lopsided opulence in one part of the world and destructive poverty elsewhere. It is intolerable—a Christian must say it is sinful—to accept simply the fact that by the year 2000 two hundred and fifty million Americans will consume a third of the most needed resources in a world of six billion people.

As Senator Mark Hatfield's chapter in this volume suggests, if we had the political will to act, we could reverse this constant accumulation and consumption of so much of the world's goods by just a minority of the world's people. Commenting on the gap between rich and poor in the world, Pope Paul VI in his 1967 encyclical letter *On the Development of Peoples,* said:

It is the responsibility of public authorities to look for a solution, with the active participation of individuals and social groups (n. 23).

Bread for the World encourages and facilitates such "active participation."

Later in that same encyclical letter, Pope Paul points out clearly that the obligation to bring about a more just distribution of the world's goods is not just a responsibility of individuals but also of nations.

> Advanced nations have a very heavy obligation to help the developing peoples. . . . Although it is normal that a nation should be the first to benefit from the gifts that Providence has bestowed on it as the fruit of the labors of its people, still no country can claim on that account to keep its wealth for itself alone. . . . Given the increasing needs of the under-developed countries, it should be considered quite normal for an advanced country to devote a part of its production to meet their needs, and to train teachers, engineers, technicians and scholars prepared to put their knowledge and their skill at the disposal of less fortunate peoples (n. 48).

> We must repeat once more that the superfluous wealth of rich countries should be placed at the service of poor nations. The rule which up to now held good for the benefit of those nearest to us must today be applied to all the needy of this world . . . (n. 49).

Bread for the World tries to remind those who represent us in the U.S. Congress, and those who occupy positions of influence in the Executive Branch, that all Americans have a serious moral obligation to help hungry people.

Assuredly, the *kind* of foreign assistance program we develop is of the utmost importance. Programs of development and food assistance must be sharply focused toward self-help opportunities, especially for the rural poor living in hunger and poverty. Aid should ensure their full participation in the development process, as well as in development gains such as higher incomes and increased food production. I would argue that it is clearly necessary to separate development and food aid from military and security-supporting assistance. Combining these different types of aid confuses the issue and confuses the public. Obviously, there should be international standards acceptable to both donor and recipient countries as the basis for determining the amount of aid. Standards would include such things as (1) proved need, (2) evidence that aid is primarily spurring development among the very poor, (3) willingness to institute basic reforms such as land reform, tax reform and anti-corruption measures that will reduce the disparity between rich and poor in the recipient country, (4) the degree of emphasis on military spending, and (5) the extent of efforts to secure human rights.

To be truly effective, it seems to me, our aid should be more in the form of grants rather than loans. Finally, we ought not to compel the recipients to spend the aid dollars in the United States, a restriction which can diminish the value of assistance and even distort its purpose.

With these and other cautions in mind, we must work to create the political will in our country to support a generous foreign assistance program. Within a matter of a few years, the U.S. assistance should return to the minimum level of the early 1960's: one half of one percent of our Gross National Product. This does not seem to be asking too much. If we could achieve that modest goal, we would have doubled our present level of foreign assistance. For more on aid, I refer the reader to James Cogswell's comprehensive treatment elsewhere in this volume.

Even though I have suggested that an effort to share what we have in such abundance is the first thing we must do, it is not enough. This conviction was urged upon Christians of the United States by Pope John Paul II when he visited this country in October 1979:

> Social thinking and social practice inspired by the Gospel must always be marked by a special sensitivity toward those who are most in distress, those who are extremely poor, those suffering from all the physical, mental and moral ills that afflict humanity, including hunger, neglect, unemployment and despair. There are many poor people of this sort around the world. There are many in your own midst. On many occasions, your nation has gained a well-deserved reputation for generosity, both public and private. Be faithful to that tradition, in keeping with your vast possibilities and present responsibilities. The network of charitable works of each kind that the Church has succeeded in creating here is a valuable means effectively mobilizing generous undertakings aimed at relieving the situations of distress that

continually arise both at home and elsewhere in the world.

But this is not enough. Within the framework of your national institutions and in cooperation with all your compatriots, you will also want to seek out the structural reasons which foster or cause the different forms of poverty in the world and in your own country, so that you can apply the proper remedies. You will not allow yourselves to be intimidated or discouraged by oversimplified explanations, which are more ideological than scientific—explanations which try to account for a complex evil by some single cause.

But neither will you recoil before the reforms—even profound ones—of attitudes and structures that may prove necessary in order to recreate over and over again the conditions needed by the disadvantaged if they are to have a fresh chance in the hard struggle of life. The poor of the United States and of the world are your brothers and sisters in Christ. You must never be content to leave them just the crumbs from the feast. You must take of your substance, and not just of your abundance, in order to help them. And you must treat them like guests at your family table.

Bread for the World has, from its very beginning, tried to focus attention on the "more" that we must do if world hunger is to be eliminated. In August 1975, BFW published a "working statement of policy" which was intended to guide our members' efforts in helping to bring about "the reforms—even profound ones—of attitudes and structures that may prove necessary. . . ."

This statement of policy is still a timely guide in trying to work toward solutions. Without reproducing the whole statement, I would like to call special attention to some parts of it that will require persistent efforts to bring about necessary changes in U.S. policies:

1. *A U.S. food policy committed to world food security and rural development, as proposed by the World Food Conference:* The United States clearly shoulders a special responsibility re-

garding global food needs. Our country controls most of the world's grain exports. U.S. commercial farm export earnings *from poor countries* alone jumped from $1.6 billion in 1972 to $6.6 billion in 1974—an increase double the amount of our entire development assistance to those countries. While this happened, U.S. food assistance declined sharply. We now need to respond in a way that reflects the more generous U.S. tradition of two decades following World War II. The World Food Conference charted the necessary path to world food security under a World Food Council that would coordinate both emergency relief efforts and long-range rural development. Bread for the World supports:

(a) U.S. participation in a world food reserve program, with reserves under national control;

(b) an increase in U.S. food assistance, especially the grant portion, to at least the level of a tithe (10%) of this country's food exports, as our share toward the establishment of a grain reserve with an initial world target of ten million tons;

(c) a substantial increase in the amount of food made available to the UN World Food Program and to voluntary agencies for distribution abroad;

(d) humanitarian, not political, use of food assistance, with assistance channeled through, or in cooperation with, international agencies;

(e) fair return to the U.S. farmer for his production, with curbs against windfall profits and special measures to assist family farmers; just wages for farm workers; and

(f) full U.S. participation in the International Fund for Agricultural Development, along with other steps that would promote rural development in the poor countries. Such development would, among other things, enable them to produce or secure adequate supplies of fertilizer and energy, and accelerate research relating to food production there.

2. *Trade preferences for the poorest countries:* Trade is not perceived by the public as a "hunger" issue, but trade, even more than aid, vitally affects hungry people. In the past, poor countries have been compelled to export their raw materials at bargain prices and to import high-priced manufactured products. The terms of such trade have progressively deteriorated over the past two decades. Recent food, fertilizer, and oil price hikes have

left the forty poorest countries, representing a billion people, in a desperate position. For them in particular trade opportunities are more important than ever. Bread for the World therefore supports the following positions, which are partly embodied in the Trade Act of 1974:

(a) the lowering of trade barriers such as tariffs and quotas, especially on semi-processed and finished products. It has been estimated that these barriers cost U.S. consumers $10 to $15 billion a year;

(b) special trade preferences for the poorest countries. These countries need markets for their products, if they are to work their way out of hunger; and

(c) greatly increased planning for economic adjustment, including assistance for adversely affected U.S. workers and industries. Without this, U.S. laborers are made to bear an unfair burden and are increasingly pitted against hungry people.

3. *Reduced military spending:* U.S. defense spending alone exceeds the total annual income of the poorest billion people on earth, the truly hungry children of God. Our thinking begins with them. During his presidential years, Dwight D. Eisenhower said, "Every gun that is made, every warship launched, every rocket fired signifies, in the final sense, a theft from those who hunger and are not fed, those who are cold and are not clothed." Bread for the World supports:

(a) the principle that each country has the right to determine its own path to human and social development, including legitimate control over outside investments;

(b) efforts to study and analyze the role of multinational corporations, especially as they regulate positively or negatively to the problem of hunger;

(c) national and international measures that seek fair means of accountability on the part of such companies; and

(d) special examination of the role of corporate farming, with a view toward adequate safeguards for low-income consumers and small family farm holders.

I often have a sense that many highly motivated people hesitate to get deeply involved in something like Bread for the World because it seems that their efforts will not really amount to very much. Also, there is often lacking much of a sense of actually doing anything that makes a difference right now. But there is something that each of us can do, and, I think, must do immediately. We must work very seriously at changing our own lifestyle. We must begin to conserve the resources which we now consume so recklessly. To do this in the United States requires strong motivation and courage because it seems counter to the basic ideology of our whole society, which is to consume more.

At the World Food Conference in 1974, Pope Paul VI closed his address with an appeal that is still urgent for each of us:

> This progressive reorientation of production and distribution also involves an effort which must not be simply a constraint imposed by fear of want, but also a positive will not to waste thoughtlessly the goods which must be for everyone's benefit. After freely feeding the crowds the Lord told his disciples, the Gospel relates, to gather up what was left over lest anything should be lost (Jn 6:12). What an excellent lesson in thrift—in the finest and fullest meaning of the term—for our age given as it is to wastefulness! It carries with it the condemnation of a whole concept of society wherein consumption tends to become an end in itself, with contempt for the needy. . . .

This appeal of Pope Paul is something that each of us can act on right now. It is in our power to change our way of living. We do not simply have to follow the trends. We can begin to be genuine stewards of the earth and all its resources. And this will begin immediately to make a difference for us. Pope Paul points this out by reminding us that a society built on consumerism deadens our spiritual sensibilities and makes us even "incapable of perceiving that man is called to a higher destiny."

Such active stewardship also is a survival value for the human race. This generation must begin to limit its use of resources or we are condemning our children and their children to deprivation and ever increasing misery.

I hope that reflection on the possibility of a change in lifestyle will cause large numbers of us to begin to do something immediately in our personal lives. When we do, this will also be a source of continuing motivation for us to undertake more zealously the role of Christian citizen advocates who will, with firm persistence, keep involved in the long-range and often frustrating effort to shape public policy and achieve legislative changes designed to eliminate world hunger.

This motivation will be strengthened if we ground it in our daily prayer and reflection on the Gospel. I have been helped to do this by recalling frequently my own reaction to part of Michael Harrington's recent book, *The Vast Majority*. On page 95 he records his deeply felt response to the poor of Calcutta:

> Then there began the Via Dolorosa of Calcutta, the Stations of the Cross. I can only evoke the miseries and infirmities I saw. The man with legs so misshapen that he walked on fours; another with wads of flesh hanging from his cheek; piteous, mumbling, muttering, dirty children; haggling cab drivers; people picking at garbage; bright-faced babies who have not yet understood that they were born condemned, convicted, sentenced; and on and on, a vast wheedling, suppurating army of the halt and the maimed. They finally led me to think blasphemies about Christ. . . . Though I left the Catholic Church long ago, I have always had an affection for Christ—which is to say the Christ of the *Catholic Worker,* of the Sermon on the Mount, of compassion and gentle love. But now I want to curse Him. Who is He to set up His anguish as a model of meditation for the centuries? He was crucified only once, that is all. If you assume that He is God, then you can say that He must have felt a terrible psychological loss as they nailed His divinity to the cross. But only one time; only for a matter of hours. Just one excruciating struggle up the hill with the means of His death on His back; just one crown of thorns. Terrible, but just once. In Calcutta, I think, people are crucified by the thousands every day, and then those who have not died are crucified again and again and again. If He were half the God He claims to be, He would leave His heaven and come here to do penance in the presence of a suffering so much greater than His own.

The first time I read this passage I was kind of shocked by it. I didn't really expect Harrington's reaction to the poor to be one of such anger, and anger against God. I really had to stop and think. And I realized that one reason I was shaken by it was that it came closer to expressing my own feelings than I wanted to admit. I too was tempted to be angry with the Jesus of the Gospels. It really does seem that his crucifixion does not compare with the agony, the suffering and utter hopelessness of the poor—the hundreds of millions of them—who are the vast majority of people in the world right now. I, too, could be tempted to doubt God. How could a loving God create a world in which the majority are condemned to this kind of dehumanized existence?

But then as I thought more about why this passage so profoundly disturbed me, and admitted to myself that the line between my belief and disbelief was very thin, I also began to see a couple of things that Michael Harrington had failed to consider.

First, getting angry at God is a kind of escape from responsibility. We don't want to be always reminded of Lazarus suffering outside the gate of our very comfortable life. And we especially do not want to be reminded that there are so many poor, and that there is such suffering among them because of what we do or fail to do.

The poor are not poor and the hungry are not hungry because of a failure on the part of God. He has not created a world which is a cruel joke; there really are enough resources for everyone. There is enough food for every person on this earth and even for many times the present population of the world. There are enough resources for every person to live a fully human life.

Second, putting down the sufferings of Jesus, disparaging his sufferings, in the face of the agony of the poor of the world, is to forget a very basic truth Jesus proclaimed during His life. We remember the dramatic words found in Matthew's Gospel: "When I was hungry you gave me to eat; when I was thirsty you gave me to drink; when I was naked ... when I was homeless ..." (Mt 25:35ff).

Jesus did not just suffer one time only. His agony was not for three hours only. Jesus is one with the world's poor. He is undergoing a cruel agony and death again and again and again. This is what our faith really tells us. The poor are not a vast, unnamed multitude of faceless people. The poor have a name. It is Jesus. They are especially loved by their Father who is God. And even as Jesus is crucified now in them, so too will the Father raise him up once more *in them.*

The final comment I want to make is a challenge to all of us. Will we share in this continuing living out of the death and resurrection of Jesus? Will we begin to listen to the cry of the poor and recognize in it the cry of Jesus? Will we begin to act courageously and boldly in response to this cry of Jesus in the poor? Will we do it by changing our lifestyle? Will we choose to become citizen advocates for the poor? For our sake and for theirs, I pray to God that we will.

Contributors

Myron S. Augsburger is pastor of the Washington, D.C., Community Fellowship of the Mennonite Church. He also serves as adjunct professor of theology at the Eastern Mennonite Theological Seminary and the Associate Mennonite Biblical Seminaries. He is past president of Eastern Mennonite College, Harrisonburg, Virginia.

Eugene Carson Blake is a former General Secretary of the World Council of Churches. He retired in 1979 after serving five years as first president of the Board of Directors of Bread for the World.

Edward J. Brady, S.J., a former missioner in Ceylon (now Sri Lanka), left the position of executive director of the Bread for the World Educational Fund in 1980 to work directly with refugees in Thailand near the Laotian border.

William J. Byron, S.J., is President of the Catholic University of America. From 1975 to 1982 he was president of the University of Scranton. One of the founding directors of Bread for the World, he served as president of the Bread for the World Educational Fund from 1974 to 1981.

John C. Calhoun, a Roman Catholic priest of the Archdiocese of New York in residence at Corpus Christi parish, is active in planning and developing social policy with human service organizations in New York City.

James A. Cogswell is Director of the Office of World Service and World Hunger of the Presbyterian Church in the United States. He previously served as a missionary to Japan, and as Asia Secretary for his denomination's Board of World Missions.

Eileen Egan is now writing a history of Catholic Relief Services, an organization she served at Headquarters and in the field for many years. Part of her work at CRS consisted of linking American women's groups with development programs in Asia, Africa and Latin America. She is an associate editor of *The Catholic Worker.*

Douglas Ensminger is professor of rural sociology at the University of Missouri. He served as Ford Foundation representative for India and Pakistan, 1951–53, and for India and Nepal, 1953–1970.

Norman J. Faramelli is director of planning for the Massachusetts Port Authority. An ordained Episcopal priest, he is coordinator of the Urban Mission Committee of the Episcopal Diocese of Massachusetts. Before taking his present position, he was director of The Boston Industrial Mission.

C. Dean Freudenberger has extensive overseas experience and has taught courses in agriculture to Peace Corps trainees. He is currently a professor at the School of Theology at Claremont, California.

Thomas J. Gumbleton is auxiliary bishop of the Archdiocese of Detroit. He serves as president of Bread for the World and also of Pax Christi/USA.

Mark O. Hatfield is United States Senator from Oregon. Before his election to the Senate in 1967, he was Governor of Oregon (1959–67).

J. Bryan Hehir is director of the Office of International Justice and Peace, U.S. Catholic Conference. A priest of the Archdiocese of Boston, Fr. Hehir is a member of the Council on Foreign Relations and a scholar in the fields of social ethics and foreign policy.

Warren P. Henegar is a farmer and county commissioner from Bloomington, Indiana. He has taught occasional courses at Indiana University.

Richard John Neuhaus is a founding director of Bread for the World. He is project director for the Council on Religion and International Affairs, and "Pastor on Assignment" for the East Coast Synod of the Association of Evangelical Lutheran Churches.

Arthur Simon is founder of Bread for the World, a movement he has served as executive director since it began in 1974. A Lutheran pastor who lives in the Lower East Side of New York City, his interest in the poor led him to recognize hunger as the most urgent form of poverty.

Kristen Wenzel, O.S.U. is an Ursuline sister of the Eastern Province (U.S.A.) who holds the rank of professor in the Department of Sociology and the position of Director of Women's Studies at the College of New Rochelle.

Jayne Millar-Wood is president of the Bread for the World Educational Fund. A member of the Sojourners Fellowship in Washington, D.C., her primary professional responsibility involves the presidency of Development Resources, a non-profit organization serving people in developing countries in the areas of agriculture, rural development and nutrition. She was formerly director of public education at the Overseas Development Council.